From Fairbanks to Boston
50 Great U.S. Marathons

From Fairbanks to Boston
50 Great U.S. Marathons

Edited by
Michaela Gaaserud & Renee Dexter

Rainmaker Publishing LLC
Oakton, Virginia, USA

ISBN: 0-9765498-2-4
LCCN: 200590179

⊗ Printed on Acid-Free Paper
Automated Graphic Systems - White Plains, Maryland, USA
Cover Design: Imaginus Designs

Rainmaker Publishing LLC
Oakton, VA 22124-3102
info@rainmakerpublishing.com
www.rainmakerpublishing.com

Acknowledgements

Thank you to new and old friends who went the extra mile for this book. The welcoming arms of the national marathon community made this effort much more fun than we imagined. A special thanks to Lenore Dolphin, Aaron Schwartzbard, Jerry Dunn, and Steve Smith, for their time and dedication. Thanks also to Pete and Clark for all of your support and enthusiasm and for putting up with the late nights, empty refrigerators, and dust bunnies.

Forward

Although they might not admit it, nearly everyone who ever laced up a pair of running shoes has contemplated running a marathon. For some, it's a fleeting thought with a headshake, for others it's a goal and yet for some, a way of life.

Choosing the right marathon can play a role in your training, attitude and, of course, the end result. It can define vacation plans, forward a goal, or present new challenges to the seasoned distance runner. A marathon is a journey and the reward of running the right race can leave years of fond memories.

There are more than 300 marathons held in the United States each year. This is the good news. There are literally dozens of great races to choose from at all times of the year. The bad news is, it can be difficult to determine which 26.2 miles you will most enjoy.

Does the idea of running through the Magic Kingdom® greeted by familiar characters under bright sunshine warm you up? Or do you prefer hoofing it through the wilderness where grizzlies may be watching? You might be someone who loves the big city and throngs of people bouncing shoulder to shoulder at the start line, or you may prefer a low key race in the country where someone says, "Hey, have we started?" Whatever your preference, we thought it was time to depart from the usual advice of how to train for your next marathon and focus on *where* to run your next marathon.

Since every runner is different, who better to turn to for advice than a successful running club with thousands of miles of experience under its collective belt? The Reston Runners Club is based in Reston, Virginia (a Washington, D.C. suburb) and is a branch of the Road Runners Club of America. With nearly 1,000 members, Reston Runners of all ages and experience levels can be found pounding the pavement (and trails) nationwide. Many club members have run marathons in all 50 states, and a surprisingly large number are ultra distance runners.

The races in this book are recommended by Reston Runners and club members authored many of the chapters. Other featured authors in this book include marathoners from across the country of all ages and experiences who graciously volunteered their time to share their fondest marathon experiences. Most importantly, every author completed the marathon they recommend at least once, but often many more times (and sometimes many, many more times!), and we are very thankful for their contributions.

We also thought it would be fun to include an introduction to the elite sport of ultra distance running, and in doing so included six sections written by seasoned endurance runners. These participants are truly special athletes (although some would argue their sanity), and we're thankful to them for enthusiastically sharing their ultra experiences in these pages.

None of the sponsors or organizations of the races written about in this book asked to be featured. Although most provided an outpouring of support, for which we are extremely grateful, we approached them, not the other way around. This book is truly a coordinated effort of advocates of the sport of running and the love for this activity is evident in each chapter.

For each race recommended for this book, we researched opinions outside of the Reston Runners and race reports from across the country to confirm that other participants shared similar positive experiences. However, each recommendation remains as such—the opinion of the author and his or her view of the race.

We also included some brief reference information at the start of each race section. One such item is a course classification. For the purpose of this book, "Flat" refers to races that describe themselves or are described by our authors as flat or flat and fast. "Challenging" is reserved for courses whose web sites indicate they are difficult, challenging, or are run through mountains. "Rolling" includes everything else from rolling to gently rolling. For further details, we recommend visiting the individual race web site or contacting the race directly.

Another piece of information we included is whether the course is USA Track & Field (USATF) Certified. USATF is, among other things, the national governing body for long distance running. The purpose of their course certification is to verify that a race distance is accurately measured. Only finishing times on USATF-certified courses are eligible for national ranking.

Additionally, racecourses and details can change from year to year. Although great care was taken to provide accurate, up-to-date information at the time of publication, please don't be surprised if the aid station at mile eight you read about —where perhaps a group of Boy Scouts handed out Gatorade—was relocated a quarter of a mile and now features a mariachi band and POWERade.

This work wouldn't be complete without thanking marathonguide.com for the valuable resource they provide in individual race ratings and race contact information. We'd also like to thank the race directors and planning organizations for the featured races for the support and enthusiasm they provided throughout the project and their willingness to provide graphics and confirm facts for this publication. This is truly a national effort, and we hope you have as much fun reading it as we did putting it together.

Whether you are running to finish or racing to win, we hope you will find this book to be a valuable resource as you select your next marathon.

Michaela Gaaserud and Renee Dexter, Co-founders
Rainmaker Publishing LLC

Table of Contents

January

Walt Disney World Marathon
David Glover... 1

HP Houston Marathon
Jonathan Beverly... 5

P.F. Chang's Rock 'n' Roll Arizona Marathon
Phillip Utterback.. 9

Carlsbad Marathon
Pony Asher... 13

February

Mercedes Marathon
Kristen Adelman.. 17

BI-LO Myrtle Beach Marathon
David Glover... 21

Blue Angel Marathon
Hope Hall... 25

March

Napa Valley Marathon
Valentine Pisarski "SKI"... 29

Ocean Drive Marathon
Todd Katz... 35

Shamrock Sportsfest Marathon
Tamra Hall
Gary Euliss... 39

Bataan Memorial Death March
Jim Eckles... 45

April

May

June

July

August

September

October

Ultra Distance Races

From Fairbanks to Boston

Yakima River Canyon Marathon

Grizzly Marathon

Crater Lake Marathon

Mesa Falls Marathon

Deadwood-Mickelson Trail Marathon

Avenue of the Giants Marathon

Napa Valley Marathon

Wyoming Marathon

St. George Marathon

Pikes Peak Marathon

Valley of Fire Marathon

Big Sur International Marathon

Carlsbad Marathon

The Oklahoma City Memorial Marathon

P.F. Chang's Rock 'n' Roll Marathon

Bataan Memorial Death March

Equinox Marathon

Honolulu Marathon

Kilauea Volcano Wilderness Marathon

50 Great U.S. Marathons

Grandma's Marathon

Mount Desert Island Marathon

KeyBank Vermont City Marathon

Adirondack Marathon

Twin Cities Marathon

Boston Marathon

Lakefront Marathon

United Technologies Hartford Marathon

Detroit Free Press/Flagstar Bank Marathon

ING New York City Marathon

The LaSalle Bank Chicago Marathon

Road Runner Akron Marathon

Philadelphia Marathon

Des Moines Marathon

Columbus Marathon

Ocean Drive Marathon

Lincoln National Guard Marathon

Marine Corps Marathon

Eisenhower Marathon

SunTrust Richmond Marathon

Shamrock Sportsfest Marathon

4-H Old Mulkey Classic Marathon

Oklahoma Marathon

Country Music Marathon

St. Jude Memphis Marathon

BI-LO Myrtle Beach Marathon

Mercedes Marathon

Kiawah Island Marathon

Blue Angel Marathon

HP Houston Marathon

Walt Disney World Marathon

WALT DISNEY WORLD® Marathon

orlando, florida

Web site: www.disneyworldmarathon.com
Month: January
USATF Certified: Yes
Course: Flat

Author: David Glover
Number of Marathons Completed: 21
Age Group: 30-34

What isn't there to like about anything Mickey Mouse? In fact, Mickey Mouse even starts the WALT DISNEY WORLD® Marathon which takes runners through all four Disney theme parks: Epcot®, Magic Kingdom® Park, Disney's Animal Kingdom®Theme Park, and Disney-MGM Studios then through Disney's Boardwalk to finish back at Epcot.

Qualifications for entry into the marathon are that participants must be 18 years of age or older and must be able to maintain a 16-minute per mile pace, finishing the marathon within seven hours. Although the race does fill up early, there are numerous charity groups, such as Team in Training, that provide an alternative means of entry into the race. The marathon is USATF certified and a qualifier for the Boston Marathon, which is a little over three months later. Due to the long qualifying window for Boston, it is possible to qualify at Disney then race Boston either the same year or the following year.

I decided to sign up for the marathon after some friends who had previously done the race talked me into it. "Come on," they said, "It will be fun. It's a great opportunity to take a mini vacation away from the snow in Northern Virginia, plus there's this really great restaurant called 'The Flying Fish.'" It sounded great at the time, but I seriously did reconsider my decision several times during the 26.2-mile run. My fiancée, Jen, signed up for the half marathon, which used to start concurrently at an adjacent location before runners merged at mile four. Now, the half marathon is held the day before the marathon along with a Family Fun Run 5K and Kids' Races.

Flying into Orlando was very easy. We caught a relatively inexpensive

and direct flight from Washington Dulles. Upon arriving in Orlando, we took the Mertz shuttle bus to our Disney hotel, avoiding the hassle of a rental car.

Disney's Health and Fitness Expo, the site of packet pick up, was one of the largest and most comprehensive race expos that I have seen. It took place at Disney's Wide World of Sports Complex. In addition to Disney race merchandise, there were running stores, product demos, and free samples. All runners received a commemorative race program, long sleeve race shirt, and entry into the Post Race Celebration and Awards Ceremony. Given Mickey started the race, it was not surprising that marathon finishers received Mickey Mouse head-shaped medals on a color ribbon. Half marathon finishers received Donald Duck head shaped medals.

Our group stayed at the Disney All-Star Sports Resort, which is a budget hotel by Disney standards. The hotel was not extravagant by any means but there was a cafeteria and swimming pool on site plus, as we were on Disney property, access to the free shuttle buses to take us around to the theme parks and other Disney locations. I highly recommend staying at a Disney hotel for the marathon as Disney will also provide early morning busing to the start line and from the finish line back to the hotel. Given that runners need to be at the start by around 4:30 a.m., the shuttle service from the hotel was very convenient. Another nice touch was that the hotel cafeteria opened several hours early to accommodate runners. Unfortunately for us, we did not realize the coffee shop opened early until we were walking out to catch the bus. In the meantime, two of our friends had gotten up an extra 30 minutes early to make a coffee run to a nearby gas station.

The race started at 6:00 a.m. The least desirable aspect of the race for me was being at the start line so early before the race start. I believe the early start was to get the runners through the parks as much as possible before the parks opened later in the morning. The early morning would be even more difficult for some flying in from the West Coast due to time zone differences.

The weather was humid and cool in the morning. Our friends who had done the race previously recommended that we go to a local Home Depot to pick up a white Tyvek painter's suit to wear race morning. The Tyvek suit was a complete body suit with a hood made of paper that we could wear while waiting for the race to start and then just throw away. The Tyvek suit was $7.00—which was well spent to stay warm. Plus, wearing the suits gave our small group team cohesion, which is what

2

my friend, Bruce, told the announcer who had asked about runners wearing white suits. Bruce said, "We're Team Tyvek." The Tyvek Company got some positive publicity out of us that morning. I imagine that the next time I do the race even more people will be wearing Tyvek suits to stay warm on race morning.

While waiting for the race to start, there was really not much to do except sit in the parking lot or walk around. I honestly have never seen as many port-a-johns in one location as there were near the start line of the marathon. So many, that if you walked down to the end of the line of port-a-johns, you could find one that had not been used yet. At some point, we were all herded to our respective race starting areas and starting corrals. The start takes place on the highway, which is actually quite nice since it's a very wide, smooth road.

As we lined up at the start, it was still relatively dark given it was January and near the shortest day of the year. I remember Mickey Mouse standing up on a lighted platform waving his arms and cheering on all the racers as the official marathon race starter. I do not remember Mickey's exact words but his words were something to the effect of: "Okay boys and girls, this is Mickey Mouse welcoming you to the Wonderful World of Disney and the Walt Disney Marathon. We hope that you have a magical experience that you will never forget ...." You get the point. Donald Duck started the half marathon on the adjacent highway. I think there were fireworks and probably cannons at the start, too.

Running the marathon, I had a chance to see a side of Disney that most people do not see, including the backstage of the Magic Kingdom and the Disney water treatment facility. Being able to look forward to the next park gave me something to think about, as the course between the parks was on somewhat desolate highways. One unique aspect of the race was the abundance of Disney characters strategically placed along the course to cheer on the runners. Each display of characters had a theme, such as the evil witch and talking mirror from Snow White or characters from The Little Mermaid. I thought it was amusing that the evil characters would have small signs on the side of the road leading up to them that said things like, "Your legs are feeling heavy," "You should quit now," "You're tired," etc. I imagine that if I were really struggling to keep running that these signs might have pushed me over the edge to start walking.

The course was well marked and well supported with water stations approximately every mile and three food stations. By mid-race, the temperature had warmed into the 70s.

I finished just as a small rainstorm blew through which rapidly cooled the air. I ate and then headed over to the buses to catch a ride back to the hotel. Jen, who ran the half-marathon, had gone back to the hotel earlier. She ran into a small fiasco when her bus driver, who apparently did not know his way back to the hotels, drove around lost. In the meantime, a runner on the bus vomited.

Disney was spectator friendly in that there were plenty of places to hang out and just watch the racers run by from in the theme parks or, better yet, at Disney's Boardwalk near the finish. There were lots of places to eat, drink and just be entertained at the Boardwalk.

From my own perspective, I had a great race and achieved a marathon personal best. Needless to say, I had to pick up my pace the last couple of miles to squeeze in just under three hours with only two seconds to spare.

Race Stats:

- Finish time: 2:59:58
- Finish place overall: 50th
- Finish place age group (M30-34): 12th

In summary, I liked the race so much that I have signed up to do it again. Like everything Disney, the race was well executed from start to finish. It is a fast course and at a fun location for family and friends. One thing to consider for those traveling from colder climates is the time of year. Running a marathon in Florida in January is good; however, training for a January marathon in northern climates may be challenging. Register early (mid-summer) as the race will fill up.

I also recommend staying a couple of days to enjoy the theme parks and everything else at Disney. We spent the day before the race at Disney Quest, which is a fun place for kids and adults ... sort of a virtual reality theme park. There are also some really good restaurants, especially the "Flying Fish," near the Disney Boardwalk, where we ate the first two nights.

David Glover lives in Reston, Virginia and works as a business analyst at Capital One. He lives with his dog, Princess, a deaf Dalmatian, on Lake Audubon where the Reston Triathlon is held in his backyard every year. An active runner in high school and college, David has completed 21 marathons, 17 of which were run as part of Iron-distance triathlons (2.4-mile swim, 112-mile bike, 26.2-mile run). He has a marathon PR of 2:53 and has finished in the top 10 overall 10 times in Iron-distance triathlons, including four overall wins. He is also a five time USA Triathlon All-American.

HP Houston Marathon

houston, texas

Web site: www.hphoustonmarathon.com
Month: January
USATF Certified: Yes
Course: Flat

Author: Jonathan Beverly
Number of Marathons Completed: 25
Age Group: 40-44

Houston has a solid reputation as a place where you go to run fast in the winter. I like training in winter, but it is difficult to run fast in the north between December and March. That being said, I dislike heat as well. Houston promised a winter marathon with spring-like weather over a smooth, fast course. It delivered on its promise.

Several small details were welcome, such as my name on the number, and a separate race tag on the back of the half marathoners, who shared the first 10 miles or so with us, so there was no confusion over who was in what race.

I stayed at the host hotel, from which I could look out at the start and finish. I believe that this convenience is very important and a significant factor in running a good marathon—you can burn a lot of energy in the logistics and stress of race-day travel and waiting on the starting line for hours.

The loop course and moderate race size created a very smooth, very convenient event. I rolled out of bed an hour before the start and looked out at a nearly empty starting line. I didn't go downstairs until 30 minutes before the start, and still it felt relaxed and uncrowded. This is a big contrast to other big-city marathons where the start is crowded and highly regulated, you have to take busses to the start, or at least arrive hours in advance to avoid roadblocks and ensure that you make it through the masses and fences in time.

The field was adequately large, so it felt like a big event as we ran through the city, and provided good company throughout the race at any pace. I hooked up with a friendly Houstonian, Paul Hernandez, who kept me company, pointed out the sites, and shared drafting responsibilities from about mile 10 through 23.

The weather was near perfect: sunny and in the mid-50s throughout the run, warm enough to wear shorts and a singlet, cool enough to feel chilly at the start, and perfect once the run was underway. This is another large contrast to much of the rest of the country in mid-January, buried in snow and braving cold fronts.

The only negative side to the weather was the wind, which buffeted us from the west throughout the race. We noticed it the most during the zigzag route from halfway to mile 18, where we turned east into Memorial Park and rode the tail-wind home.

The course is a figure-8 loop through mostly residential streets of Houston (all paved, all urban, and all relatively flat — conducive to fast times).

Having visited Houston once before, and after spending a few days there before the race, I had very low expectations for the course. Driving in Houston, you spend your time on large freeways shuttling between stadiums, shopping centers, theaters, and parks; all remote from each other and seemingly stranded on their own access roads and parking lots. The racecourse was a pleasant surprise. Starting on the eastern edge of downtown near the Astro's baseball stadium (I did my pre-race run and pick-ups around the stadium the day before), we ran over a long bridge and then were plunged directly into street-level, residential Houston. The first six mile loop is through a Hispanic neighborhood with storefronts painted in bright, primary colors advertising "Herbiceria," "Novedades," "Panaderia." The residents called "Varnos" as we went by. Having spent time in Latin America, I relished in the memories as the miles clicked off.

Miles 7 through 10 passed through a fairly generic, mixed residential and business urban district on a divided four-lane road. Fortunately, the top half-marathoners were coming back on the other side, and cheering for them provided distraction. Miles 10 through 15 took us into the southern elegance of Rice University and the River Oaks neighborhood. I recall an impressive fountain where we turned toward the university, heard the sounds of a bag-piper, and enjoying the shade of old oaks on increasingly smaller and more intimate roads. In neighborhoods, were signs to cheer for family and friends and, in front of a school, "Good luck, Ms. Martin."

The scenery deteriorated toward construction, underpasses, and ramps as we turned in a series of zigzags heading for the famed Galleria shopping center. We skirted the edge of the Galleria under its entrance archways and lights, then continued onto oak-overhung Tanglewood Boulevard between million dollar homes. This high-class neighborhood, where George Bush, Sr.

reportedly lives, provided a pleasant mile along a winding, divided suburban drive.

At mile 18, we made a right angle right turn, and started enjoying the tailwind home. After crossing under the interstate at mile 19, the course wound through Memorial Park, providing welcome quiet and greenery, and even a soft surface if you chose (as I did) to jump up onto the grass and dirt border along the course.

The high rises of downtown that I could see from mile 20 on got closer and closer with each view. We briefly paralleled a pretty path alongside the river, passed under and over a few ramps and were soon in the midst of the towers with only one mile to go. Through the canyons, eerily quiet on a Sunday morning, I spied the trees in front of the convention center, then the crowds, including my wife, lining the curve that took us to the festive finish line. Having run faster than expected, I crossed the line with a smile, like the many Boston qualifiers around me.

Any negatives about the race were minor. The time and distance through the convention center after the finish, before you could meet your family and friends, seemed long, dark, and difficult. Mile splits, while consistent, were always given as pace, not elapsed time, nor were there any time clocks to see elapsed time. Sometimes this is nice, but I tend to keep the current mile on my watch, and rely on the race for the overall time. If you know your elapsed time at the moment, for example, with "1 Mile to Go," it can help if you are shooting for a specific time. The only other negatives that come to mind are items of preference. For example, I was automatically signed up for charity fundraising when I registered, and started to receive emails about raising money—I found this pushy and would prefer to have been asked. Another annoyance for me was the big pack of runners in a pace group who took up the road and clogged water stops—I'm a loner and prefer to set my own pace and have some room to both step and think. In both instances, I easily remedied the situation: deleting emails and accelerating just enough to pull away and not see or hear the group again.

The location of the race expo was convenient and near the race start and host hotel in the heart of the city. The size was typical of a mid-size marathon, not the mega-production of New York City or Chicago, but enough to be interesting without spending too much time on your feet in crowds.

Without a solid public transportation system, spectating at the race was essentially limited to the start and finish for out-of-towners like me who didn't know the city well enough to want to try and drive to locations on the route. That being said, the start/finish area is a nice place to hang out.

Houston prides itself on technological advancements. With Hewlett-Packard as their title sponsor, they were the first to offer web and email-based tracking systems, and in 2004 offered a web-based interactive map for spectators to follow up to five runners around the course. After the race, results options on the web included a number of interesting statistical calculations and charts derived from your placement in the field, plus a computer-generated image of you and runners around you as you finished.

In all, Houston was a well-organized, smooth-running, big-city marathon. Registration through the web site was seamless. The course was fully closed to traffic and well marked. Water and Gatorade were available every mile; gels in later miles. The neighborhoods were diverse and interesting and spectators were plentiful and polite. This is the only marathon where I've heard, "Way to go, Ma'am" to a woman running alongside me.

Jonathan Beverly is the Editor in Chief of Running Times *magazine. He has been running competitively since high school cross-country in the late 1970s. He has run 25 marathons since 1980, with a best time of 2:46.*

P.F. Chang's Rock 'n' Roll Arizona Marathon

phoenix, scottsdale, tempe, arizona

Web site: www.rnraz.com
Month: January
USATF Certified: Yes
Course: Flat

Author: Phillip Utterback
Number of Marathons Completed: 6
Age Group: 25-29

Having trained, and successfully completed two marathons with The Leukemia & Lymphoma Society, I decided that it was time to run a marathon on my own. What better way than to run the inaugural P.F. Chang's Rock 'n' Roll Arizona Marathon? The first race in Elite Racing's Grand Slam Challenge, this marathon is a great way to kick off the four-race event. Held on the second Sunday of January, this race also proved a great way to kick off the year as a whole.

I decided to do this marathon as I was walking through a race expo and came across Elite Racing's booth. Upon seeing the medal that was given to people who completed the Grand Slam, I decided that I wanted it. So I immediately signed up for the Arizona Marathon. A representative from Elite Racing helped me complete the paperwork, which made the process very easy. By signing up at the expo, I even got a free t-shirt and camera — which I would later drop at the end of the race having used up the whole roll.

My first instinct after the excitement of signing up for another marathon was to figure out how I was going to get there. The second thing I had to do was find a place to stay where those coming to watch me could easily get to the course, since the marathon causes most of the streets to be blocked off on the day of the race. Fortunately, the designers of the marathon created it so the racecourse forms a box. This puts all the spectators in one of two positions — inside the box, in which case they can drive around to different points within, or outside the box. Travel outside the box is also fairly easy, it just takes a little longer because they have to drive around the course.

Aside from making travel plans to Arizona, the first part of any race experience is the letter received with your race confirmation. Since the race is sponsored by P.F. Chang's, a gift certificate was sent out with the confirmation as was a new menu created with the help of professional marathon runners and Team in Training® (The Leukemia & Lymphoma Society's marathon training organization). The menu was created for people running marathons and was specially designed to show the number of carbohydrates, proteins, and fats that were included in each dish. P.F. Chang's even had a challenge with their workers to support the race and run the marathon.

The second part of a race experience is the race expo. This race expo was probably one of the best that I've seen. It was skillfully laid out within the Phoenix Civic Plaza Convention Center with tons of booths and an easy to maneuver bib and packet pick-up. While many of the booths were similar to other expos, there were several things that I haven't seen anywhere else. In retrospect, I should have bought some stuff at the expo because it would have saved me several hours of searching the Internet for the same products.

Within the race program were several maps. These helped inform runners where bands, water, and first aid stops were going to be, and also provided spectators with clear directions as to how to get to spots throughout the course while avoiding the roads that would be closed for the race.

Since our hotel was on the outside of the course box, travel to the start line was fairly easy, and conveniently, only two miles away. Elite Racing also provided shuttle buses from the finish line, where you could park your car, and then ride to the start line. The shuttles, however, proved to be the one flaw in the master plan. Although I didn't use them, I heard through word of mouth, that there were problems with the organization of the buses. I did, however, receive a post-marathon letter, that assured me that this problem would be fixed for upcoming years.

The late running buses caused a slight delay in the start time, which caused much grumbling throughout the starting corrals. Not being a super runner who has a whole routine outlined before every race, the delay didn't really bother me. It actually turned out to be a benefit because the bathroom lines were empty when the second announcement, saying that the start was going to be delayed, was made.

The course itself was fairly flat, and while it was spotted with the occasional hill, none of them were particularly steep. It was a nice scenic run through Phoenix, Scottsdale, and Tempe with plenty of water and Gatorade stops to counteract the warmth of an Arizona January. I would recommend carrying a fuel belt, or some form of water container. Although the farthest distance between water stops is a

Courtesy of Elite Racing

mile and a half, there is never one when you want water the most, as it always seems to be in any race.

With three other races under their belts, Elite Racing seemed to have learned how to pull off a marathon. The race registration was easy, there were first aid stops scattered throughout the course, the race expo was great and the race support was just terrific.

Dubbed a Rock 'n' Roll marathon, one would expect some form of music on the course, and Arizona did not disappoint. Probably my favorite part of the race was the more than 50 bands and cheerleaders that were spread throughout the course to help motivate the runners along. Having music not only seemed to make the race go faster, but it also provided the desire to keep running, if only to hear the next band, or see how the next cheer squad was going to be dressed up. The music part of this race is something that Elite Racing has clearly worked on, pulling in local bands from every genre including country, bluegrass, reggae, house, and of course, rock and roll.

Aside from the bands and cheerleaders provided by the race, spectators were plentiful throughout the entire course. Arizona natives and friends and families of runners were at every turn cheering the runners on. There were only a few sections that were lacking in the spectator department and this was only because there was only one road into the area and we were running on it. But overall, there was almost always people screaming and cheering for us.

If the race expo was good, the post race party, or festival as they called it, was even better. With a band playing as you sprinted toward the finish line, hundreds of people cheering you on, and plenty to eat and drink once you crossed over, the feeling of accomplishment provided by the race was tremendous. With 15,000 participants, it took very little time to find my family in the meet up area, which was a definite plus. Although I didn't go, nothing beats a free concert of a major musical group. This time the Goo Goo Dolls, finished off your day of running.

Looking back, it was one of the most fun races that I've ever done. With such a nice course, good spectators, and great support from Elite Racing, there was very little to complain about. There were no long stretches without spectators, as is frequently the case, the water stops were regular and plentiful, and the pre- and post-race experiences were fun and exciting.

Another favorite part of the race for me was a series of signs placed on the course by Reebok that said "Seek The Rock," which, I assume, refers to the mountain next to the Wells Fargo Arena, the marathon finish line. The signs were so motivational throughout the race; it was like Reebok was cheering us through to the finish.

The weather, spectators, support from Elite and the race layout made this a fun and festive race. This was only the first year of the race, as well. I can only imagine that as the number of people racing will increase, so will the number of spectators. This race will only get better over time. So go out, have some fun, and "Seek the Rock."

Phillip Utterback is a six-time marathon runner, although he only ran two of those before Arizona. Running at about a 10-minute mile places him right in the middle of the pack. If you're running and hear someone screaming and cheering from within the runners, it's probably Phillip.

Carlsbad Marathon

carlsbad, california

Web site: www.carlsbadmarathon.com
Month: January
USATF Certified: Yes
Course: Rolling

Author: Pony Asher
Number of Marathons Completed: 17
Age Group: 45-49

The Carlsbad Marathon is held in Carlsbad, California, and for several years it was called the San Diego Marathon, not to be confused with the Rock 'n' Roll Marathon. Last year, the name was officially changed to the Carlsbad Marathon, aptly named as the course meanders through the quaint beach city of Carlsbad. This race is held in January, usually mid month.

This was my first marathon. I had only run one 10K and that was about three months before the marathon. I guess you could say I jumped in with both feet. I was 38 years old when I ran this race for the first time. In my 20s I used to run about five miles a day, smoke cigarettes, and have a couple of drinks in the evening. When I started training for this marathon, I was 45 pounds overweight and completely out of shape. On my first day of training it was all I could do to walk/jog the one-mile workout. But six months of training and crossing that finish line completely changed my life. I have since run 16 marathons and 1 ultra distance race.

Typical weather for this race begins in the low 50s with clear skies, warming up to the high 60s by the end of the race. I have either run the race or coached runners for this race for the past 11 years and it has varied only slightly. No qualifications are necessary for entry. However, it is a sanctioned race, one that can be used as a Boston qualifier.

This race, from registration until you cross the finish line, is incredibly well organized. The race director carefully oversees a well-trained crew of volunteers. There are pace teams during the race and volunteers are

13

available to watch over your gear bags so they are handy when you finish the race. Family presentation of medals is even available at the finish line.

Registration is available online and chip timing is used. Entry limits ensure attention to detail for every participant. There are plenty of volunteers along the course. Usually the local high school cheerleaders volunteer and have ample encouragement to pass along to the participants. This race is also walker friendly, with an early morning start.

Most of the race is along the coastline of Southern California. The view doesn't get much better than this. The sound of the ocean as you run long miles provides for a very nice experience, and the view provides some of the best scenery around. The ocean breeze feels wonderful. There are many local bands that come out and play along the course, and we all know that music is a great motivator as it picks up your spirits and lets you have some fun along the way.

The course is rolling (the highest elevation is 308 feet, which is gradually reached from miles five to nine). The Marathon begins at the Westfields Shopping Town Plaza Camino Real in Carlsbad. Runners head for the coast, passing the Buena Vista Lagoon by way of the village of Carlsbad to Highway 101 (Carlsbad Boulevard). From there, the course heads south on 101 to Palomar Airport Road. After running three miles inland, the course returns to the coast and south on 101 to a U-turn near La Costa Avenue. From there runners go back up the coast to the finish.

During the last few miles, many of the spectators, particularly kids, line the route with hard candy, oranges, and lemonade for the participants. Just to see them, wanting to give you a high five and a piece of candy, made those last few miles fun.

Aid stations are available at every single mile, something I absolutely loved. As a first time marathoner, it was great to know that every mile I would see a smiling, cheering face. Electrolyte replacement drinks were available at the aid stations, usually every other mile. That drink changes over the years, depending on the sponsors, I believe.

I have never been bored running or coaching this race. There are always the running Elvis's, someone running barefoot, and someone running backward. There are also armed forces running in their groups.

The race expo starts on Friday afternoon and continues on Saturday for the day. You can pick up your race packet and enjoy some great shopping. The expo also continues on Sunday so family members supporting participants can get in a little shopping at the expo, as well as at the mall, located in the same parking lot.

At the expo, there is a terrific selection of apparel with the Carlsbad Marathon logo on them, such as sweatshirts, singlets, t-shirts, hats, visors, polo shirts, etc. There are also a variety of vendors with new items on the market. This is where I buy my running shorts and singlets for the coming year, as the prices are the lowest anywhere in town or online. Anything you might want related to running is available.

On Saturday, there are many different events, something for everyone, at any fitness level. There is a kid's mile race for those who are age 12 and under. There are separate divisions, based on age, and different distances. Medals are provided for every finisher. Saturday also features one-mile races, for men and boys, women and girls. Medals are provided for the first three finishers in each age group. Saturday evening features a pasta party, which is great for carbo-loading.

I stayed at the Del Mar Hilton the first time I did this race in 1994. Now there are many closer places to choose from, including Inns of America Suites, Holiday Inn, Best Western, La Costa Resort, Hilton Garden Inn Carlsbad Beach, and Grand Pacific Palisades Resort. Most of the local accommodations will provide a late checkout for race participants.

What I liked most about the race the first time I ran it, was that it was in my hometown—perfect for a first time marathoner. I could train on the course as much or as little as I wanted. I could drive the course just about any time I wanted to help with my visualization of the race. The best part about the marathon for me was that all my family and friends could come out, and they did, to cheer me on at different locations.

This is an extremely spectator friendly course. There are many places for spectators to see the runners. Some spectators choose to stay in town, have breakfast, and step outside to the curb and cheer the runners on. Shuttle service is provided for spectators so they can get out to different parts of the race, cheer the runners on, and then catch the shuttle for a ride in to the finish line.

One friend rode her bike the last several miles alongside me rooting me on. Another friend ran several of the last miles with me. Another friend was at mile 20 with a fresh pair of socks for me. All of my family was at the finish line, and they surprised me by wearing t-shirts with my name on them and congratulations written across them. The race announcer was spectacular. He called out my name as I crossed the finish line, making the day even more memorable.

Finisher medals are provided for marathoners and half marathoners and age group medals for the top three finishers in each age group.

Carlsbad is a great place for a family vacation. The ocean is right at your back door and Legoland is nearby. Disneyland is up the road, and the San Diego Zoo is down the road. The world famous La Costa Resort is also in the area as is the Torrey Pines Golf Course.

The first time I ran this race, I was a member of The Leukemia & Lymphoma Society's, Team in Training®. My patient, a three-year-old girl, and her family, were also at the finish line. That was a very special moment for me. My friends also had a cooler with ice-cold beer in it so I could have a toast with them when I crossed the finish line (as I had chosen to abstain from beer during my training period). As soon as I crossed the finish line I was planning my next marathon.

I first ran this race because it was one of my life's goals. I joined The Leukemia & Lymphoma Society's Team in Training group and this was their featured race. I liked the idea of running for a patient, a child with leukemia. I knew that I would need motivation to keep going through the training. The idea that a child had leukemia and was fighting that battle provided the motivation for me to train for this race. There are now many charities that provide training for this particular race.

Pony Asher ran track and field in high school and then returned to running 20 years later for recreational, short distance runs. In 1994, she decided to tackle her dream of running a marathon and completed the Carlsbad Marathon (formerly called the San Diego Marathon). She was hooked, and during her third marathon, she qualified for the 100th Boston Marathon.

After a bad skiing accident in 1985, Pony was told she would never run again. "They" were wrong, and in 1996, Pony ran with the Olympic torch when it came through San Diego. Pony is a self-employed paralegal, and has been the assistant coach for several marathon training programs in the San Diego area. She lives with her husband of two years, and has three daughters and two granddaughters.

Mercedes Marathon

birmingham, alabama

Web site: www.mercedesmarathon.com
Month: February
USATF Certified: Yes
Course: Rolling

Author: Kristen Adelman
Number of Marathons Completed: 15
Age Group: 30-34

The Mercedes Marathon is a great event. The race is mid-sized (about 5,000 runners), it is well organized, the volunteers are superb, and the course is scenic and challenging.

The race takes place in February in Birmingham, Alabama. A friend of mine lives in Birmingham, which is how I learned of the race. There were no qualifications necessary to enter, and registration for the race is completed easily online.

I absolutely love a challenge. This is why I run marathons. So the Mercedes Marathon was a great race for me. February in Birmingham is a bit chilly and the temperature at the start was about 27°F. It did get into the 40s by the end, but it was definitely cold.

The course starts in downtown Birmingham and was gently rolling. The first hill was around mile six where there was a gradual incline along a four-lane highway. This highway was cut into a mountain, which made it very beautiful and the climb well worth it. Reaching the top meant a nice reward since a great downhill followed. People complained about the downhill, but I disagreed. It's nothing but fun to me, when you can let your legs just go, stretch out your stride, and let gravity do the work!

Following, were some mild ups and downs through mile 16. The course wound through the scenic campus of Samford University, which, according to their web site, is the largest independently supported university in the state of Alabama. There were also many beautiful Georgian colonial buildings that I really enjoyed seeing along the way.

Up to this point, there were numerous rumblings about a monster hill at mile 17. "How bad could it be?" I wondered to myself. Challenge is what it's all about! Finally, there it was. The infamous "monster" of a mountain, and actually quite worthy of the earlier remarks I'd heard! In fact, as I looked up, I can't even recall being able to see the top! I heard many discouraging remarks as people complained their way up the incline muttering how they couldn't understand how this could be a part of a race. I bit my lip and wondered, "Why wouldn't it be?" Please, put a mountain in my way and just watch me go right over it! I disregarded their discouraging remarks, put a smile on my face, and climbed step by step. I started with little steps, not looking up but right in front of my feet, and after about a mile of climbing, I reached the top.

There were plenty of spectators on this hill cheering us on and up. This truly helped a lot. Looking back, I'm glad this monster was there, and I'm glad it was tough. Isn't that what this is all about? Pushing ourselves past the point we think we can go? Fortunately, I was forewarned of this climb, and I am glad I was. It was good to have saved some energy for it.

As intimidating as the "monster" was, I still managed to glimpse the million dollar homes that lined its streets. They were amazing and this kept things interesting. There was an equally challenging descent to follow, but as I said before, just let gravity take over and enjoy the ride.

From mile 17 to mile 21, there were a considerable number of sharp climbs and descents. Not impossible by any means, but I definitely felt accomplished after getting through it. Especially since during the last five miles my feet cramped up and tried their best to lock in a twisted position. This made each step quite painful. In spite of the pain and fatigue I focused on the finish line.

I used to run races to win, to beat my last time and to beat anyone in my age group. That was the biggest thrill for me and that greatly motivated me. However, since ending a 2 1/2-year battle with Non-Hodgkin's Lymphoma just a year before this race, my focus changed entirely. I quickly learned to appreciate being a part of the race no matter what the time on the clock read at the end. Crossing the finish line alone represented a personal victory in itself, more so than any first place medal could have ever meant. When you are told more than once that you have less than a year to live and honestly believe you won't run again, perspectives change.

So whatever your reason for running, always hold it close and realize you are an absolute winner for even making the attempt. Another thing to remember is that race day is your day and your event, so enjoy every part of it.

The Mercedes Marathon provides excellent runner support every step of the way;

including plenty of aid on the course, water stops at almost every mile, medical tents, gels, oranges and a variety of other things. The post-race party was also really nice and they had plenty of food that everyone enjoyed.

The race expo was fair. There wasn't a lot of space and depending on what time people checked in, they might have experienced some long lines. Because I went in the evening, I had no trouble and everything went smoothly.

At the expo, there wasn't a lot of race merchandise to purchase; in fact there was only one apparel vendor there. It was a bit crowded and tough to get to see things. I did manage to get a very nice fleece jacket, which I wear proudly! There were some race day articles such as disposable jackets for race day morning, gels, gloves, socks, etc. All of the volunteers at the expo, just like on the course, were very friendly and helpful. So the expo, although only fair, accomplished what needed to be done.

On the other hand, I thought the race t-shirts they gave away were really great. All participants receive the official long sleeve t-shirt, and finishers receive an additional long sleeve running shirt.

The finisher's medal was absolutely gorgeous. It was a silver medallion with the Mercedes-Benz logo on it. Stunning, to say the least and definitely well earned and worth every step. As an added bonus, through a random drawing, one lucky marathon or half-marathon finisher walked away with a new Mercedes Benz M-Class!

Another unique thing about this race is that they let you switch between running the marathon and half marathon not only until the start of the race, but actually during the race. But, if you're reading this, then that's probably not an option for you!

While in Birmingham I stayed with my friend. However, if you don't know someone in town, there is a complete listing of hotels on the race web site.

Overall, I had a lot of fun. This was my 15th marathon, and I managed to finish in about four hours. This race is a Boston qualifier; however, I believe it would be challenging to PR here. To sum it up, if you are looking for a flat easy race to set a PR, this is not the right one. On the other hand, if you are looking for a race that is a top-notch event, fairly low key, very challenging, very rewarding — all sprinkled with a touch of southern hospitality — this is the one for you!

Kristen Adelman teaches Algebra, Science, and PE at an elementary school in Elkridge Maryland. She began running in 1997 and has been running ever since, even throughout her three-year battle with cancer. She has completed 15 marathons, several triathlons, as well as 8 ultras, one of which was a 100-mile trail run. Her focus now entails completing a marathon in every state, as well as many more ultras.

BI-LO Myrtle Beach Marathon

myrtle beach, south carolina

Web site: www.mbmarathon.com
Month: February
USATF Certified: Yes
Course: Flat

Author: David Glover
Number of Marathons Completed: 21
Age Group: 30-34

The Myrtle Beach marathon is a relatively small marathon with just under 1,000 participants on a flat, breezy course through the oceanside town of Myrtle Beach, South Carolina. The course route is a figure eight shape with two 13.1-mile sections (the first section is also the half marathon course which is run concurrently with the full marathon). There are no qualifications for entry in the race, but there are a limited number of race entry slots. In 2004, the marathon did not fill up ahead of time (I was able to register online within two weeks of the start), but the half marathon did fill up early. The marathon course is USATF certified and is a qualifier for the Boston Marathon. Because the race is in February, it's possible to qualify for Boston at Myrtle Beach then race Boston two months later. The race has a cutoff time of eight hours.

I think that this is a great marathon for runners of all experiences and any family they may bring along, as there is both a 1-mile fun run and 5K race the day before the marathon as well as the half marathon. The marathon also allows relay teams with up to five runners (5 transition points every 5 miles for the first 20 miles then a final leg of 6.2 miles to get to the full 26.2 miles). Three bicycle rides are being planned for future races, the day after the marathon. Because it's Myrtle Beach, there are also restaurants, shopping, miniature golf, and the beach to enjoy.

I had an unexpectedly fast race and a new PR! For me, the challenge of this race was to push through a reasonably fast time without having a solid running base.

My race stats:

- 13.1 Mile Split: 1:21:42
- Final Time: 2:53:31
- Place: Fourth OA, First AG
- Total Finishers: 1,148

The year had not started out too well for my training due to injury and bad weather. I had been nursing a sore left Achilles for many weeks which I think was caused by overstraining my Achilles tendon while running on ice/snow. It was a nagging injury that never seemed to get worse but just would not go away. Consequently, I had backed off my running volume quite a bit.

The decision to do this marathon (and the associated road trip from the Washington, D.C. suburbs to Myrtle Beach) was a last minute decision. My fiancée, Jennifer, had signed up to do the marathon relay with three other friends (Lindsey, Hope, and Cindy, AKA the "Tator Tots") and Lindsey's husband, Gary ("Velvet Elvis"), who was doing the half marathon. The women decided to go with a pink theme, so I wore a pink bandana during the race (I missed out on the pink Elvis t-shirts that everyone else was wearing).

About a week and a half before the marathon, I tried to sign up for the half marathon, but it was already full. Since I had committed to the seven-hour drive, I figured that I should probably at least run something more than just the 5K which left me with the option of the full marathon. I signed up for it thinking that the best thing about not really focusing on this race meant little pressure and low expectations.

I had been an active runner since high school (about 16 years). This was my fourth standalone marathon, but I had also completed 14 marathons as part of Ironman distance triathlons. My previous marathon PR was a 2:59 at the Walt Disney World Marathon.

We stayed in nearby Murrell's Inlet about a 15 minute drive south of Myrtle Beach. Given that Myrtle Beach was a beach town in the off season, beachfront hotels were readily (and cheaply) available if we had wanted to go that route.

Per the race web site, the average high temperature for February is 58°F and the average low is 38°F. Race morning in 2004 was windy and unseasonably warm, it was probably in the high 50s at the start then quickly warming up to the low 70s. I opted for running shorts and a race tank top, and I was quite comfortable while running although it was chilly standing around waiting for the race start. There were some very windy sections along the beach and the last long stretch toward the finish line seemed like it had a headwind the entire time.

I felt that the race was very well-organized from online registration to onsite packet pick-up to race day logistics. There was no race day packet pick up. The race expo at the host hotel was the site of packet pick-up for runner bib numbers and long sleeve t-shirts (bonus!). I felt the race expo was more than adequate. Marathon sponsors and merchandise vendors were represented with clothing, accessories, nutritional products, and free giveaways. Official marathon merchandise was available as well. If I had forgotten anything critical like shoes, they were available. There was a pre-race pasta dinner, which we did not attend, that was reasonably priced at $15.00 a person.

The race started at Coastal Federal Field (minor league baseball stadium) which was across the street from an outdoor mall so parking was not an issue. The runners had access to the stadium bathrooms although there were long lines. Port-a-Johns were also available at the Start/Finish and every two to three miles along the course. The Port-a-John that I stopped at near mile 16 was very clean and had not been previously used. This actually posed a problem when I stopped, because the toilet paper was still in its wrapper requiring an extra few seconds to get to the roll.

The race has a fun, low key atmosphere with a field of runners that thinned out relatively quickly in spite of the marathon and half marathon being run on the same course simultaneously. Because of the time of the year, it was dark close to race start. Crowding was never an issue. I placed myself about two rows back from the front at the start and did not experience the jostling typical of a larger race. Maybe there was a little bit of Southern hospitality in play, too.

BANG! I took off. Because the half marathoners started with the marathoners, it was difficult to see who was in what race unless you could see the race number on the front of their shirts. I ran with my heart rate monitor with the intent to try to hold a 6:30+/- pace for as long as possible. I felt reasonably comfortable with this level of effort at the beginning of the race. My pace and effort were fairly consistent for the first 18 miles with my pace dropping slightly lower in tail winds and creeping up higher in headwinds. The course was well-marked with mile markers at every mile.

During the race, Dasani water and lemon-lime POWERade sports drink were available approximately every two miles along the marathon course and at the finish. Food stations with gel were also available at miles 16 and 22 and at the finish. The aid stations were adequately staffed with volunteers, and I had no problems picking up food and drink as needed.

The course seemed very spectator friendly. Because the "Tator Tot" women were doing the marathon relay, the non-running legs had to drive to the different hand off points. The race provided maps for spectators to plan their driving routes and meeting points.

My split at the half marathon point was 1:21:42. At this point, I was thinking I could possibly break 2:45 and almost certainly break 2:50 even if I was forced to slow down a little (which seemed inevitable). I remember also thinking that the smart thing to do would be to stop now since my left Achilles tendon had been hurting since about mile six. I decided to keep going with the notion that I could always walk if I felt the need.

In the end it was not the "runner's wall" or "bonking" that slowed me down, but general muscular fatigue, a very sore Achilles tendon, and the associated discomfort of running 20+ miles on an inadequate volume base. Since the last five or six miles seemed to be in a steady head wind across a desolate highway of ugly asphalt and strip malls, the scenery did not help. This last straight section was definitely the most difficult and least enjoyable portion of the race for me.

There were a few runners gaining on me toward the end that I managed to hold off (the 5th place finisher was only 23 seconds back).

I somehow managed a vertical jump to touch the timing clock as I crossed the finish line. Another marathon finisher's medal! Awards were presented to the top three male and female BI-LO Myrtle Beach Marathon finishers in the age groups 19 & under, 20-24, 25-29, 30-34, 35-39, 40-44, 45-49, 50-54, 55-59, 60-64, 65-69, 70 & over. I received my finisher's certificates and official results about one month after the marathon. Results were also available online immediately following the race.

Overall, I had a great experience at the BI-LO Myrtle Beach Marathon and achieved a marathon PR. I would love to do the race again and would recommend it to anyone, especially a first timer who wants the comfort of a well run, flat race but not the large crowds.

David Glover lives in Reston, Virginia and works as a business analyst at Capital One. He lives with his dog, Princess, a deaf Dalmatian, on Lake Audubon where the Reston Triathlon is held in his backyard every year. An active runner in high school and college, David has completed 21 marathons, 17 of which were run as part of Iron-distance triathlons (2.4-mile swim, 112-mile bike, 26.2-mile run). He has a marathon PR of 2:53 and has finished in the top 10 overall 10 times in Iron-distance triathlons, including four overall wins. He is also a five-time USA Triathlon All-American.

Blue Angel Marathon

pensacola, florida

Website:
www.naspensacola.navy.mil/mwr/current/bam2000/bam_2004.htm
Month: February
USATF Certified: Yes
Course: Flat

Author: Hope Hall
Number of Marathons Completed: 7
Age Group: 35-39

M y father was an avid runner. He took up running when cigarettes were forcibly removed from his list of consumables. Running was the healthy habit by-product from his self-devised smoking cessation program. I still have the framed photo of him grimacing through his first marathon in the mid-80s. He was my distance guru, and I took as law all running advice issued from his lips.

My dad once told me that you only have to train half as far as you intend to race. Let me say that again: You only have to train half as far as you intend to race. Train 13, race 26. Sounds great! He may not recall telling me this if you pressed him about it today. He's much wiser now. But, for whatever reason, this one fleeting comment struck a chord and made me believe running a marathon was possible. Now, this preparation scheme may work well if your goal is a 5K or maybe even a 10K, but as it turns out, running only 13 miles before your first marathon is a really, really bad training plan. It was this philosophy I embraced for my very first attempt at the 26.2-mile distance at the Blue Angel Marathon.

My friend, co-worker, and eventual training partner, Debbie, was a collegiate swimmer. I was a collegiate gymnast. I was 24 years old and Debbie was 23. To say that we were new to distance running would be a grave understatement. I once read that gymnasts, while strong and quick, have greater endurance than only two sets of athletes: marksmen and yachtsmen. If you ever watch Wide World of Sports, you know that gymnasts breathe hard after a two-minute floor exercise routine! Running 26 miles is out of the question. For swimmers, speed and agility in the water does not always translate into running aptitude. Ask a group of high school swimmers what "punishment" their coaches devise and running may just be the answer. But, what Debbie and I lacked in experience, we made up for in tenacity. We were both in for a rude awakening.

Debbie and I were Naval officers, stationed at a helicopter squadron in Mayport, Florida. We had always been involved in sports and missed the camaraderie of collegiate athletics. To combat the onset of a sedentary lifestyle, one in which you reminisce about the "good ole days" when you were young, fit, and stood atop the podium, we began running together. I think it was probably Debbie's idea to run a marathon. She was a classic overachiever, good at everything, and I was easily swayed. We looked around for available races, talked to some of the pilots in our squadron and decided that the Blue Angel Marathon was the one to do. We were both familiar with Pensacola, and we knew it was the very definition of FLAT. At the time, this race was still relatively small, but was heavily attended by members of the Armed Forces. In fact, it was and still is the Official Marathon of the Navy. Debbie's husband, Pete, was going through Naval flight school, so we had a free place to stay. When you're young and fresh out of college, free is good!

Debbie and I now had our target race and we started to get semi-serious about our training. I don't think we ever wrote anything down, we never had a well-defined plan of attack and we both banked on my dad's methodology being accurate. I had never heard of Jeff Galloway or his book on running. Fartlek was just a funny word to me. And the only speed work I incorporated was chasing a poorly thrown Frisbee on the beach. We just ran. Every morning, as sure as the sunrise, Debbie and I ran along the Jacksonville beaches. We figured out a nine-mile out and back course and rarely deviated from this regiment. On the weekends, we upped the mileage to 13 miles, following Dad's sage advice. Using his methodology, after three months of this schedule, we figured we were more than ready for a marathon. But, we were young and naïve and terribly under trained. Of course, we would not come to realize the flaw in our training strategy until race day.

Like I said, the marathon was held in late-February. If this were Chicago, New York, or Boston, February would be reserved for long hours at the local pub. But, this was Florida, the Sunshine State. The temperature for this time of year is typically in the low 60s and absolutely perfect for running. In fact, the race web site says that they have NEVER had rain on race day! The course is USATF certified and is a qualifier for the Boston Marathon.

While it draws a large military contingent, the Blue Angel is open to the public and provides an opportunity to take an up-close tour of an operational Naval base. Did I mention that the course is flat? There is a hill on the course in the form of a bridge, which is crossed twice during the marathon. Other than that one feature,

Courtesy of Blue Angel Marathon

this coastal course is very forgiving for those of us who entered somewhat un-indoctrinated. The racecourse weaves its way through the Pensacola Naval Air Station before entering the downtown Pensacola area. At the time that I ran the race, the "running for a cause" boom had not yet struck, so the field was rather small and the course wasn't exactly lined with cheering spectators.

Today, the Blue Angel Marathon field numbers about 600 runners, which is large enough to have company throughout the race but still small enough to get personal attention by the volunteers and race organizers. If you desire a race with a hometown feel, look no further than Blue Angel. I don't recall attending a race expo the year I ran, but knowing the precision of Naval Aviators, I would wager that the Blue Angel expo is top-notch, top gun, complete with well-known vendors and a carb-loading dinner before the race.

Debbie and I toed the line on a slightly overcast but warm February morning wearing cotton t-shirts and running shoes boasting 13 miles as the longest distance traveled. I remember not having a full appreciation (or fear) of the event I was about to undertake. Debbie and I ran together, laughing and joking as we always did in our training runs. The early miles of the race passed without incident and we settled into a rhythm we told ourselves would carry us through to the finish line. Appreciation of the marathon discipline didn't settle in until about mile 18. This was the part of the race where I first started to question my dad's training advice. He had fibbed about Santa and the Tooth Fairy. Had he just played a huge joke on me? My legs ached, and I was beginning to wish I had a few more long runs under my belt.

Eight more miles seemed like an insurmountable distance, and I was ready to unlace my running shoes and call it a day. If it weren't for Debbie, I probably would have. I began to understand the bond training partners share. We had gotten up early every morning, shared secrets, made up songs, taken potty breaks behind the sand dunes, and convinced ourselves that we each had a marathon runner in us. The pace slowed and we plodded along, speaking to each other only in a series of grunts. We took whatever the volunteers manning the waning miles' aid stations passed to us. I recall thinking that the volunteers got t-shirts, too, and this might have been a better role for me to play. I was fairly certain I could hand out water to runners for several hours without "hitting the wall."

The final three miles of the marathon are a little fuzzy in detail. When the finish chute finally appeared in front of us, I was more than ready to be finished. I remember a volunteer pulling the tag off my number (way before timing chips were in vogue) and giving me an encouraging pat on the back. This was plenty congratulations for me. I had just completed my first marathon, and I knew it was not going to be my last.

Debbie, Pete, and I made our way as quickly as possible to the nearest Shoney's Big Boy. We had talked extensively about Shoney's during the marathon. It's amazing what a motivator pancakes can be. I slept like a baby that night. When I returned home to Jacksonville the day after the race, I immediately put the Blue Angel Marathon poster up in my tiny apartment. For years, it served as a reminder of several lessons learned:

- Always consult sources outside of family for advice.
- You make your best friends when working to achieve a common goal.
- Running is as social as golf.
- Deviations from the norm can produce wonderful and unexpected results.
- Nothing on the planet beats a plate of syrup-drenched pancakes.

Hope Hall is a 38-year-old Construction Manager for Nextel Communications in Reston, Virginia. She was a competitive gymnast at the United States Naval Academy in Annapolis, Maryland. She discovered her passion for long-distance running and triathlon in the early 1990s and plans to continue competing until they run out of age groups. She has completed seven marathons and seven Iron-distance triathlons.

Napa Valley Marathon

napa, california

Web site: www.napa-marathon.com
Month: March
USATF Certified: Yes
Course: Rolling

Author: Valentine Pisarski "SKI"
Number of Marathons Completed: 101
Age Group: 60-64

The Napa Valley Marathon is held on the first Sunday in March and traverses the Valley from Calistoga to Napa, California. It is a fully-certified USATF course. It is also an extremely beautiful and scenic course, and is well suited for the first-time marathon runner, or the seasoned veteran. The event headquarters, host hotel (The Napa Valley Marriott Hotel and Spa), expo, number pick-up, and finish line are located in north Napa. Runners are transported by bus from Napa to the start line at Calistoga. Entries are now limited to 2,400, and are usually sold out by early January. The only requirements to qualify for entry are your signature on the waiver attesting to your medical condition (and maybe mental also) and payment of the entry fee.

Event organizers Rich Benyo, Gard Leighton, and David Hill and their committee have done a superb overall job. The expo is small, but covers all runners' pre-race requirements and has a very diverse offering of products and literature.

The Napa Valley Marathon Pasta Dinner serves a very good pre-race meal and includes presentations on the course and some well-known motivational speakers. If you are staying in or near the host hotel, the dinner is worth the investment and probably costs about the same or a bit less than one of the many fine restaurants in the area.

The Napa Valley Marathon has had a number of different types of t-shirts, from short sleeve cotton and 50/50 to long sleeve dri-fit. Each year the committee provides each registered participant with a very nice carrying case, backpack, or running travel bag filled with some smaller goodies, such as a lapel pin and sponsors items. All finishers receive a very nice medal.

The Napa Valley Marathon presents what they call the Napa Valley Marathon College, and throughout the day on Saturday they present seminars at the host hotel. Members of the College Faculty include Dick Beardsley (course record holder and 4th fastest U.S. men's marathoner ever), Joe Henderson (author and writer for Runner's World), and Helen Klein (world age-group record holder). Other various running experts join in on the presentations, and give runners there for the complete marathon weekend something to digest.

If you don't have an interest in the entire marathon hullabaloo, then I would certainly suggest a tour of a few of the superb wineries in the valley. This may not enhance your performance during the event, but will certainly avail you to some of the finest wines in the world and definitely enrich your visit to the beautiful Napa Valley.

The host hotel is normally the Napa Valley Marriott Hotel and Spa, but it is usually sold out in early December. However, the Hilton Garden Inn is located immediately adjacent to the Marriott, and is generally about $35.00 per night less. Accommodations are also located up and down the Napa Valley for rates anywhere from $69.00-$500.00 per night. Many runners chose to stay in Calistoga, so they can walk to the start. There is a Comfort Inn within easy walking distance of the start. However, there is no transportation available from the finish line to return you to the start. For more reasonable accommodations, there is a group of budget motels on I-80 near the Highway 12 turn off to Napa. The community of Suisun has several reasonably priced motels. They are all within a 30-minute drive of Napa on race day morning.

Along the course there are three portable toilets at each of the 12 aid stations, but as is usually the case, they will not be where you need them. Although there are no gel energy replacement stations along the course, most of the later aid stations do have pretzels, oranges slices, bananas, and/or pieces of candy. At about 23.2 miles, a friendly bed and breakfast, the Oak Knoll Inn, passes out mini-paper cups of sorbet. The aid stations in general are very well run and their spacing seems to be just about right. All of the volunteers greet you with a smile and seem to be happy to be helping.

Friends, family, and supporters can reach the course at many easily accessible crossroads from Highway 29, which runs parallel with the course anywhere from two to five miles to the west of the Silverado Trail. Seeing your runner two or three times along the course is easily within reach.

During its first 27 years of production, the Napa Valley Marathon has covered the same course without change. Some people are inclined to say change is good, but when you have a great course to begin with, why make any changes?

The course is very user friendly. From its start in Calistoga to its finish at Vintage High School on the north side of Napa, the course is dotted with some world renowned wineries. It is also dotted with several small hills. The first 22.8 miles of the course are run on the Silverado Trail. The course drops 331 feet in elevation, has several gentle turns, and is quite undulating for the first 21 miles. The ups and downs are not severe, and thus give the different muscle groups in one's legs time to share the effort. Though some of the hills seem to be quite steep (this may be the case for the extreme flatlander), they are really just part of the beautiful terrain of one of the greatest grape growing and wine producing areas in the world. The largest hill appears to be from mile 19 to mile 20. When you are running (or walking) this portion of the course, the degree of difficulty of the 19-20 mile hill is certainly multiplied. After having run the course on 18 occasions, and having driven it several other times, I believed that the 19-20 mile hill was relatively significant. However, on the day after my wedding in 2003, we took a bike ride along that portion of the course, and during the ride up this hill, I noted very little effort was required. I now believe that the 19-20 mile hill is really quite insignificant in grade, just a bit long for bewildered legs.

During the first 13 miles, up to Highway 128, the runners can run on the entire width of the road. So don't hesitate running the tangents. From about mile 13 through mile 22.8, runners are restricted to running on the right side of the Silverado Trail. As you turn off of the Silverado Trail and wind your way to the finish, you once again have the entire road on which to run.

The course profile is certainly very friendly, and is highly recommended for the first time marathon runner. Oh, by the way, this event is for runners only, and has a 5:30 time limit.

Start time is at 7:00 a.m. The Fahrenheit temperature at the start is generally in the 40s. I have seen it as cool as 33°F and as warm as 50°F. The high temperature by noon is normally near 60°F, but I have seen it reach 75°F on one occasion. The threat of precipitation is about one in seven, but don't try to fool with Mother Nature, and certainly don't count on the National Weather Service. Of the 20 times I have run the event, it has rained significantly only once, and the other two times the precipitation was more of a light drizzle. On that one stormy day, the rain was persistent throughout the event, heavy and in sheets at times. There were 30 to 50 mile per hour headwinds, and there was abundant thunder and lighting. During my jaunt up the 19-20 mile hill, a bolt of lighting struck a power pole just to my right producing an adrenaline surge that reduced my time by a minute or two.

The first time I ran the Napa Valley Marathon, I intended to use it as tune up for a May marathon. I planned on running a leisurely nine minute training pace. However, at the 19-20 mile hill I was still quite fresh. So I decided to push a little to get in a good workout. I ran the 19-20 mile hill in under seven minutes, and cruised to the finish in 3:21. I must admit that last three miles were very tough, even though they were flat. I was quite surprised at how easy the course seemed on that March Sunday in 1985. Since that event, I have enjoyed each of my additional 19 Napa Valley Marathons.

My most memorable Napa Valley Marathon was the year I chased the phantom to the finish. We started on an ideal weather day, about 38°F, mostly sunny, and a very light breeze. I was running with a training partner. At about seven miles, we were passed by a young woman I would eventually end up marrying about 10 years later. As she cruised through the course ahead, I thought it would be nice to catch up with her and run the final 15 miles or so together. So at about 11 miles I picked up my pace significantly and the chase was on. By mile 15, I came upon a friend that was waiting along the course to join the run with another friend. I asked if he had seen the young lady I was trying to catch. He stated he had not seen her, so I then assumed that she was having a Personal Record (PR) type day. I again picked up my pace in an effort to make the catch. But it turned out to be a Catch-22. I finished the marathon in 3:04 on that perfect day, and never made "the catch." As it turned out, she had ducked into a roadside toilet near 13 miles, and I had unknowingly passed her at that point. The phantom pacer pulled me to my fastest Napa Valley Marathon. Even though the official race committee rules say that pacers are not allowed, no one says you can't chase your dream, and still run a course best time or PR. The "biggest little marathon in the West" has been the PR for many a runner, and there are many good reasons to run your best there.

This course could be rated as one of the five fastest I've ever run. My best time at the Napa Valley Marathon is 3:04, but I have also cruised to a very pleasant 4:22 finish. The cruiser pace is much more enjoyable, and gives you the time to absorb the beauty of the valley. I ran my first ever marathon here in 1985, and my 100th in 2004. The beauty of this course ranks right at the top with Rotorua, New Zealand.

Since 1985, I have completed 101 marathons, with Napa Valley being my first, 100th, and 101st. I have run the Boston Marathon on 16 occasions, and have been coaching marathon runners since 1988. In the realm of marathon running, Boston is one of those events that everyone would like to run, but they do not have a lottery and the qualifying standards are not always achievable for all of us. If I was given a choice as to which one marathon I would like to complete, it would certainly be the Napa Valley Marathon. It is just a great marathon course, set in a beautiful location, run by a down to earth organizing committee, without all of the high octane participants. That suits the average or middle and back of the pack runner to a tee.

Valentine Pisarski "SKI" is a 60-year-old retired Air Traffic Control Specialist from Reno, Nevada, who continues to run marathons and coach marathon runners. He began running marathons in 1985, has run the Napa Valley course 20 times, and plans to continue as long as he's able.

Ocean Drive Marathon

cape may, new jersey

Web site: www.odmarathon.org
Month: March
USATF Certified: Yes
Course: Flat

Author: Todd Katz
Number of Marathons Completed: 6
Age Group: 35-39

I was all set and my fitness level was exactly at the point where I had an outside shot at qualifying for Boston. I was supposed to run the 2nd Annual Washington D.C. Marathon. However, on the Thursday before the race, officials from H2O Entertainment, the race company for the short lived D.C. Marathon, cancelled the event. The problem for me and about 5,000 other runners was what to do? Most of us had been training diligently all winter to run a marathon. Not only did I want to run, but I was looking to qualify for Boston. My goal that Thursday afternoon was to find another race within one week, because I didn't want to lose any fitness due to a longer than expected tapering process.

I checked online and found there was a race not too far away from my hometown in Reston, Virginia. It was in Frederick, Maryland and only about a 30–40 minute drive. I should have signed up immediately. Within two hours of the cancellation of the D.C. marathon, this race filled up, and I missed the boat. The next closest alternative was Ocean Drive. A race that starts in Cape May, New Jersey and runs in a point to point fashion north through a variety of little beach towns and settings. I quickly signed up, fearing another race closure.

As it turns out, the Ocean Drive Marathon had a huge influx of people, and although I think it caught the officials a little off guard, it remained very well organized. The cancellation of the D.C. Marathon proved to be a big talking item during the expo and pasta dinner. I must have met a half a dozen people at the race who were in the same situation as me.

The Ocean Drive Marathon is a very scenic and fairly flat course that starts out in Cape May, New Jersey and runs north to Sea Isle City. Unfortunately, the weather gods were not with me and there were 25 mph head winds for about 20 miles.

There is a two-mile stretch where you run on the deserted Wildwood Crest boardwalk. Runners who grew up on the East Coast and spent any time at the Jersey shore may feel some kind of nostalgic moments while running along this isolated stretch. There is always something peaceful about the ocean, the beach, and the boardwalk. What is it in our minds that fully loves the beach scene in the summer? I found that the beach in the winter is just as peaceful. Even an isolated beach and an isolated boardwalk conjure up memories of my youth. This section of the course was fun to run, and easy on the feet. It also had the largest number of spectators since it was also the finish for the concurrent 10-miler. As you continue your run, the runners and the spectators look on with awe because the pace you're running is the same as many people running the shorter 10 miles. The crowd at this point gives you a little shot of energy.

The race actually felt a little more like an average size 10K. There were only about 800 people in the race, and I'd say almost half of them were doing the concurrently sponsored 10-mile event. As stated previously, the weather on this particular race day was almost the worst you can get for a race. Extreme heat is probably the worst, but after that, hard rain and heavy headwinds are a close second.

We lined up right on Ocean Drive in Cape May in the pouring rain. There were puddles everywhere, and I tried as hard as I could to keep my feet dry. After about five miles it didn't matter. The sloshing couldn't be avoided, and I didn't waste any effort missing puddles. The first five miles weren't so bad because I found a guy who was about a foot taller than me and running the pace I was looking for. Perfect. I just tucked right behind him and let him cut the wind for me. A few other people had the same idea and before I knew it we had a nice little pack of runners all shooting for the magic 3:15 (my age group's qualifying time for the Boston Marathon). So we just clicked off 7:20 miles, just slightly ahead of pace. Then at mile six, the roof caved in. The wind picked up and took the sails out of our six-foot-nine inch wind-blocking friend. We went through mile six in just over eight minutes. I knew I'd have to ditch the group if I wanted to stay on pace. I took off by myself, but the wind was inescapable.

I ended up running the next few miles with a couple of 10-mile participants. As I mentioned, the best part of this race is running along the Wildwood Crest boardwalk. Very cool! It's only about 2 1/2 miles, but it was a nice little distraction to traditional street running.

After the 10-mile mark, it got lonely. I saw a couple of runners ahead of me that I eventually caught around mile 22, but essentially from mile 10 until mile 26 I ran alone. The volunteers were braver than the runners this day. There was no way for them to stay warm and dry, yet they remained helpful and friendly.

I spent the time focused on my pace and tried to maintain even 7:20 to 7:25 miles. At mile 22, I was on pace, but then the wind got even stronger. It became a struggle to maintain an 8:00 minute mile. I knew at mile 25 that a 3:15 would not to be achieved this day. I finished in 3:18:36 which was good enough for 13th place overall, and although I didn't qualify for Boston, I knew that I had given every ounce of energy my body had to go for it. I am proud to say that despite the bad weather, I finished with a 12-minute personal record. I knew that Boston qualifying times would be attainable another day.

The scenery was what I most enjoyed about this race. It was a beautiful course, and I would love to go back and run it again. In addition to the ocean and the boardwalk, the course goes over several inland bridges. It's a classic beach atmosphere and the scenery is very nice.

I also enjoyed the pasta dinner. For such a small race, I wasn't really expecting that much, however, of all the pasta dinners I've attended (Boston, Chicago to name a few) this was the nicest one with the best food. I think I went back for thirds.

The course is also great for spectators. It's easy for friends and family to get in their cars and drive north several times in the race to cheer you on. My wife, who is probably the most directionally-challenged person on earth, found it easy to get around and she did it with our 2-year-old daughter and my 60-year-old father.

The registration process was fast and efficient. I registered online and it was straightforward. The expo was held in a small high school gymnasium that was probably built in the late 1940s or 50s. It was another nice piece of nostalgia. Everything else about this race was small and well organized.

I stayed in Cape May near the start of the race. However, my recommendation is to stay near the finish area. The starting area is easy to reach if you have someone to drop you off, since there is very little hassle with road closures. The one change I think would be an improvement to the race would be to change the direction of the race and end in Cape May.

I love the location of this race. We drove up from Virginia the Friday before the race. It took about five hours to get there and we got a little lost, but it's definitely one of those nice out-of-the-way destinations that have a lot of character. Instead of driving back the whole way, we took the ferry out of Cape May, which dropped us off in Lewes, Delaware. The sea was a little rough, but it was a great experience.

Todd Katz is a Senior Manager at Nextel Communications in Reston, Virginia, where he runs a performance engineering organization. Todd was an ice hockey player for over 20 years before turning his attention to running. A member of the Reston Runners, Todd, who competes in the 35-39 year age group, has run in six marathons with a time of 3:18 at Ocean Drive and a personal best of 3:02 at Columbus. In addition to running, Todd loves spending time with his wife Melissa and daughters Gaby and Calleigh.

Shamrock Sportsfest Marathon

virginia beach, virginia

Web site: www.shamrockmarathon.com
Month: March
USATF Certified: Yes
Course: Flat

Author: Tamra Hall
Number of Marathons Completed: 3
Age Group: 45-49

Author: Gary Euliss
Number of Marathons Completed: 11
Age Group: 45-49

"May the shamrock winds always be at your back" are some of the last words you will hear from the announcer as the starting gun signals that the Shamrock Marathon is underway. The notice served by this final salutation is that winds can be a significant factor in a race that is otherwise described as flat and fast.

The Shamrock Marathon is an annual event run in the family-oriented resort city of Virginia Beach, Virginia. The race was ranked among the top 20 marathons in the country by *Runner's World,* and is one of the oldest marathons in the area. The race has been run for more than 30 years.

The marathon is part of the Shamrock Sportsfest, which includes the very competitive Checkered Flag 8K in which three world records have been set. There is also a marathon walk, two-person marathon relay, children's marathon (26.2 yards), and children's one mile fun run—all on the same morning. This creates a family atmosphere with something for all ages and fitness levels. As the name implies, the event has an Irish theme and is held in the spring near St. Patrick's Day, typically on the third Saturday in March. However, Irish ancestry is certainly not necessary to appreciate the fanfare surrounding the event. Many runners don festive attire to show their green. Kermit the Frog has even been spotted running at what can only be described as a competitive pace for someone in a full frog costume. The potential embarrassment of losing to a frog can provide a lot of motivation.

The experience of managing a successful event for over 30 years is evident in the race organization. The registration and packet pick-up process is usually quick and easy. The race atmosphere is fun, but mostly very laid back and relaxing. As a mid-sized race, the field of marathon runners is typically no more than a couple of thousand which means that most runners will have no problem finding the camaraderie many of us seek to help us through a marathon. On the other hand, the problems that can be encountered in much larger races, particularly at the starting line, will not be found. No qualification is required and in previous years the race has not filled up. Runners can typically register right up to and including the day before the race, eliminating the pressure to make a commitment several months in advance, all contributing to a great event for first-time marathoners.

Virginia Beach is a popular vacation destination with all the amenities that typically accompany a resort town. There is no shortage of lodging and since this time of year is considered the off-season, look for bargains at beachfront hotels. The weather in March is generally not ideal for the usual summertime beach recreation, but afternoon temperatures are typically warm enough for other activities like walking on the beach and building sandcastles. There are lots of restaurants—some with all you can eat buffets—to load up before the race, or replenish the body and soul after.

The weekend begins on Friday with the Shamrock Sports and Fitness Extravaganza, an expo held in conjunction with registration and packet pick-up that is also open on the day of the race. It is boasted to be one of the largest associated with East Coast races. At the expo, you can find a wide selection of fitness apparel and other accessories, including some last minute items such as hats, gloves, and nutrition supplies for race day. A local artist creates a poster for the race each year that makes a very nice, inexpensive souvenir that can also be purchased at the expo to go along with the (usually long-sleeved) t-shirt you will receive at packet pick-up. Race day events conclude with an evening post-race party, with a live band and dancing if you have the energy. Rumor has it that the post-race party is a fun event, but we have never ventured back out after hot showers and a seafood dinner. Opting instead for March Madness which provides an alternative post-race activity for basketball fans. Best of all, the crowds that converge on the resorts during the summer months are nowhere to be found. So consider arriving early, bringing the family, and spending the weekend.

If you do not like logging a lot of miles in the summer heat, a March marathon is a good option. This was a factor that motivated both of us to pick this race for our marathon debuts, albeit in different years. The race is also spaced conveniently on the calendar to avoid conflicting with several of the marquee races in the region held in the fall, including the Marine Corps and New York City Marathons, as well as the Chicago Marathon. More serious competitors might want to consider using this race as a tune up in their final preparations for the Boston Marathon a few weeks later. Or, if still seeking that qualifying spot for Boston, Shamrock serves as a flat, fast qualifier. However, because the race is run so late in the year with respect to the Boston Marathon, qualification must be applied to the following year's race.

Weather often defines a marathon experience and may be the only thing a runner remembers, particularly if it is bad. Virginia Beach has a relatively mild climate owing to the city's location near the ocean. The weather can vary considerably this time of the year, however. In the seven combined years that we have entered and completed this race, we have seen starting Fahrenheit temperatures ranging from the 40s to the high 70s, and light rain as well as brilliant sunshine. Temperatures at the finish can approach 90°F, although that is unusual. The start time was moved up a couple of years ago in response to a particularly hot day the previous year that took a toll on a number of participants. More often than not, however, the weather is ideal for running—dry, temperatures in the 50s, and tolerable winds coming off the ocean. Nonetheless, it is highly advisable to check the weather forecast and come prepared for a range of conditions.

Have we mentioned that this course is flat? An out and back that generally follows the geography of the Atlantic Ocean and the Chesapeake Bay shorelines, Shamrock is likely to be one of the flattest courses you will ever experience. So this is a good opportunity to hook up with one of the pace groups, and take a shot at clocking a personal record.

Traditionally, the race has started and finished at the Virginia Beach Pavilion located a few blocks from the ocean. The Pavilion is convenient and provides shelter, but it is just a convention center and certainly not a highlight of the course. In 2005, race organizers changed to an oceanfront start with the finish line located at the boardwalk—a move we view as an improvement. This course description does not reflect those changes. From the Pavilion, the course heads directly to the south end of the boardwalk. "Boardwalk" is a misnomer in this case, since the entire length is actually concrete. The city of Virginia Beach has invested significant effort over the last decade to renovate the tourist area along the beach and create a family-oriented vacation destination. Results of these efforts can be seen as the course proceeds north along the boardwalk. The ocean view dominates the scenery along the approximately four-mile section of boardwalk. Dolphins can often be sighted along this stretch of ocean, as well as large ships heading to and from ports via the nearby mouth of the Chesapeake Bay. Some may find this section to be rather harsh because of the hard surface, but the scenery serves as a nice distraction.

As mentioned, Virginia Beach is a tourist town, and this event draws visitors during an otherwise slow time of the year. So local support for the race is strong with residents turning out both to watch the race as well as volunteer. Some water stops are manned by local groups and the race organizers provide a reward for the water stop voted by race participants to be the best. Volunteers are motivated and enthusiastic with themed costumes, decorations, and inspirational music. Special treats like gummy bears and salty pretzels can usually be found along the course. Unofficial "aid stations" have even been known to offer a beer to any runner so inclined. Official stations provide water and sports drink about every two miles, with items such as energy gel packs at select stations later in the race. Medical attention is available to help deal with unexpected issues from blisters to dehydration, or in the event of a more serious problem.

The racecourse leaves the north end of the boardwalk and rejoins Atlantic Avenue. The stretch of four-lane road is shared with vehicular traffic for the next few miles, although the far right lane is restricted to runners only. At the north end of Atlantic Avenue, the course makes a turn to the left and onto Shore Drive. Proceeding along the tree-lined section of Shore Drive, runners are treated to the entire westbound side of the divided roadway and some of the only shade they will find during the race. The flavor of the course changes dramatically after making a right-hand turn into historic Fort Story. Runners are now fully exposed to the sun and the wind that often accompany this race. On an unseasonably warm day, this is where the heat can become a factor. Entry into the fort is strictly controlled, which tends to limit the number of spectators. But depending on your pace, this is also where many runners will begin meeting the race leaders on their way back to the finish followed by a steady stream of other participants—an advantage of out-and-back courses. Runners are treated to views of the original Cape Henry lighthouse as they pass through the fort. The old lighthouse is located on the shore of the Chesapeake Bay and began operating around 1792. The replacement for the old lighthouse was built in 1881 and can also been seen nearby. Runners proceed all the way through the fort, exiting briefly from the gate at the opposite end. Without access to the fort, this offers the only opportunity for most spectators to see the runners near the halfway point of the race as they make the turnaround and begin the return trip back through the fort.

Most of the out-and-back course is accessible with the exception of the section passing through Fort Story. Spectators can find a number of good vantage points reachable by walking or driving. Speaking from experience, bicycles work well as transportation to various locations on the course. A paved bike path runs the length of the boardwalk and can be used to follow the race. The section along Shore Drive is a nice ride as long as you use caution around the runners. Anywhere along the boardwalk is a good option for spectators on foot. Be sure to bring a camera and take advantage of the photo opportunities provided by the ocean backdrop as the runners pass by on the boardwalk. For less ambitious spectators who prefer a more relaxed approach to watching the race, the boardwalk is lined with ocean view cafes and snack shops for a respite from the occasional inclement weather as well as an opportunity to get coffee and a pastry, or lunch. Window-shopping along Atlantic Avenue is another way to pass the time as you wait for runners to return, or stroll out on the Virginia Beach pier. But you should make your way to the finish line area well in advance to enjoy the party before your runners arrive. Because, as we know, the rest of the day will have to be all about them!

Perhaps the best testimonial for any marathon is provided by answering the question: Would you do it again? Needless to say, with eight finisher's medals either displayed or stashed away in various places at our house, we think this one is worth repeating. May the luck of the Irish be with you!

Tamra Hall was introduced to running when her husband strapped a heart rate monitor to her and proclaimed "You will run." Ten plus years of happy marriage and many miles later, she has three marathons and numerous triathlons under her belt. Her weekends are spent running, biking, and socializing with friends in the Reston Runners.

Gary Euliss is strictly a middle-of-the-pack runner and has been running marathons for nine years, beginning with the Shamrock Marathon in 1996. He is also a recreational triathlete and enjoys hiking and backpacking with his wife Tamra. An active member of the Reston Runners, Gary can usually be found running with the club on weekends near his home in Northern Virginia.

Bataan Memorial Death March

white sands missile range, new mexico

Web site: www.bataanmarch.com
Month: March
USATF Certified: No
Course: Challenging

Author: Jim Eckles
Number of Marathons Completed: 1
Age Group: 50-54

I am not a distance runner, but there is one marathon I have always wanted to do. It is the Bataan Memorial Death March held annually at White Sands Missile Range in southern New Mexico.

As an employee at the missile range, I have worked the event for years. Watching the thousands of marchers and runners each year only made me want to be part of the group, to share that special camaraderie that accompanies a really special event.

Last year, I asked for the day off so I could enter. Permission was granted.

I run for fitness, but I knew my four to five miles every few days wasn't going to cut it. So, I decided to walk it.

This marathon is unusual because of the theme and the terrain. It started out as a march sponsored by the ROTC unit at New Mexico State University in 1989 to honor a special group of World War II military personnel who suffered and died at the hands of the Japanese in the Philippines.

These soldiers were responsible for defending the islands of Corregidor and Luzon as well as the harbor defense forts of the Philippines. Among the tens of thousands of personnel surrendered to the Japanese on April 9, 1942, by General McArthur, was the 200th Coast Artillery, New Mexico National Guard.

45

These soldiers survived on a fraction of normal rations, in a malaria-infested region with outdated equipment and very limited medical help. After the surrender, the soldiers were marched through the Philippine jungle for days in devastating heat. Thousands of soldiers died. Others were wounded. Those who survived went on to the hardship of prison camps.

In 1992, the White Sands Missile Range and the New Mexico National Guard became sponsors of the event and it was moved to the White Sands Missile Range for better support. Over the years, the course was tinkered with until it was stretched and bent to its present 26.2-mile route through the desert. The event has grown as well. White Sands now caps the event at 4,000 participants.

Because it is a tribute to WWII veterans, the event starts with a military ceremony recalling their sacrifice. Present are several survivors of the Bataan forced march of 1942. Many of these same men sit at the finish line and shake hands with participants, thanking them for remembering. It'll give you goose bumps—even after finishing 26.2 miles.

The event has all kinds of categories for entrants split between military and civilian participants. There are the usual age blocks but teams can also compete and there is a special "Heavy" category. In the Heavy division marchers and runners wear 35-pound packs, combat boots, and fatigues over the course.

It is very impressive to see a team of five guys (and some women) running through the desert in the heavy category helping each other to the finish line. They are required to finish together and they will encourage, pull, and even carry a weak member to get there.

I ran into one heavy team that used short ropes with handles and clips to assist anyone in the group having trouble. They hooked two ropes to a person's pack with a strong runner on each side. The three would then jog along with the other two members offering encouragement. Then they would trade out.

This event has become a way for many participants to honor relatives. At the starting line, I stood behind two women dressed in matching t-shirts. The shirts had a picture of the same man but a slightly different message under it. One shirt said, "In honor of my father ...." The other said, "In honor of my grandfather...." They were a mother and daughter marching together.

Nearby, I noticed a team of adults and youngsters from a small New Mexico town. All of the members wore matching shirts that proclaimed they were marching to pay tribute to their community minister who had survived the Bataan march in 1942.

Because of this aspect of the race, there are probably more walkers than runners on the route. It means I didn't stand out like a sore thumb in my cruise through the course.

I knew I wouldn't have any trouble walking the route, but I did want to do it as quickly and as painlessly as possible. So I trained. In addition to my regular running, I made progressively longer walks into the desert every week. By the time of the race I was easily striding along at four miles an hour for 16 miles.

Some of that training included a quick trek up a local peak. I did this because the Bataan route at White Sands is grueling. The race starts on the paved streets of the main post but within two miles follows a sandy two-track road. This stretch can be nice and firm or soft and nasty depending on whether or not it has rained recently.

When you leave this section, you are on asphalt for miles. However, it is uphill with an elevation gain of over 1,000 feet. Toward the top of the climb the route turns onto another two-track which is alternately sandy or rough and rocky. It is then downhill back to the pavement on the other side of a small mountain called Mineral Hill. By the way, the local elevation is about 4,200 feet, so the climb puts runners/marchers a mile high.

Eventually, you get to the "sand pit" which is a dry arroyo that you have to ascend to get to the home stretch. For those not in very good shape, this section proves challenging since it is similar to beach sand and comes along as many hit the wall. Once out of the pits, you finish on a good packed gravel road.

Because of the sand and gravel, the missile range advises participants to take several pairs of good socks and change them after going through the gritty areas. The medical support folks see a lot of people with blisters and other foot problems that can be avoided by frequently putting on clean socks. Every piece of grit stuck in wet socks can abrade and cut skin.

Speaking of medical support, all the support is superb. There are water points every two miles. Participants can get cups of water and Gatorade, orange slices, etc., but many stops have water tanks so marchers can fill their hydration packs. Also, given the demanding, rough course and the possibility of warm, dry conditions, there are several medical support points and a helicopter "med evac" capability.

Since the course is through the desert on an Army post, there are no spectators. However, each water point is manned by volunteer organizations such as the Boy Scouts, local churches, and civic organizations. Typically, they are boisterous and encouraging. One outfit was grilling and selling real food. Boy, did it smell good.

Last year, the race was run in late March, which is now the goal of the organizers. The day was partly cloudy so the temperatures were cool. Originally, the race was held in early to mid April and temperatures were sometimes hot. Dehydration was a real problem for the inexperienced.

My training worked. I finished in 6:50. Given my stops to change socks, drink, snack, and talk to friends, I averaged right at four miles an hour. Plus, there were no blisters or other problems.

At the finish line, in addition to shaking hands with some of the Bataan survivors, I was given a finisher's dog tag instead of a medal. It was very appropriate given the nature of the event.

A word of warning for serious marathon runners—this route is not certified. According to the organizers they have measured and adjusted the course to get it as close to 26.2 miles as possible. However, they have no intention of perfecting it. For the average participant, given the peculiarities of the course, being off a few yards will not be noticed since times cannot be compared to any other route.

The race is fairly well organized, but given that it is on a military installation some of the requirements may be inconvenient. Registration can be accomplished on the Internet as well as by mail. Participants must pick up their bib number, chip, and other materials during the two days before the race. The ceremony and start take place just before sunrise, so there is no pick-up on the morning of the race.

There are no motel rooms on post but participants can pitch a tent in the park or drop a sleeping bag in the gym. There are plenty of motels in Las Cruces that offer reasonable rates for the event. The only problem is that it is about 25 miles away and there is no public transportation to White Sands. Out-of-towners need to rent a car or catch a ride with someone else.

Jim Eckles has worked in the Public Affairs Office at White Sands Missile Range since 1977 and is noted as the local historian. He runs and rides his mountain bike in the desert around Las Cruces, New Mexico and hikes the mountains in the Southwest.

Yakima River Canyon Marathon

yakima, washington

Web site: www.ontherun.com/yrcm
Month: April
USATF Certified: Yes
Course: Rolling

Author: Bob Dolphin
Number of Marathons Completed: 350+
Age Group: 75-79

As someone who has run in over 350 marathons/ultras, I've participated in marathons of all kinds and sizes. Over the years I've run some that I've preferred more than others, but my favorite is one that is small in numbers (around 400) but big in everything else. It's the Yakima River Canyon Marathon in south central Washington. This is a weekend event with the camaraderie of mega-marathoners, regular marathoners, and many first timers that is highlighted by the 26.2-mile point-to-point race on an awesome course.

Fourteen months prior to the inaugural Yakima River Canyon Marathon on March 31, 2001, my wife Lenore and I joined fellow Hard Core Runners Club members at a marathon planning meeting in Yakima, Washington. I had run a lot of marathons, and Lenore had been a volunteer at many, many races. We came to the meeting to share our ideas for a proposed marathon in the beautiful Yakima River Canyon ... and left as co-directors of a new race!

At the meeting, I asked for the concession that I be permitted to be a race participant as well as co-director. Subsequently, we learned that being race directors is a year-round job, but on race day only one director is needed. I would be able to participate as another marathoner while Lenore "ran" the marathon.

Before that first marathon, we spoke with many race directors, and we paid more attention to race management at the 20+ marathons we attended before our race date. Participation in the Race Directors Workshop at the Portland Marathon in October 2000 was also quite useful to us.

After a busy 14 months, the day of our first marathon arrived. Lenore and I arose at 4:00 a.m., hurriedly dressed, ate, roused our runner houseguests, and left for the marathon race headquarters at the Civic Center in the nearby town of Selah. We opened the center to provide shelter for the runners until school buses arrived from Ellensburg, where the point-to-point race would start.

By 6:00 a.m. the bus convoy had arrived and all runners requiring a ride to the starting area were transported 35 miles north to the Ellensburg Best Inn, the race start staging area. The runners who gathered there were animated in anticipation at the prospect of participating in an inaugural marathon in which the whole field was running an unfamiliar course for the first time. The Best Inn, a race sponsor, was handy for late packet pickup, drop-bag checking, and as a place to meet and stay warm.

As the 8:00 a.m. start drew close, the field warmed up by walking or running to the starting line about 1/3 of a mile away. The famous running author, Joe Henderson, greeted them there. He made announcements and introduced Fenny Roberts of Salem, Oregon, who sang the national anthem while Boy Scouts in the background held flags from the United States, Canada, and United Kingdom, the countries of the participants. At 7:55 a.m., Joe started the two competitors in the wheelchair race.

At 8:00 a.m., the runners had a surprise. A diesel engine on a nearby railroad track started the race with a blast of its air horn. The Burlington Northern/Santa Fe Railroad provided the engine that made a 70-mile round trip from Yakima to be part of the race starting ceremony!

As the runners raced down the flat, two-lane state highway, the sky was overcast and calm with temperatures in the 40s. The front-runners made a right angled turn, and those of us in the back of the pack could look across a pasture to admire the swiftness of the leaders. The first three miles were in the flat Kittitas Valley, an agricultural area with livestock, pastures, and fields of grass or alfalfa hay and scattered houses and farmsteads.

After 5 kilometers, the runners entered the 23-mile Yakima River Canyon. It was quite a contrast from the first three miles. The canyon is a curving, deep valley, and the racecourse road parallels the winding Yakima River with its clear, calm-to-turbulent water.

Mount Baldy, a treeless peak, is prominent mid-course, and tall hills, ridges, and lava cliffs are prevalent on both sides of the river for most of the marathon. Ponderosa pine, cottonwoods, willows, and other trees and bushes find moisture close to the river. In contrast, the drier hills are covered with sagebrush and other desert shrubs.

With less than a mile of ranchland, housing, and recreational areas, the canyon is a federal nature reserve occupied only by native plants and animals such as deer, mountain sheep, waterfowl, bald eagles, great blue herons, and other wildlife.

Because the state highway that serves as the racecourse is closed for over seven hours (except for official and local vehicles), the runners had solitude and were able to appreciate the ever-changing scenery. They engaged in animated conversations and appreciated the friendly and enthusiastic volunteers at the 11 aid stations. Water and sports drink were plentiful at these stations, and solid food was available at miles 14 and 23.5.

Due to the road closure and absence of laterals in the canyon, spectators had access to the course only at the start, mile three, and at the finish area. At a pep rally for the volunteers the week before the marathon, it was explained to them that THEY would be the cheering sections on the course. I was pleased that the volunteers were indeed friendly and in a festive mood. Some even wore costumes and had music at their aid stations.

The course proved to be average in difficulty with many flat or gentle downgrade sections. A 300 foot loss of elevation and cool running conditions contributed to many Boston qualifying times on this USATF-certified course. However, there were some challenges that two major hills presented. Most runners negotiated the first one in the 14th mile without difficulty. A down slope on the backside of the hill allowed me to make up some of the time I had lost on the ascent. Near the Roza Dam at Mile 22, a gradual climb for 1 1/2 miles presented the major challenge of the day. After that, it was all down hill!

As I crossed the finish line, Joe Henderson announced some of my stats on his microphone as he did for all of the finishers. A hug from Lenore was most welcome as I stopped my run and my timing watches. She greeted all of the finishers as they crossed the line and hugged the first timers as they finished, before they received their medal with the Yakima River Canyon Marathon logo on it.

Food, drink, and space blankets were available to the runners beyond the finishing chute. Medical and massage tents and the drop bag claim truck were in the finish area as well. I appreciated finding a much-needed chair for me to rest on! Shuttle buses transported runners about five miles to Selah with a stop at a junior high school for free showers (with soap, shampoo, and towels provided) and then to the Selah Civic Center for post race activities.

The Civic Center is key to the race management of this marathon. On Friday, the day before the marathon, packets were picked up there, and registration was permitted for those who hadn't registered online or mailed in an entry form.

At the small expo, Yakima River Canyon Marathon and 100 Marathon Club North America merchandise was available; Joe Henderson autographed his books as he sold them; and editor Martin Rudow, promoted his Northwest Runner magazine.

Joe was also the guest speaker at our pasta dinner as the participants gathered for a pre-race meal, and Lenore gave "Nuts to You Awards" to thirty five, 50 Staters and to some other special people.

Now that the marathon was over, many of us returned to the Civic Center for a post-race awards ceremony/meal. The awards were first class. Framed pictures of canyon scenes went to the first place man and woman, and beautiful, colored, acrylic awards were presented to the first three age division winners. Fourth and 5th place winners received ribbons. The age classes were in five-year increments from "19 and under" to "80+".

First-time marathoners wore a foot sticker on their bibs, and now at the awards ceremony each first-time finisher received a certificate of completion from Lenore. Door prizes provided by our many sponsors were awarded, and all in attendance were eligible to win.

Steve Christofferson, our course photographer, sold individual pictures at the finish area and later at the Civic Center. Our computer timing system worked well, and progressive results were posted at the finish area during the race. Later, the final results were posted at the Civic Center, and within a day they were posted on our web site.

The next morning, some of us gathered at the West Coast Yakima Gateway Hotel (now the Red Lion) for a no-host breakfast where we compared notes on the inaugural race and read all about it in the *Yakima Herald-Republic* newspaper. For 14 months, a great committee of dedicated people worked hard to make the inaugural marathon in our beautiful Yakima River Canyon such a success!

We are now on race number five, and 39 runners will compete in the marathon for their 5th time. This is more than 10 percent of the field in any one year. We like to believe that their loyalty is a result of the friendly committee, volunteers, and sponsors who provide a wonderful marathon weekend on a beautiful course. Yes, I'm prejudiced. But of the 351 marathons/ultras I've run since 1981 (20-22 each year), the Yakima River Canyon Marathon is still my favorite!

Bob Dolphin has been running marathons since 1981. This native of Worcester, Massachusetts, was 51 when he ran his first one, the Heart of America Marathon, in Columbia, MO. Ten years later, while living in Yakima, as a retired entomologist, he returned to Columbia to run his 100th marathon. Bob ran his 200th marathon in London in 1997, when he also became the first American added to the 100 Marathon Club United Kingdom. Bob formed the 100 Marathon Club North America at the inaugural Yakima River Canyon Marathon in 2001. He and his wife Lenore are co-directors of this marathon and of the 100 Marathon Club North America.

Bob ran his 300th marathon (this includes 44 ultras) in 2002. He served in the U.S. Marine Corps for 6 1/2 years, so he's proud of completing his 350th marathon at the Marine Corps Marathon in 2004. Bob is a member of the 50 States & D.C. Group, 50 States Marathon Club, three 100 Marathon Clubs (UK, NA, and Germany), Marathon Maniacs, Hard Core Runners Club, Fort Steilacoom Running Club, Interurban Running Club, the Oregon Road Runners Club, the Columbia Track Club (MO), and the Sedalia (MO) Road Runners Club.

Bob's marathon record is 3:00:12 at age 58 in 1988. In the same year, he ran a 3:04:30 at Boston for 7th place in the 55-59M division. At age 75, he runs 20-22 marathons per year.

Eisenhower Marathon

abilene, kansas

Web site: www.eisenhowermarathon.com
Month: April
USATF Certified: Yes
Course: Flat

Author: Allen Griffiths
Number of Marathons Completed: 32
Age Group: 55-59

Run the historic Chisholm Trail at the
EISENHOWER MARATHON

Kansas is flat. Abilene, Kansas is flat. The Eisenhower Marathon is flat. From the route 170 overpass, which is the highest hill in town, you can see the whole city. So much for the discussion about the course terrain.

I chose to run the Eisenhower Marathon because my son Derek and I are a little more than halfway through our goal of running a marathon in all 50 states and we both needed Kansas. He lives in Denver, and I live in Ohio. Derek publishes Colorado Runner magazine, and the Eisenhower Marathon advertised in the magazine. Kansas is between Ohio and Colorado, so we both could drive to it.

It took me two days to drive to Abilene, and Derek was able to make it in one day. My first day of driving ended in St. Louis at the Tap Room of the Shafley Brewing Company, which had great pasta and great beer. If they can survive in the shadow of Anheuser Busch, you know they have a good product. The second day ended up being a leisurely drive across Missouri and eastern Kansas.

The Eisenhower Marathon is a small marathon with a few hundred runners. They have enough runners that you don't run alone, but you aren't crowded either. Accommodations are not difficult to find, but you need to plan ahead.

Abilene, Kansas is not a large town, but if you like museums, there is the Eisenhower Museum that contains all sorts of memorabilia concerning President Eisenhower. If you like Victorian house museums, there is the Lebold House Museum, which is complete with gas lights, draperies at the windows and doors, Victorian furniture, and an eccentric curator who can explain everything from why the house has a tower, to how the basement was used as a kitchen by the servants.

This was the first race I ran with music. The race allows it so I ran with an Apple iPod mini. It is light enough to carry during the race, and has enough capacity to not repeat songs for an extended length of time. The iPod has a recommendation to keep it away from water. As you will read, that wasn't possible, but the iPod did a magnificent job while just cruising or seriously trying to mentally block out the weather, and it didn't skip a beat. Several weeks later though, it succumbed to the moisture infection and had to be replaced. But running to music was enjoyable and made the miles pass much more pleasantly. I've run with an iPod ever since.

The course is paved, and makes its way through an area that cattlemen brought their herds through to Abilene in the 1800s on the Chisholm Trail. In addition to stationed nurses and a roving emergency response vehicle, horseback riders and bicyclists provide security along the course and carry cell phones and emergency contact numbers.

The race begins at 7:00 a.m., early, but not too early. There were dark clouds to the west. A mental note here, beware of dark clouds in Kansas, Auntie Em. The race itself was great, with frequent water stops, a well marked course, and it was manned by people who, as we found out later, were willing to risk their lives to provide us with whatever we needed to finish the race.

We began by running south for what seemed like a long time because the weather system was arriving and the weather didn't like us running south. It provided us with a 30 mph head wind, and later, there was hail, small biting hail, at first, then larger. Of course about the time we turned off the southern branch of the Chisholm Trail, the weather front came through and the wind shifted. No, it wasn't a tail wind. By the time I had reached the 20-mile mark, the storm hit full force with strong winds, heavy large hail and lightning, lots of lightning, very close, which of course was accompanied by loud thunder.

The volunteers were wonderful, standing in the hail and lightning to help us. Aid station personnel are even encouraged to develop a theme for their rest stop and wear costumes. The storm was so fierce it would have closed all other outdoor athletic events, but those volunteers stayed until the final runner was out of danger.

Of course, my son Derek didn't experience most of the hail as he had finished, and was enjoying the post-race party. My experience with post race parties is there is rarely anything left by the time I finish, but this one was much better as I was able to eat all I wanted.

All in all, the Eisenhower Marathon was an excellent race and an enjoyable experience. It was even broadcast live on a local radio station, allowing friends and family to follow racers worldwide on the Internet. I'd give it four stars out of four, for organization and race support before, during, and after the race. The course was very scenic if you like running in rural areas. Very few spectators watched our race, but if you take the weather into account, that was understandable.

Allen Griffiths is an optometrist in Washington Court House, Ohio. He was a sprinter in high school and at Wittenberg University in Springfield, Ohio. Allen has been running distance races since 1976 and is working to complete marathons in all 50 states with his son Derek (the Publisher of Colorado Runner *magazine). The Eisenhower Marathon was his 32nd marathon.*

Boston Marathon

boston, massachusetts

Web site: www.bostonmarathon.org
Month: April
USATF Certified: Yes
Course: Rolling

Boston Marathon®

Author: Aaron Schwartzbard
Number of Marathons Completed: 13
Age Group: 25-29

In 1896, members of the Boston Athletic Association attended the first modern Olympic Games in Athens. When they returned to Boston, they brought back reports of an exciting new event: The Marathon. Though mainly track and field events, those first Olympic Games included the marathon to commemorate the Greek heritage of the games—specifically, the legendary run by Pheidippides from Marathon to Athens to bring news of the victory of the Athenian army over the Persians in 490 B.C.

The first Boston Marathon (inaugurated as The American Marathon) took place on April 19, 1887. The course was 24.5 miles from Ashland, Massachusetts to Copeley Square, in downtown Boston. John J. McDermott finished with a time of 2:55:10 to beat the 14 other people who started that first race. It was not until 1924, when the race was lengthened to the now-standard distance of 26 miles, 385 yards, that the starting line was moved to Hopkinton, Massachusetts.

Today, the Boston Marathon is the oldest annual marathon in the world. (The Olympic Marathon, which is one year older, is run quadrennially.) With over 100 years of history, the Boston Marathon has transcended its status as a sporting event to become an institution. Every year on Patriots' Day, a Massachusetts state holiday on the third Monday in April, roads are closed so that runners can race the clock and each other from Hopkinton to Boston.

Compared to other modern marathons, Boston is unusual in several ways. The course was originally designed to evoke the original Greek course from Marathon to Athens. The straight line, point-to-point, hilly course is one that few race directors today would consider for a new race. The distance between the start line and the finish line presents logistical challenges to organizers of the race, and the hills present a competitive challenge to racers. Further distinguishing Boston from other marathons is that it is

Courtesy of Aaron Schwartzbard

a Monday race. Patriots' Day — race day — is a state holiday, which leaves most of the residents of Boston and the surrounding suburbs free to cheer for the runners, cheer for the Red Sox (who traditionally play a home game on Patriots' Day), or, judging from the hand-drawn score boards that some spectators post along the race route, both.

The final distinguishing feature of the Boston Marathon is the one that, perhaps more than anything else related to the race, gives it its mystique. Getting into the Boston Marathon is not as simple as sending in an application. It is even more difficult than achieving good fortune in the sort of lottery that some other large races use to grant entry. To be accepted into the Boston Marathon, each racer must meet qualification time standards on a USATF-certified marathon course. Qualification times are not lax, but they are within reach for many marathoners. The promise of running a historic race among thousands of experienced, competitive marathoners from around the world gives Boston an appeal unmatched at any other race.

The magnitude of the event is striking even when stepping out of Logan Airport in Boston on race weekend. It seems impossible to turn around without seeing a billboard or a poster or a sign on a bus or a banner hanging from a light post proclaiming that the marathon is about to happen.

The race expo is a giant swirling mass of merchandise, free samples, video demonstrations and, if your timing is good, celebrity appearances. Someone could easily spend several hours wandering past the booths, looking for some spectacular deal. The most serious racers would be well advised to avoid the expo, with all its excitement, as much as possible. Packet pick-up is at the expo, and some form of photo identification is required, so it is impossible to avoid the expo completely. However, packet pick-up is usually isolated on one side of the expo, so it is possible to get in and out with minimal hassle. Those runners who don't want to miss the experience of the expo, or who need to make some last minute purchases, should try to get to the expo when it first opens. Before 10:00 a.m., it's possible to stroll through the rows of booths. By noon, every aisle is packed booth-to-booth with runners, and it only gets more crowded through the afternoon.

Race day is no less of a logistical challenge. If you mention how difficult it is to get to the start of the Boston Marathon, a runner who has never done Boston might assume that you are talking about achieving the qualifying standards. However, a Boston veteran will know that it is just as likely that you are talking about the literal process of reaching the starting line on race morning. The course is straight and point-to-point, which means that the Boston Athletic Association must transport many thousands of runners from the middle of Boston a full 26 miles to Hopkinton. In case of snafus, the last scheduled busses are supposed to arrive in Hopkinton several hours before the start of the race, which means that despite the noon start time, runners still face an early morning. Those runners who believe they can "beat the system" by recruiting a friend or family member to give a ride to the start will learn that due to road closures, for all but the drivers with an extensive knowledge of secondary and tertiary routes in and around Hopkinton, taking the bus is the only tenable option. Of course, the bus ride itself is a part of the Boston experience that should not be missed. The entertainment starts when the bus is still 10 miles from Hopkinton. Invariably, at least a couple of racers will have made poor calculations with respect to bladder size, expected time on the bus, and the timing of an aggressive (excessive, even) hydration strategy. As long as you are not one of the unfortunate few suffering for want of a port-o-john, the scene can offer some entertainment on what is otherwise a long, unremarkable trip.

Hopkinton itself is a small town. Racers come to know the athletic fields behind Hopkinton High School as The Athletes' Village and they come to know Main Street as The Starting Line. As noon approaches, the mile between The Athletes' Village and the corrals at the starting area becomes a river of people. Even those runners in the crowd who can maintain six minute miles from start to finish of the marathon find that 30 minutes might not be enough time to cover the mile from the Athletes' Village to the buses that will transport bags back to Boston, then to reach corrals full of runners, stretching west from the starting line.

The corrals are pens that keep runners segregated by qualifying time before the race. In most marathons, only elite runners are seeded — elites are given race numbers reflecting their expected finishing position and they are given a preferential starting position. Every runner at Boston has a seeded race number, and those numbers determine which corral (that is, how close to the actual starting line) a runner may enter. Therefore, before the race, there is no need to guess how fast a competitor is; simply look at his number. A runner with a low number ran a faster qualifying race than a runner with a higher number in the prior 18 months. When it comes time to line up for the start, race numbers confer not just status, but privilege as well. Racers with numbers in the 1000s may pass by the gate keepers of corral #1 to line up immediately behind the starting line. Runners holding numbers in the 2000s may enter corral #2; 3000s may enter corral #3 ... 12,000s thousands may enter corral #12 ... 17,000s may enter corral #17.

During the last few minutes before noon, racers start to take off their final layer of "throw away" clothes, or not. Weather in Massachusetts in April is highly variable. Racers could face lows in the 30s with rain and a head wind, or highs in the 80s with sun and a tail wind. (The weather is a concern for racers not just for its effects during the race, but also for its effects during the hours leading up to the race.) Usually, however, the reality on race day lays somewhere between those two extremes, with at least some variability along the race route.

The start of the race is a spectacle unto itself. Television cameras record from the side of the road, a swarm of helicopters hovers overhead and cheering spectators occupy every inch of real estate with a view of the starting line. From there, the race goes downhill, literally. From start to finish, the racecourse drops almost 500 feet in elevation; a full quarter of that elevation loss comes in the first mile. So exactly when runners are already trying to deal with the incompatible goals of settling into an appropriate pace and spreading out as a group, they must also handle the stresses of running down a notable descent.

Then a funny thing happens: nothing. The Boston Marathon is known for, among other things, the crowds of spectators who line the course. But after the first steep descent out of Hopkinton, runners find themselves on a wooded, two-lane, country road with no spectators at all. A runner might start to wonder if they are at the wrong race. Runners should expect those first three miles between Hopkinton and Ashland to be two things: deserted roads and downhill. (By the fourth mile, half of the race's elevation loss has passed.)

After the stretch leading to Ashland, the course is less purely downhill. While the elevation still trends generally down, the next 10 miles are the flattest of the race. There seems to be as much uphill as downhill as runners pass through Ashland then Framingham then Natick. But as runners near the halfway point, they should prepare for something significant: Wellesley. Sure, the halfway point is in Wellesley, and that is significant. There is also some noticeable downhill to precede the infamous Hills of Newton, also significant. However, neither of those is the first thing to come to mind when considering Wellesley during the Boston Marathon. The spectator support during the race is great from beginning to end. From the leather-clad bikers enjoying barbecue in front of a biker bar to the bluegrass band jamming in front of an auto body shop to all the kids who compete with their friends to see who can give out the most orange slices or get the most high fives, everyone has positive energy to offer. But there are three places where the people on the sides of the road are perhaps more noteworthy than those in the middle of the road: the start, the finish and Wellesley. The women of Wellesley College line the right side of the road, three, four, even five deep, for a quarter mile, creating what can only be described as a wall of noise.

A short distance later, the course crosses the timing mats that mark the halfway point. Two miles later, the race crosses the Charles River as the course heads into Newton. In the 16 miles before Newton, despite the occasional uphill, the race is generally a downhill race. Newton is where the race starts to trend upward. Anyone trying to devise a strategy for this race would be well advised to break the race into three sections. First, there is a generally downhill (aside from a few rolling hills) race from the start to mile 16. Then, there is the uphill race from mile 16 to mile 21. Finally, from mile 21, through Brookline to the finish in Boston, the race is either downhill or flat. An experienced racer will run each of the first two sections with the next section in mind.

More than 17 miles into the race, the right turn at the firehouse in Newton comes as the first turn of the race. The next several miles take the race through one of the more expensive Boston suburbs, past million-dollar houses with perfectly manicured lawns. Through these neighborhoods and up the hills, those racers who paced themselves well earlier in the day will wonder what all the fuss concerning "the hills of Newton" was about. However, most people—especially those who started the race unaware of what was to come—find sufficient reason to despair in Newton. The crux of the marathon may very well be Heartbreak Hill. Heartbreak Hill received its sobriquet after the 1936 race in which Johnny Kelley passed Ellison Brown to take the lead for only a moment before Brown repassed Kelley—all on that one hill.

Today, that hill is a favorite location for spectators to spend an afternoon. And the top of the hill is a favorite place for many runners. The top of Heartbreak Hill is the end of the climbing. The final five miles of the Boston Marathon are where experience and patience pay off. Runners who try to run even mile splits through the race might get flustered through the hills between miles 16 and 21, running them too hard in order to stay "on pace." But the experienced, patient racer will maintain a steady effort through Newton, even if it means falling behind the goal pace. The experienced, patient racer knows that if they can reach mile 21 without overextending themselves, they will be able to make up lost time, and more, over the last five miles of the race.

Finishing times aside, the last five miles of the marathon course are some of the most exciting. Some people struggle through dead quads and cramping calves, some people move quickly down the road as they enjoy the fruits of their patience in the hills, and everyone enjoys running past the crowds of spectators that cover the sidewalks along the city streets. The mile markers tick by and the sidewalks grow more and more dense with people until the course turns right on Hereford Street for a short block. Then, the home stretch: Boylston Street. No matter how difficult the prior 26 miles had been, no matter how many times a racer might have cursed the name of Boston between Hopkinton and Boylston Street, with that left turn, all is forgiven. The road opens up to four lanes, with crowds 10, 15, or 20 deep on either side of the road, and the archway of the finish line rises above the road only a couple of hundred meters away. Halfway to the finish line, the packed sidewalks give way to packed grandstands and television cameras. The noise and sights and emotions on Boylston Street can be almost overwhelming. But if there is one piece of advice I would hope to offer to someone who plans to run the Boston Marathon, it is this: Whatever else you do during the day, do not forget to appreciate and enjoy those final, fantastic steps to the finish line.

Aaron Schwartzbard is a 2:37 marathoner who has competed in ultras as long as 100 miles and triathlons up to the double Iron distance. He finished his first race in 1999. When not on the roads or trails, he does software development. He has run the Boston Marathon five times.

QUALIFYING FOR

B O S T O N

AGE GROUP	MEN	WOMEN
18-34	3:10	3:40
35-39	3:15	3:45
40-44	3:20	3:50
45-49	3:30	4:00
50-54	3:35	4:05
55-59	3:45	4:15
60-64	4:00	4:30
65-69	4:15	4:45
70-74	4:30	5:00
75-79	4:45	5:15
80 & Over	5:00	5:30

Bonus Feature

A Means to an End? Or, the End to the Means?

Aaron Schwartzbard

All right, here's the deal: The Boston Marathon doesn't start until noon. Twelve o'clock p.m. - in Hopkinton. Due to road closures on race day, it is near impossible to sleep late and drive out to the start, arriving with only minutes enough to lace up your shoes and elbow your way to the starting corrals. No, despite the noon start, the alarm clock rings at some cold, dark hour so that you can catch an official race bus out to Hopkinton. In Hopkinton, the two options available for the wait for the race start are: 1) sitting on a large, grassy field, or 2) standing on a large, grassy field. (Actually, there is a third option. In the center of town, near the starting line, there is a small fair. You could sample the funnel cake and smoked sausage. I don't, however, recommend option #3 if you value your stomach.)

No doubt, many a runner has found himself sitting (or standing) in Hopkinton, thinking, "What a lovely morning for a run! What a shame it is that I'm wasting it just standing (or sitting) here!" So let us delineate the salient points here:

- On race morning, you're going to have to get up early no matter what you do

- You have to get to Hopkinton by noon

- Aside from the task of getting to Hopkinton, you have nary an obligation to occupy your time in the hours between waking and racing

When drawn so explicitly, with such lucidity, the question hardly needs be asked: Why not run to Hopkinton? Such a course of action could not have been more obvious to my companions and me as we stood on the line that proclaimed, "FINISH," amongst the empty grandstands on Boylston Street, in the early morning on Patriots' Day. Glancing at each other, we seemed not to know how to start our little jaunt. One member of our hearty band finally said, "Well, I suppose we should go." The other three of us agreed, and a moment later, we were heading west on Boylston Street.

We made it through almost a quarter of a mile before striking the first notes of discord. Which road is it that the marathon uses to cut over from Comm. Ave to Boylston? We debated for several blocks until we arrived at the proper street. Our discord was immediately replaced by harmony as each of us immediately recognized the correct road. After that, there was no question about where we were supposed to go. It was the same marathon course that we all knew, only everything was in reverse: forward was backward, uphills went down, the end grew farther away and the start approached.

Most roads were not closed yet, so we ran on the sidewalks. Where there were no sidewalks, we ran on the shoulder. Where there was no shoulder, we ran on the median. And where there was no median …. Well, there was always one of those things.

While heading out of the city, we could stop into a cafe or shop and ask to refill our water bottles. Upon explaining our morning's journey, not a single proprietor refused our requests. In fact, the only time we were unable to beg, borrow, or finagle water from someone with water to spare was late in our trip. In the miles before Hopkinton, where the course travels through very rural areas, there are long stretches of road with nothing but trees on either side. Much to our happiness, we came across a marathon aid station that was in the process of setting up. Certainly, we believed, they would be all too eager to offer aid. After all, we did have official marathon numbers pinned to our shirts, and we were miles from the nearest population center. But skepticism prevailed, and our request for water was refused at one aid station, and accepted at another only after several minutes of persuasion that we were, in fact, running from Boston to Hopkinton before the marathon proper.

Our arrival at our end point (or our mid point, depending on perspective) proved anti-climactic. Arriving in Hopkinton along the marathon course, we were no longer the marathoners going the wrong way. We quickly became engulfed in the packs of runners, jogging up and down the road, preparing for what would surely be a PR marathon for each and every one of them.

As for our gang of four double marathoners? Not only did we make it to Hopkinton in time to turn around and jog back to Boston with 20,000 runners who failed to realize that there were better things to do than spending all morning sitting (or standing) on a field in Hopkinton, but we also had a lovely time getting there.

Aaron Schwartzbard is a 2:37 marathoner who has competed in ultras as long as 100 miles and triathlons up to the double Iron distance. He finished his first race in 1999. When not on the roads or trails, he does software development. He has run the Boston Marathon five times.

Big Sur International Marathon

carmel, california

Web site: www.bsim.org
Month: April
USATF Certified: Yes
Course: Rolling

Author: Steve Smith
Number of Marathons Completed: 3
Age Group: 35-39

As you drive south along Highway 1 and enter into Carmel, California you will see the following sign:

Big Sur	26
San Luis Obispo	132
Los Angeles	337

Well, not quite. Someone, a runner, one of our ilk, our clan, stuck a nice, clean piece of graffiti on that road sign. Right next to that "26" is one of those small, reflective mailbox numbers, the number "2." With that small act all is right in the world, because if there was ever a stretch of road worthy of a marathon effort it is this stretch of curvy asphalt ribboned along the majesty of vast ocean meeting coastal mountains.

What runner doesn't see 26 miles and think, 26.2? Jack-Jill; Salt–Pepper; Peanut Butter– Jelly; 26–point 2. And, given the scenery since arriving in Monterey, Carmel's northerly, larger neighbor, I relished the opportunity to run 26.2 miles along this fabled road.

Three years before the 2002 Big Sur International Marathon, I ran the Marine Corps Marathon in Washington, D.C., my first marathon. Independent of my own middle-age crisis decision making (I would turn 30 the day before the race), two friends from work also chose the Marine Corps as their first marathon. Scott would prove to be the center of our training trio, a little slower than me, and a little faster than Beverly. Scott and Beverly would train together occasionally, and so would Scott and I. We all finished the marathon that day and we all enjoyed ourselves. More importantly, we found that having a common goal made the training more fun, more communal, even if we did much of our training by ourselves.

With this in mind, the decision to run another marathon as a group was easy. In 2000 I had to watch Scott run his second marathon (and break four hours at Maryland's Marathon in the Parks) after injuring my calf six weeks before the race. In 2001, I lotteried into the New York City Marathon without my marathon buddies. By the end of the year, Scott, Beverly, and I were looking forward to aiming for another marathon as a group.

Why Big Sur? Well, before Scott, Beverly, or I had ever run a marathon, I'd put the idea into their head that the Big Sur Marathon would be a fun time. As an avid backpacker and traveler, I'd always had my eye on Big Sur but had never made it there. I'd driven hundreds of miles along Highway 1 north and south of Big Sur, but I had somehow never made it to Big Sur itself. Sure, I told them, it's a little hilly, but the view … ahh, the view.

What drew me to the Big Sur International Marathon itself was a brief conversation I had with a guy with the coolest job in the world. While attending a course at the National Outdoor Leadership School in the wintry northwest corner of Wyoming, I made friends with my instructor. I'd started running road races the previous year and was thinking about the Marine Corps Marathon later that year. We started talking about running and he mentioned that he ran the Big Sur International Marathon. Big Sur? Holy cow, I didn't know they had a marathon. (At this stage in my running career I figured there were 10 or 12 marathons like Chicago, New York, Boston.) Yeah, he said, they have one, and it's a bear. They say take your marathon time and add 15 minutes to it. I think he ran a 3:12.

Now, you have to realize, the guy telling me this story has climbed some of the most serious mountains in the world. He's hiked 20 miles with 60 pounds on his back. He's dragged a 100-pound sled through a blizzard for 15 hours. Tough? Heck, I thought, if you say so … sign me up! So I tucked the Big Sur Marathon into the back of my mind.

Many people were introduced to the Big Sur race in a similar way. If you know anything about the Big Sur International Marathon you probably know these two things: 1) the course is stunningly beautiful, and 2) there's a hill, its name is Hurricane Point, and it will hurt. If you've been paying attention, you've probably also heard there's a piano at a very pretty bridge, but I'm getting ahead of myself.

What the course gives out in toughness—double that for beauty. If you've seen a car commercial in the last 15 years, you know a little bit of the course's scenery.

The picturesque Bixby Bridge, in addition to serving as the backdrop of one in five car commercials, is one of the icons of the Big Sur International Marathon. It is a stunning piece of architecture beautifully set into the curving hills and ravines of the California coast, and while most Americans dream of cruising these tight turns in a convertible performance car, there's a group of us that see this scenery and want to spend a little more time with it, or at least have it as a quiet companion as we push ourselves.

Monterey is the usual home base for the traveling marathoner. Carmel is smaller, quaint, and much pricier. To give you some idea of the area around Carmel, realize that Clint Eastwood did a spell as the mayor of Carmel and the legendary Pebble Beach golf course is just outside of town. Big Sur itself offers camping for the adventurous and little else. If you're flying to the race, a car rental is an excellent idea given all to do outside of Monterey. However, the budget minded can easily live without a car if they simply want to take in Monterey itself (and don't mind waiting for the shuttle bus after the race). If you are flying to the race, consider flying into San Francisco; as a major international airport it will offer more flexibility with flight scheduling and the drive to Monterey is beautiful.

I arrived in Monterey on Thursday to share a room with Dave, a friend from Ohio. My co-workers arrived later that night after having some connection woes in San Francisco. They made an unscheduled drive from San Francisco to Monterey, but had to do so in the less scenic dark of night.

The group of us previewed the racecourse on Friday. It was the first time any of us had seen Big Sur. But, more importantly, it was the first time we'd seen Hurricane Point. The talk for the rest of the day was about "that hill." It was big, but not too big. Yeah right, it was huge. Nah, it wasn't too bad. Besides (rationalization) it comes at just the right spot, miles 10 through 12. Not too soon. Not too far into the race. About Hurricane Point (a.k.a. mountain) this was universally agreed: If it has to be somewhere, miles 10 through 12 is a fine spot.

Monterey, like most coastal California towns, is a diner's haven. Mexican, coffee houses, seafood, stylish breakfast joints all await the hungry tourist. We ventured onto the Pier (of course) for dinner and dined more for Monterey than for the marathon. With bellies full of wondrous seafood dishes and minds full with shadows of Hurricane Point, we hustled into bed as early as we could. Because after the scenery and after Hurricane Point, the next major point of interest for this race is that you have to be up at an hour not fit for print. Shhh, lean over, and I'll whisper … It begins with three, yes, a three.

Like most things about this race, it's a double-edged sword. Highway 1 is a two-lane ribbon through paradise. It's not known for its shoulders. To run 4,000 runners 26.2 miles up the coast requires the closure of at least one lane (in my opinion, two would do better). In order to get everyone to the start before the road closes, the race organizers shuttle most people from Monterey to the race for the 7:00 a.m. start. (Those adventurous, cheapo folks camping in Big Sur don't look so silly now, do they?)

Waking up at 3:00 a.m. violates one of my cardinal rules in life: I don't wake up at 3:00 a.m. If something requires me to be awake at 3:00 a.m., then darn it, I'll just stay up. However, given the modern miracle of jet travel, I found a loophole. In Washington D.C. it would already be 6:00 a.m. when I woke up, so I managed a few hours of sleep without violating any essential ethic policies.

Beverly, Dave, Scott, and I stumbled out of bed and over to the shuttle pick-up area. Like all early-morning bus rides to a race, we had the Nervous-And-Loud-Good-Natured-But-Annoying-Guy. You know the type. "Hey! Why does everyone look so tired? Ha!" and "Mr. Bus Driver! Could you just park here at mile 10 and wait for me? I sure could use a ride up THIS!" That it was three in the morning was bad enough, but as we drove onto the best stretches of Highway 1, it was a draw.

For outside the bus window was something I imagine is rare: a sharp, clear night with a full moon above the Pacific Ocean. (Every previous morning was foggy and drizzly.) Given the height of the seats in our luxury travel bus, I had a clear view over the guardrails, and I stared at the amazing night for what seemed like seconds, but turned out to be hours until the race start. The ocean was calm and the moon lit a pathway from the ocean's edge into the horizon, and I wouldn't have traded a wink of sleep for the bus ride.

I seed myself waaaay back in the line. I promise myself that this is a training run, a jaunt with friends. Waaaay in the back, as we're all packed into the narrow two-lane road of Highway 1, I see the most bizarre thing. The banner with the five-foot letters that spell "START" waffles, waivers, and then falls into the crowd. Some runners reach up to prevent it from hitting the ground, like concerned citizens keeping the Stars and Stripes clean. There's some commotion, a rising of the banner, and a few moments before the race starts! Finally. It isn't until I pass the Start line that I realize the seriousness of the situation. A man is on the side of the road, his head bleeding slightly. Man. How bad is that? You spend months training for a marathon, probably a long drive or a plane ride to get to California, and finally wake up at three in order to get to beautiful Big Sur ... and WHACK! The Start line slaps you upside the head.

I'm finally on my way, thankful that nothing hit me on the head or anywhere else. The first few miles are through some dense forest, on a gentle downhill slope. The race organization shows early. Each mile is clearly marked, with a helpful volunteer calling out your time. Just beyond that volunteer is another volunteer calling out your predicted finish time given your current location and time.

After several miles we break out into the clear coastal fringe, with the Pacific stretching forever to the west and the mountains looming to the east. We run by a spectacular lighthouse. I think about the beautiful day—lucky? I don't know, but the three days prior to the race were all foggy mornings followed by sunny days; today we had a starry night, sunny morning, and calm winds. I think that I'm holding my pace down quite well, walking a few aid stations even this early in the run.

I'm running along at a comfy pace, and I think about the amazing bus ride to the race start. I think about my friends and all our training. I think about … dinner. Uh oh. Maybe seafood wasn't such a great idea. Soon I find myself approaching mile eight. No more thoughts of starry nights, friends, or calm winds, only unpleasant thoughts of dinner and my stomach (did I mention that there are plenty of portable potties on course?).

Given the complexities of closing down one lane of Highway 1 for 5.5 hours, the Big Sur International Marathon organizers make the most of their efforts and stage several races during the day. There's a 5K race featuring some very fast people, and a relay race for the marathon that gets some competitive teams. When I first heard this I thought, "Cool!" but as I approached mile 10 (We all remember what looms at mile 10, don't we?) I felt that this wasn't so cool. I start pondering the relay teams. There are five people per team, and the unlucky soul running the third leg gets to sit at the base of Hurricane Point for a few hours and stare up the two-mile climb that awaits him or her. I come closer to the base of the mountain and my pity for the third-leggers turns into jealousy. Lucky dogs with their fresh legs; two miles up, a few miles down and some rollers for 6.9 miles.

Finally, mile 10 arrives, and it's time to climb. I make my first competitive decision of the race, nobody passes me. This isn't as competitive as it sounds as I've seeded myself well outside of my peers. I slowly make my way up the hill, my heart rate slowly rising as well. After about 10 minutes, I realize that I'm getting along just fine. All my limbs are still attached, and all my vital organs are still inside my body. This hill isn't so bad. The road starts to curve around, and I again notice the Pacific Ocean. As we rise up the road more of the ocean takes over my world. I find out after the race that Hurricane Point is named for its winds, but we are lucky today; it's clear and not even breezy. Just as I begin to feel victorious in this climb (no walking, no one passing me, I actually feel good) the road takes a very sharp turn, both around the hillside and toward the sky. The last few minutes of the climb are the worst. To this day, I'm not sure if it's the actual pitch of the road at that point, or if it's the two miles of climbing that precedes the "summit."

Mile 12 arrives and, for the first time, my predicted finish time reaches my brain—3:18. Wow, this surprises me. I generally felt pretty good.

The descent of Hurricane Point isn't as bad as I feared. In all our pre-race worries we even found time to worry about the downside of Hurricane Point. As if getting up the darn thing wasn't bad enough, we'd hemmed and hawed about how downhill running can actually do more muscle damage. Great, we thought.

But here I was on the other side of the Point, and I was still alive. Heck, not only was I still alive, I felt good. Like most people, we managed to talk-up Hurricane Point in order to diminish it. Well, obvious or not, the strategy worked for me.

As I descended the backside of the point, I was treated to one of the hallmarks of the Big Sur International Marathon. Each year, they fly in a grand piano to sit at mile 13. That's right, they chopper in a piano. Not only does mile 13 mark the (almost) halfway point of the race, it happens to sit in front of the scenic Bixby Bridge. Best of all, it's at the bottom of Hurricane Point, so even if your legs ARE sore from descending, you are treated to some pleasant music and one heck of a view.

The remainder of the course is rolling hills, nothing compared to Hurricane Point, but nothing easy. At some point in time someone will joke that the course has a net elevation loss. Listen to the half-hearted chuckle that follows and believe it (the half-hearted chuckle).

After passing mile 14 and regaining normal pace and gait, I started to do the math. My mile 14 predicted finish time was 3:16. I still felt fresh. As I approached mile 15, three things occurred to me: 1) Starting out easy is a good marathon pacing strategy, especially for a training run (even-splitting is generally the best option for a PR, or at least a close positive split); 2) I really wanted to be done running; and 3) If I was really feeling good, and not faking it, I could snag a Boston Qualifier time of 3:10. So it was decided. At mile 16, the jets would go on.

I approached mile 16, walked some of the aid station, got myself a few drinks and an orange slice, and hit the split button on the watch. Time for a fast Sunday morning 10 miles!

The remainder of the run course is rolling hills as you approach Carmel. There is more housing along the coast and more spectators. The point-to-point nature of the course doesn't make for a spectator-friendly course. The race organizers make up for this with musicians at every mile. But as you approach the end of the course, more and more spectators appear as they travel south from Carmel along Highway 1, seeking out friends and family.

Somewhere, mile 20 I think, there are a collection of drag queens. Or were they belly dancers? Or both? But mostly I remember the rolling hills and the harder pace. By the time I am running by the drag queen belly dancers (wait a second, one of those is a lady! Or am I just getting tired?), my predicted finish time is 3:12. Six (point 2) miles to go. Two minutes. Mmmm, yeah, this can work, I think. Of course, given my conservative early pacing and the pacing of your typical marathoner (too fast to the wall at mile 20), I am passing a LOT of people as I run on.

Mile 22 brings me to a nice downhill, and I start approaching someone slowly. This is new. Most people over the last six miles have come into sight, and left sight, quickly. It takes nearly a mile for me to catch up with this fellow. We run together, silently for two miles before he begins to fade or I begin to speed up, concerned with hitting my 3:10. Too bad, it would have been nice to finish up strongly together.

There's a last small hill at mile 25 and then the finish is on a slight downhill of about one mile, and the finisher area is a big party. I have something to celebrate: 3:09:12.

The finisher medal for Big Sur is really something else. The year I ran, it was a baked ceramic medallion with the Bixby Bridge, highlighted with hand-painted colors. I've done a lot of races, and I have a lot of medals, and this one is the most impressive. Much like the race itself.

Steve Smith contracted a serious case of adult-onset athletics at age 28. He has spent the years since avoiding potential cures. He's glad to have a name that Googles poorly, or effectively, depending on the purpose. He spends his days searching the web for results that he can claim.

The Oklahoma City Memorial Marathon

oklahoma city, oklahoma

Web site: www.okcmarathon.com
Month: April
USATF Certified: Yes
Course: Rolling

Author: Mark Bravo
Number of Marathons Completed: 25+
Age Group: 45-49

THE OKLAHOMA CITY

MEMORIAL
MARATHON

Each year as April gives way to May, runners in increasing numbers appear before daybreak in front of the Oklahoma City National Memorial, to take part in an event that will almost surely call for character and a depth of physical effort unprecedented for many of them. What I witnessed, though, at the inaugural Oklahoma City Memorial Marathon in 2001—and have seen validated in each event since—is a sense of sheer gratefulness for simply being there. I've not encountered that depth of emotion in any of my other marathon experiences. With the plethora of marathon offerings worldwide, why would these feelings prevail in Oklahoma, hardly a state known as a marathon mecca? Furthermore, why has such an embryonic event reached "destination" marathon status?

Ask the two founders of this race, who formulated the concept one Sunday morning while traversing the streets of Oklahoma City on a long training run. The answer is most paradoxical. Both are quick to say this race is NOT about running. The race is about life.

Oklahoma City Memorial Marathon President Thomas Hill and Race Director Chet Collier had a vision in early 2000 to celebrate how far the city had come since that April day in 1995 when the Alfred P. Murrah Federal Building was the sight of the senseless tragedy that altered the course of so many lives here. Hill, an accomplished marathoner, emphasizes the theme of the race, "Find a Reason to Run." Collier's passion is evident as he reiterates their goal for everyone who participates, whether running or walking: that this last Sunday in April will continue to be a "Run To Remember" for all who take part.

A race with tremendous purpose—in this case to raise money for the Memorial, and to remember those victimized by this act of terrorism—can sometimes thrive for a year or two on emotion alone. For a marathon to persevere, however, it must be carried off with precision and efficiency. In this department, accolades abound. After only three years on the marathon "map," the Oklahoma City Memorial Marathon was accorded by *Runner's World* magazine as one of the 12 greatest marathons in the world, a "Must Run" singled out as "Most Memorable" and introduced into an exclusive circle with the likes of marathons in Rome, Stockholm, Pikes Peak, and Vancouver. Bart Yasso, veteran race and event promotion director at *Runner's World*, wrote the article and has run marathons on all seven continents, numbering over 150 worldwide. He describes this marathon as, "A very moving marathon … it starts right next to the memorial; you can see the different-sized chairs that symbolize the kids and adults. After the race, runners leave notes and bib numbers on the remembrance wall near the finish. It's amazing. You never forget it."

Race day brings a groundswell of excitement, mixed with awe and reverence, but also pomp and pageantry. The best way to describe this race is that it's an event, a classic triumph-over-tragedy story that continues to grow and be nurtured by an entire city that embraces this day. In memory of those lost and in honor of the survivors, runners take to the streets and are shocked by the support shown by throngs of onlookers looking for friends and family. Many spectators are simply there to lend support to the masses of runners, walkers, and wheelchair athletes who have gathered. Keeping with the theme of inclusion paramount in this race, the Oklahoma City Memorial Marathon offers a half-marathon, a five-person relay (distances from 5K to 12K), and a 5K walk. A Kid's Marathon, which promotes motion and fitness by having youngsters log 25 miles in the months leading up to race day, finishes with a 1.2 mile dash around downtown Oklahoma City which starts moments after the marathon. With 3 1/2 hours of live television, those not able to hit the streets to cheer can possibly catch a glimpse of their race "favorite" as the morning unfolds.

Marathon Sunday morning has graced Oklahoma City each of its years so far with clear skies and a groundswell of nervousness and anticipation apparent at all starting lines. Yet there is a certain ease in many of the runners' approach. Sometimes wind is a factor. Those factors simply aren't as paramount at Oklahoma City, for this isn't just another athletic endeavor. While indeed the presence of elite runners is more evident each year—witness two-time winner and 18th place finisher in the 2004 U.S. Olympic Marathon Trials, Conor Holt—the factors that fuel the popularity and nationwide exposure of this race have everything to do with triumph of the human spirit whatever it takes. What better forum for these lessons to be displayed than on the streets of the city that witnessed this horrible terrorist act?

Courtesy of The Oklahoma City Marathon

In 2003, the Oklahoma City Memorial Marathon posed an enduring wind in the face of the athletes as they headed back toward the Memorial from Lake Hefner, which marks the halfway point of this citywide tour. Even by Oklahoma standards, it was an inordinate obstacle that day, as normally this slightly rolling course is conducive to fast times. Miles 14 to 17 offered an ample dose of Lake Hefner's grandeur, but also the day's most brutal wind. Well-wishes from spectators and teams of volunteers were never more welcome. The character needed at this time in the race reminds me of the reason this event has gained acclaim as a "Must Run." Accounts of runners coming from all over the country, young and old, fast and not-so-fast, have a common thread that echoes through their word: Emotion.

Simply put, it brought 63-year-old Dick Esselborn here. A veteran of marathons in the upper echelon of the sport in his age group, Esselborn has raced internationally, and sets his sights on 3:30 as a finishing time when he embraces the marathon. The severity and consistency of the wind that day in 2003 was unprecedented in his marathon pursuits, but to hear him describe his experience is to witness the essence of what runners aspire to glean from the sport. "I told myself to cope with it; in Oklahoma City there was a sense of obligation," Esselborn stated. "To know that these people died mercilessly, you wanted to do your best to honor their memory. I found myself grateful I had the ability to work that hard. This marathon combines the beauty of everyone coming together for one cause." Esselborn hopes to make Oklahoma City an annual trek, and says the race symbolizes the words of legendary runner Roger Bannister to "…give a little more than you think you've got." Thirteen miles of stiff wind on the back end of a marathon leaves a range of epitaphs—usually none too complimentary—but with sentiments such as Esselborn's dictating this most unusual feeling at Oklahoma City, most runners wouldn't have had it any other way.

That marathon in '03 is still widely talked about, but you feel year after year that race organizers aren't resting on their laurels, attributing to a great number of "repeat performances" by veteran marathoners, as well as those who made it their inaugural. I can only compare the Marine Corps Marathon (one I've run five times) in terms of this race event feeling like a citizen's race. By that, I mean the volunteers (2,500 strong) seem as excited as the runners to be a part of the day. The volume of the crowds cheering as you're led from the race start, only steps from the emotion and reverence of the Memorial, leave a lasting impact. Make no mistake though;

this is not a depressing day, but uplifting beyond wildest expectations. Even the days leading up to this last Sunday in April are brimming with excitement, with appearances by running legends Dick Beardsley, Frank Shorter, and Bill Rodgers. The two-day expo has become another source for bragging rights, where pre-race chatter is full of anticipation. The difference is the unprecedented purpose that brings everyone together for this race and seems to hold the promise of something unique each year.

Proving the emotional power of this race, a race director of another event changed the date of her race so she could run the Oklahoma City Memorial Marathon. Co-race director Geneva Hampton's efforts moved the Little Rock Marathon in Arkansas to early March after missing the 2003 race to stage the inaugural Little Rock event. Hampton grew up in Oklahoma, and though she hasn't lived in the state in over two decades, felt an unwavering emotional tie in the aftermath of the bombing. When the marathon was established, she wanted to be part of that first race. Experienced with the distance and with race credits including Stockholm and Chicago, that first Oklahoma City hooked her. The perseverance shown that day in her first Oklahoma City Memorial race is nothing short of the perfect embodiment of this race, and why it came to be.

"I actually ran the last three miles of the first race with a broken foot," Hampton recounts. "I stepped off a curb and something didn't feel right. I stopped to stretch, and that was a mistake. But I wanted to finish that day so badly, and kind of carried my leg the rest of the way." Hampton, who is slight in stature, but determined as she is physically tough, now brings a contingency of marathoners of all abilities to the event annually. Bearing in mind all that she faced in the 2001 race, to say it was a positive experience for her doesn't do justice to the exuberance she brings to conversations about this race, "It was the best race I'd ever been to."

We all have been in situations where no matter what the surroundings or history of that particular race present to us, all we're thinking is, "Where are the aid stations? Where is the crowd?" Anything to provide that much-needed lift so often searched for in the latter stages of a marathon. In Oklahoma City, you notice the plethora of water stops with ample and varied refreshment and volunteers not only emotionally-charged but efficient, a key ingredient especially at "crunch time" when inspiration and fuel are most vital. As you wind through the city to live bands, and through diverse neighborhoods, something truly unique to Oklahoma City's race becomes evident, lining the streets throughout much of the race are banners bearing the names of the 168 people lost in the bombing, as poignant an experience when first noted as you can imagine. It's quickly realized what those names represent, and more than a few have credited the sight of those names for finishing the task on a day that may otherwise have been unconquerable.

While Holt's winning time of 2:23 is certainly worth noting, this race is anything but geared to "elite" racers only. The 2004 Female champion Tracy Evans, a finisher of every Memorial Marathon, ran the final six miles having aggravated a hip injury to the point that it altered her gait dramatically in those final miles. The memories she counts as most important? Not her perseverance, her time, even her victory, but this, "One lady ran out of her house ... she had been watching the race on TV, and she runs toward me yelling, 'Thank you for running; I'm so proud of you,' and you find out that maybe these people lost someone on that day in 1995, or knew of someone who did, and you know there's a special reason you want to run this race."

One of the running world's true diplomats, who is seemingly unaware of his celebrity, Bill Rodgers' unbridled joy for the sport is visible with every word, and the importance Rodgers attaches to this race is clear, "Running is one of the ultimate affirmations we can have in our lives. Running the Oklahoma City Memorial Marathon brings people together in goodwill and friendliness. It is an act of non-violence, something I believe we can never have too much of, especially with what happened there."

The overriding message of this marathon and everything leading up to it is one of promoting inclusion. The passion of Hill and Collier is infectious, witness the array of volunteers and competitors from all 50 states and multiple countries. That passion was also evident in 2003 when service personnel from our armed forces in Saudi Arabia paid homage to lives lost by emulating the Oklahoma City Memorial Marathon with their own 26.2 mile trek (complete with official race numbers sent to them by race officials).

The theme is pervasive everywhere you turn, kids scurrying down Robinson Avenue in the Kids' Marathon, walkers accomplishing their mission, special-needs athletes enjoying enthusiastic cheers, and relay runners taking in the emotion, revelry, and camaraderie of the day. Of course, there's the main attraction: Over 2,000 marathoners, both novice and serious-minded taking on the 26.2 mile challenge in whatever manner they're able.

One is hard-pressed to be part of the proceedings as a walker, runner, volunteer, or onlooker and not be touched in a lasting manner.

Simply put, this race was established, "To Honor Their Memory, Celebrate Life, Reach For The Future, and Unite The World In Hope."

Oklahoma City's an easy place to travel to and get around in, and you'll find you're greeted with warmth and appreciation. As well, you may learn and grow in ways that far transcend the sport of running.

Mark Bravo is a freelance writer, running coach, and veteran marathoner in Oklahoma City, having run over 25 marathons.

Country Music Marathon

nashville, tennessee

Web site: www.cmmarathon.com
Month: April
USATF Certified: Yes
Course: Rolling

Author: Tracy Whittlesey
Number of Marathons Completed: 3
Age Group: 30-34

Author: Lewis Goldberg
Number of Marathons Completed: 5
Age Group: 55-59

It all started with the challenge to run two marathons in six weeks. My boss, Lew Goldberg, and I first decided to run the San Diego Rock 'n' Roll Marathon. It would be my first marathon and Lew's fifth. While registering for the San Diego Rock 'n' Roll Marathon, I noticed the advertisement for the Nashville Country Music Marathon. Not only would there be a marathon with bands at every mile, but also if we ran both the San Diego and Nashville Music Marathons we would also get a special medal in the shape of a music note—and, of course, I wanted the music note, so I approached Lew with the idea. He agreed, and we were off.

Training for the marathon was a little harder than I anticipated. The farthest distance I had run previously was 10 miles—with very little training. But, Lew and I ran when we could and prepared ourselves for both marathons. Our basic training plan was two weekday runs of about three to six miles and one weekend long run. During our training, our longest run was about 15 miles. I learned later that we should have gone a little farther in our long runs. The biggest hole in our training program was the hill work. If you are running the Country Music Marathon don't skip out on the hill training. We trained on two courses that were fairly flat. It really hurt us in the end.

Lew and I lived about two hours away from Nashville in Huntsville,

Courtesy of Elite Racing

Alabama, so we did not have a long trip to the race. On April 28, we packed up our family and friends, found a nice hotel on the outskirts of Nashville, found some spaghetti downtown, and prepared for the big day.

It was beautiful in Nashville on race day. The Fahrenheit temperature at the start of the race was in the upper 40s with highs expected in the 70s. It was a little overcast, but perfect for running.

The Country Music Marathon organizers did a great job getting the runners in place for the start of the race. There were plenty of shuttles to get runners to the start and parking was not hard to find.

Lew and I were just hoping to finish so we started in the corrals at the back of the line. The race started on West End Avenue at Centennial Park. Centennial Park is well known for the Parthenon that stands in its center. The Parthenon is a replica of the original Parthenon in Athens, Greece and serves as the city's art museum.

From Centennial Park we headed toward Demonbreun Street, which took us to Music Row. This was the first of the hills during our 26.2 miles. Demonbreun Street was the start of a five-mile long hill—tough, but manageable. Don't skip out on your hill training!

Music row was a great part of the run. The street is lined with record companies and the Country Music Hall of Fame. Nashville made sure the city was ready for the marathon. The neighborhoods were beautiful, and it was a great feeling to see families having breakfast on the front porch and cheering on the runners.

At mile six, we passed Belmont Mansion. The mansion was built in the 1850s and was, at separate times, home to an art gallery, a bowling alley, and even a zoo. The mansion eventually became a part of Belmont University. We continued through this beautiful campus for a couple of miles.

Almost halfway there, at mile 12, we started through the Tennessee Bicentennial Capitol Mall State Park. The park covers 19 acres and is an outdoor history museum. It is a great place to learn about the history of Tennessee. The park includes famous sites such as the Capitol building (which was built in 1845), the zero mile marker—which is the start point for all state mile markers, and a variety of other interesting facts about the city of Nashville and Tennessee.

The next couple of miles were probably the toughest miles from a mental standpoint. There wasn't a lot to look at, the course was fairly flat and it seemed to go on forever. We found our way back to the Bicentennial Park and at mile 20 headed back downtown.

With only six miles to go, mile 20 took us to Shelby Park (a beautiful park, with rolling hills, playgrounds, baseball diamonds, and tennis courts). From Shelby Park we headed home on Davidson Street toward at the time, the Adelphia Coliseum, but now just "the Coliseum" which is home to the NFL team, the Tennessee Titans. The run down Davidson Street wasn't the prettiest part of the course, but with just a few miles to go we found a way to keep pushing toward the Coliseum.

Finally, there it was — Adelphia Coliseum! What a great feeling to see it and know that we would finish! That was the motivation we needed to pick it up and cross the wire.

Once over the finish line, the Country Music Marathon volunteers greeted us with space blankets, water, food, and our finisher's medals. The Country Music Marathon was well organized, a wonderful course and a fantastic experience.

The bands and the cheerleaders along the course were great! At least every mile had a cheerleading squad that did a terrific job of motivating the runners. Bands were spread out every mile or so, playing a variety of music including country, blues, and rock and roll. At mile 18, the music was the only thing to get us through.

Six weeks later, Lew and I ran the San Diego Rock 'n' Roll Marathon, and we got our special medal — the music note.

In 2004, Elite Racing, Inc., and Country Music Marathon Officials redesigned the course in an effort to eliminate some of the hills. It was the first time the course was altered since its inception in 2000. The new route meant fewer hills by eliminating three sections, but some neighborhoods were left out of the race experience. The Demonbreun Street hill, which was run between miles two and three, was removed, resulting in the elimination of the downtown portion of the run. Next to go was the use of Granny White Pike, and 12th Avenue South and Woodlawn Street. Now runners have a more scenic route, but they retrace their steps north on Belmont Boulevard and 16th Avenue South before reaching the half-marathon turn-off. The third change, at mile 20, cut out most of the Woodland Avenue hill, known as the killer climb. The Woodland Avenue hill consisted of a 125-foot climb over three miles. With all the changes, the finish line remains in the same place it has been since the start. Based on recent runner reviews, many still consider the course hilly. Did I mention not to skip out on your hill training?

Tracy Whittlesey is an analyst for the Department of Defense in Washington, D.C. She is an accomplished equestrian and enjoys running, golfing, and snow skiing in her spare time. The Nashville Country Music Marathon was her first marathon. Since then, she has completed the San Diego Rock 'n' Roll Marathon and the Marine Corps Marathon. She trains with the Capitol Hill Running Club.

Avenue of the Giants Marathon

eureka, california

Web site: www.theave.org
Month: May
USATF Certified: Yes
Course: Rolling

Author: Bill Turrentine
Number of Marathons Completed: 45
Age Group: 55-59

The Avenue of the Giants marathon is held each year in Northern California, 45 miles south of Eureka, on the Avenue of Giants highway. The race is held in May and is arguably one of the most scenic marathons in the U.S. and is my favorite of the 45 marathons I have done. This is not a run for those who enjoy the urban atmosphere and large crowds associated with some of the larger marathons like New York or Marine Corps. Instead, it is a chance to enjoy a run among the Giant Redwoods, with potentially a lot of time for solo reflection.

Although the race was first held in 1972, it is still a small, but well run event. Six Rivers Running Club sponsors the race as it has for the past 30+ years. The race was originally born out of the need for a local race in Humboldt County where athletes could qualify for the 1972 Olympic Trials. After its first successful year, the club decided to make it an annual event. The race has a history of attracting quality runners and also has its share of unforgettable stories, including a marathon wedding that took place at the start line, under the Dyerville Bridge.

I first ran the older course in 1978 on too little distance training and not enough long runs. It was harder than the current course with an uphill finish in the last several miles. We started and finished in a downpour that day, and I spent the last few miserable miles having hit the wall at mile 18. Since then, I returned to the changed course, which is the same as the current one. Part of the reason for the change was the increase in the size of the field, which approached 2,000 (and remains in that range today).

The early springtime is fairly cool with Fahrenheit temperatures typically in the 50s, but the forest can be somewhat humid. The course starts at the Dyerville Bridge on the Avenue of the Giants in Humboldt Redwoods State Park. The overflow parking is on the gravel by the river with a steep climb up the bank to the start. The course is paved and consists of two out-and-backs. After 6.55 miles and a bit over 300 feet of gradual elevation gain, the course turns back and retraces its path to the start/finish area. With the largest amount of climbing completed in the first half, it does not seem as hard as it would in the later part of the run.

The first leg of the race is on the narrow winding Bull Creek road, which goes through the majestic Rockefeller Grove. The road is lined with Redwoods like huge columns lining the aisle of a cathedral, and Bull Creek makes an appearance from time to time on the left side of the road. There is a feeling of enormous space between the canopy of treetops and the ground. Somewhere in Rockefeller Grove is where many biologists believe the tallest tree in the world lives. The floor of the forest is covered with red dirt from the decomposing wood, moss covered logs, and bright green ferns. This is one of the most beautiful sections of the course. Most of the first segment is shaded with a couple of open spots that can be sunny and warm. The first open area is near mile four.

There were a few small steep hills in the first five miles and then the course began a gradual climb to the turn around aid station. After another sunny open section between miles five and six, we worked our way to the turn-around aid station. By the turn around point I was in cruise mode and was able to enjoy the long gentle downhill from the turn around.

The crowds cheering the runners at the start/finish provide a burst of energy. The second half of the course travels down the Avenue of the Giants and has some small hills with the largest being the freeway overpass. The course is mostly shaded and parallels the Eel River. It rolls gently to the town of Weott near mile 15. After the town, the cover of the Redwoods again shades the course. The turn-around is at 19.55 miles and the course retraces itself back to the start/finish. The freeway overpass hill is encountered again just after mile 25, but after cresting the top, the remainder of the run is downhill.

I ran the Avenue of the Giants marathon twice as my second and third marathon efforts. It is not the flattest course and probably will not result in a PR, although my second time was a PR at that time by 11 minutes (3:05). However, The Avenue of the Giants is an excellent choice for a spring marathon. It has a fairly challenging, beautiful course and cool weather. The second time I ran, I remember the weather being cool with some early morning humidity and a couple of gentle rain showers. There are few spectators along the course and most are seen at aid stations or the finish area. I enjoyed the quiet shade of the trees while running the course.

The t-shirts and medals are colorful and nicely detailed. Due to the natural surroundings of the event, each year a unique design of flora and fauna are featured on the shirt. The web site shows the t-shirt designs from the past few years. The evening before the race there is a spaghetti dinner put on by the local fire department and a bake sale.

There is a fall marathon, the Humboldt Marathon and Half Marathon, run in October on the same course except that the two legs are reversed. The first leg is on the Avenue of the Giants and the second leg is along Bull Creek Road.

The nearby towns are fairly small. Accommodations close to the race are limited and fill quickly. One of the closest towns with accommodations is Garberville, 25 miles south of the park. We enjoyed the drive to the race from the San Francisco area (about five hours) and took the opportunity to do some sightseeing along the way.

It is sometimes difficult to concentrate on the run and not be distracted by the 300-foot trees lining the course. One such tree, which is said to provide inspiration to runners at miles 14 and 26, is the Dyerville Giant. The Dyerville Giant was over 1,000 years old when its root system finally gave way in 1992 and it fell. The tree was left in the woods, and is said to have an ephemeral quality. Even though it is now dead, some feel that the spirit of the tree still watches over the race.

Bill Turrentine started running during his active duty tour in the Navy when there was a physical fitness push. At the time, he was stationed in Hawaii and the runs at work were through pineapple fields. In 1974, he moved to California and began running road races. In December 1975, he did his first marathon and began running a variety of other distances. His wife's Navy career took them to Naples, Italy and they enjoyed many local Italian races as well as various marathons in Europe. One of his best runs was a win at the Stra Ischia in May 1982, a run of 33K finishing in 2:34. Bill and his wife moved back to Monterey, California in 1982 where his wife ran a 50-mile run. Inspired by her, Bill ran his first 50-mile run in April 1983 at the American River 50 miler and has been doing ultras ever since. Bill currently has 45 marathon finishes and 100 ultra finishes.

Lincoln National Guard Marathon

lincoln, nebraska

Web site: www.lincolnrun.org/marathon.htm
Month: May
USATF Certified: Yes
Course: Rolling

Author: Paul Van De Water
Number of Marathons Completed: 8
Age Group: 50-54

You may not find a lot of hype about the Lincoln National Guard Marathon, but you will come away from the race with the feeling that you were very special and well taken care of. That is because you, as a runner, are the center of this marathon weekend with all finishers receiving a medal and all female finishers receiving a rose.

My first Lincoln Marathon (the 10th Annual) was in 1987, which was a culmination of three years of trying to quit smoking and getting back into shape. Over those years, I was determined to see what my 30+ year-old body was still capable of doing after years of neglect. Running in circles at my local YMCA on the indoor track, led to running outside, which led to running five-mile races, which led to 10Ks, and then to half-marathons. There were no records set, except those that I had set for myself. It was me against me!

So far my training had consisted of help from a friend. I'm not sure what inspired me to even think I could run a marathon, but I did know that I was going to need more help than what my friend could provide. I decided to join a class on marathon training offered at the YMCA. When you have decided to run your first marathon, I cannot stress enough, how important a running group is in getting you through the stages of training for that marathon. Some of my best friends are people I have met in marathon training classes. To this day, even though I know what to expect while running a marathon, I still need that support group. They are the ones listening to my failures and successes. They are the ones keeping me going when running isn't fun at 6:00 a.m. on Saturday mornings in Lincoln, Nebraska, in a 0°F wind chill.

After a long winter of training, spring in Nebraska brings beautiful flowering shrubs and trees, which are in full bloom by the first weekend in May (race day is the first Sunday in May). Race temperatures average in the 40s – 50s. You'll see boulevards and trails lined with lilacs, spirea (bridal wreath), pink flowering crab, white flowing pear, and many, many more.

The Lincoln Marathon is a weekend event for runners and their families. The week prior to the marathon, the Lincoln Journal-Star publishes a paper insert that tells about the marathon, shows the course map, and lists all of the participants. It is amazing how many people will wish you good luck after seeing your name in the paper.

Saturday is the Mayor's One Mile Kid's Run. Last year, during the 17th annual run, there were 3,400 kids from 26 elementary schools. This run is held around the State Capitol Building and also offers awards to the schools that have the largest number of participants. As much as $1,700 was raised (50 cents per entry) and donated to a local youth organization. Also on Saturday, is the race expo, which offers talks on running related topics, clothing, shoes, and packet pick-up (which includes your chip timing and t-shirt).

Saturday evening is the "Pasta-thon" and Sunday after the race is the post-race lunch. Family members are welcome to attend both meals. A massage tent is located near the finish line, with free massages donated by local massage therapists. There are no extra charges for most activities during the marathon weekend—your entry fee includes *many* extras.

If there is inclement weather on the morning of the race, there are plenty of areas for runners to go inside on the University of Nebraska campus. These facilities also offer a generous number of restrooms, changing areas, and showers for before and after the race. Upon lining up for the 7:00 a.m. start, in front of the beautiful University of Nebraska Memorial Stadium and Coliseum, you can hear the Army National Guard Military Band playing various patriotic songs. There is no gun start for this race, it is instead signaled with a cannon blast!

The Lincoln Marathon is the host for the National Guard Marathon Trials. This means that Guard members nationwide compete for National Guard Marathon Team positions. Most states and Puerto Rico have teams that participate, which make up about 200 of the total 3,000 half-marathon and marathon numbers. It is fun being able to identify each state's runners by the state name on their shirts.

The marathon course is relatively flat, with only two to three short hills. Spectators can be found on all areas of the course. Some can be seen, still in their night attire, enjoying that first cup of coffee of the morning. Then there's a neighborhood group that sports elephant and pig noses, standing on the boulevard, waving to every runner. The course, being two separate loops, allows for supporters to rendezvous with their runner at numerous points without getting caught in traffic or being blocked by the course. Although not encouraged, after mile eight, there is even adequate room for bike support. This, I have found, is a tremendous boost, especially during the last six miles, when a friend can help take your mind off the fatigue.

There are water and sport drink stations every couple of miles. These are staffed by various organizations, like the YMCA and Bryan LGH Medical Center. Also, at these aid stations, you will find ice, Vaseline, first aid, loud cheering, and lots of encouragement. All cups are served with a lid and straw, which unless you are a runner, doesn't sound like a big deal. It is much easier to drink, while running, when you have a straw and the lid keeps you from spilling sticky sports drink all over yourself. There are ample liquids at every station, since there are several tables set up on both sides of the course.

Local police officers and other volunteers man each street crossing. Throughout its history, volunteers have played a huge roll in the success of the Lincoln Marathon — more people volunteer than run! One especially notable volunteer was a good friend to the race, Roger Ogea, who for 20 years was the "voice" at the finish line. Roger suddenly passed away in 2004. He will be greatly missed at the Lincoln Marathons and other local races sponsored by the Lincoln Track Club.

In my 20+ years of running, I have participated in 8 marathons (five Lincoln) and 10 half-marathons (seven Lincoln), and I can truly say that none of the others were as well organized as the Lincoln Marathon. From the expo on Saturday, to the last orange cone picked up on the streets; the race is superbly run by veterans who have put on the marathon for many years. From my first Lincoln Marathon in 1987 to my most recent in 2003, there has been the same consistent quality year after year. This shows in the participant numbers, which increased by 77 percent during that time (from 1,700 to 3,000).

Other noted festivities during race weekend include special recognition of the Lucky 13 Club. This "club" is for any runner completing their 13th Lincoln Marathon. The Harry Crockett Lunch, which is held on Saturday, gives special recognition to those runners who have completed a Lincoln Marathon after their 50th birthday. Now that I have attained membership in that "exclusive" club, I am beginning to understand what Harry meant went he said, "We don't have to let age be a barrier to a healthy, active life."

A few other things to note are that the sponsoring hotel hosts the race expo, which makes it very convenient for out-of-town travelers, and also offers discounted room rates. Registration for the race can be done online. With the chip timing, you can also track a runner's progress on the Internet.

Any suggestion for additions or changes to this marathon would be considered on the picky side, but I guess there is always room for improvement. The following would be my suggestions:

- Hold a competition amongst the various aid stations, so they become more creative with their themes. This gives runners something to look forward to at the next aid station.

- Receive the results booklet sooner, it currently takes about six months. Also the print could be a little larger (this may just be an age thing)!

You won't find a better way to begin your running season than by running the Lincoln Marathon while enjoying the hospitality of Lincoln, Nebraska. I guarantee you will be back to do a second!

Paul Van De Water is the Fiscal Director for Region V Systems (a management organization of behavioral health services), located in Lincoln, Nebraska. He started running 21 years ago, at the age of 31, and ran his first marathon at the age of 34. Although the Lincoln National Guard Marathon is his favorite of eight completed marathons, Chicago was an experience of a lifetime. At the age of 52, he considers himself a "social runner," and running for him has become a way of life. He continues to run just because he still can!

KeyBank Vermont City Marathon

burlington, vermont

Web site: www.vcm.org
Month: May
USATF Certified: Yes
Course: Rolling

Author: Jill McManus
Number of Marathons Completed: 1
Age Group: 30-34

The challenge was presented to me in an email just a couple of days after Thanksgiving 2003, "I turned 50 this year and you're turning 30 … I may be crazy, but what do you say we do the marathon (KeyBank Vermont City Marathon) in May? I mean the whole thing … 26.2 miles." I was at home when I read this. Happily sipping my coffee, still feeling quite full after proving that I could succumb to my share of gluttony, I thought to myself, "Yes, Mary has indeed gone crazy."

Mary, who had turned 50 two months earlier, and I participated in the marathon relay the year before, an option for those who want to partake in the marathon experience, but prefer to divide the course between a team of individuals. We had talked about putting a team together for the upcoming year, so when Mary's idea of doing the full race was unveiled, needless to say I was quite surprised.

I grew up with parents who were avid marathoners and triathletes, both mom and dad being veterans of the Boston, New York, Marine Corps, and Maryland marathons. Unfortunately, I was too young to appreciate, or even fathom their accomplishments. As I sat that November morning, contemplating this invitation, I thought how great it would be to share this experience with the two of them. This thought, along with my personality quirk of thriving off personal physical challenges, prompted me to reply to Mary's email with a "Sure, why not? Let's do it." We both agreed to sign up online at that moment and within 20 minutes of pouring my first cup of coffee that morning, I had committed myself to running 26.2 miles on Memorial Day Weekend, 2004.

I admit I was a little terrified at the thought of having to run that many miles. For the past 10 years, I had considered myself a runner, doing three to four miles on an average of four to five days a week. I considered five miles a long run. Once in a blue moon, I'd do a whopping six, which made me feel like a superhero. If I could do six miles, I could probably lift a car over my head — that was my mentality.

Courtesy of KeyBank Vermont City Marathon

Thinking about clocking 26.2 during one outing, pretty much blew my mind. Thankfully, that crazy woman who offered this challenge to me also proposed a great idea. Mary suggested we enroll in a class called Marathon 101. The organizers of the KeyBank Vermont City Marathon offer this training course for first time marathoners, and it turned out to be one of the smartest things we could have done.

I was anxious prior to the first night of class, which took place in late January. I had no idea what to expect. With whom would I be embarking on this journey? How experienced were the runners going to be? Due to my idea of a five-mile long run, I feared I might not have as much of a base as other participants. But it turned out that there were a lot of individuals just like me in class. There were some who had completed several half marathons, and others who had never run more than two miles at one time. After only 10 minutes, my doubts about registering for the race subsided, but soon fears of injury and maintaining good health appeared. I was quick to learn that once one worry about doing a marathon dissipates, another moves in to fill that void.

The KeyBank Vermont City Marathon takes place in Burlington, Vermont on Memorial Day Sunday, which means that most training is done from January to April. Simply put, these are rough months. It's cold, it's snowy, and it's icy. My first long run was a 7.7-mile loop in mid-January. Here's the journal entry for that one: *Sunday 9:30 a.m. Temp. 22 degrees. Windy. Snowing. Felt good for 7.7 despite two falls on ice.* This was only the beginning of my slipping on ice, I took the next two days off to rest my twisted ankle. It was these types of experiences at which I could only laugh. I soon considered the weather to be part of the challenge of my marathon training. In my mind there was nothing I could do but bite the bullet and brave the beast of old man winter face to face.

Some excerpts from my training log that winter: *SO COLD! Two degrees … but felt okay. Thighs were freezing. Not wearing wind tights. Other than freezing, felt pretty good.* There was also: *Mary and I had to check each other for frostbite every few miles, but overall good run.* I swear, after reading these entries I sometimes think I might have been a little crazy myself.

Something that kept me going out in that cold were thoughts such as, "These are great conditions in which to train because, come race day, the weather will have warmed and nothing could be as harsh as what I've been through." These thoughts were validated each week in class, where it seemed everyone else was experimenting with similar mental strategies. Marathon 101 had become a bona fide runner's therapy session. For 17 weeks we bonded over long runs, injuries, race day fears, and consuming more food than we ever thought possible. We learned from each other, we made each other laugh, and we even shed some tears together.

When Memorial Day Weekend finally approached, I wanted to make sure I took in the entire marathon weekend experience. The Friday before the race, I entered the doors to my first marathon expo. It was incredibly inspiring — all of the runners, all of the vendors … the excitement and energy that filled the walls of the convention was infectious. There were hundreds of runners who had gone through a similar winter of training, with one identical goal to accomplish, to be in Burlington that weekend to take part in the state's largest sporting event. I received my bib, shopped around a bit, and held myself back from buying anything I might have been tempted to wear the next day.

Saturday evening, I attended the marathon's pasta dinner, which was sponsored by a local Italian restaurant. Again, inspiration ran through my veins as the director of the marathon introduced the staff and the volunteers who, through dedication and passion, made the weekend happen. As I left the dinner, I knew this was something special … not just for me, personally, but for the city of Burlington. I had been told this several times, but as a first time marathoner, and a first time participant to all that the weekend encompassed, I knew I had chosen the right race to take me through my first 26.2 experience.

I woke Sunday morning after a surprisingly restful sleep. The moment of truth was about to happen — the revealing of marathon day weather. I looked out the window and saw that there was not a cloud in the sky! Unbelievable. Old man winter had taken me for a ride over the past couple of months and it all paid off for this day of sunshine in the high 60s. Our class had agreed to meet at a gas station right at the start line about an hour before the start. As I walked down the street at 7:00 a.m. that morning with Mary, the city was already alive. There were runners making their way to the start and families planting themselves on their porches ready to cheer on the participants. Signs of support were hanging from windowsills and, already, spectators were jockeying for position along the course. We, the runners, were the show, and the audience was packed. Marathon day truly is a day of celebration in Burlington.

The start of the KeyBank Vermont City Marathon sits atop a hill overlooking Lake Champlain and the Adirondacks of New York state. On this day, you could clearly see the details of the mountains hovering over the sun-sparkled water. I positioned myself among the 6,500 marathoners and relay participants at the start. With butterflies dancing in my stomach I took a moment to let the experience sink in. I could barely wipe the smile from my face … that is until I realized that I had not eaten anything for breakfast and my backpack with my energy bar was still making its way to the start with some friends who were to send us off.

Panic briefly settled in … what was plan B going to be? I had three gel packs pinned to the inside of my shorts … I could down a couple of those and rely on the food along the course to get me through, but I had never done that and I was told not to, under any circumstances, try something new on race day. With 20 minutes to the start, Mary and I found our friends and my energy bar! Next time I'll pin a whole bar to my shorts, I thought as I devoured the solid mass.

At 8:05 a.m., the gun went off and a sea of nylon shorts, performance shirts, and fancy colored running shoes flowed around the first corner and headed up a short incline. From my position near the back of the pack, I could see the throng of runners ahead. This was one of the most memorable images of race day for me. We, the participants, were beginning our journey together. My senses were triggered by the sight of the runners making their way up the small incline, and the many sounds that filled the streets of Burlington; cheering friends and family, horns, whistles, music, and the rhythmic shuffle of thousands of rubber soles hitting the cool morning asphalt.

The first segment of the KeyBank Vermont City Marathon takes runners through downtown neighborhoods. The house-lined streets of Burlington were alive with supporters of all ages. Handmade signs were present at every turn; some scribbled in children's handwriting that read, "Go Mom! We are so proud of you!" and others that only adults would have the nerve to hold up that read, "Only 25 more to go!"

Soon the course led us to the "Beltline," an out-and-back six-mile stretch on a closed highway. I heard rumors that this was one of the more difficult parts of the race. Not that it was hilly, just that it was a long and tiring stretch. As I started out onto the highway, I was able to catch a glimpse of the lead runners since they had reached the turnaround point long before I could see it. I was amazed at the speed of these runners, and I was jealous that they had already gone out and back on this section, which meant they would be long gone by the time I crossed the finish line. They probably would have gone home, showered, eaten a nice meal, maybe caught a movie … my mind had a tendency to wander like this during the race. Thankfully, it was along this segment that I heard the first of many volunteer musicians who were planted along the entire course. A funky local percussion group, situated in the median strip, emanated some great vibes that snapped me out of my drifting thoughts.

After the Beltline, we wove through the heart of downtown Burlington, and ran down Church Street, the popular outdoor pedestrian marketplace. The brick-lined street was packed with spectators three rows deep! This multiple block section provided a surge of energy, I'm sure, for every runner in the marathon. I felt as though I was running through a party on the street, and the party was for me, and several thousand others, but I pretended it was for me.

At the halfway point, marked on the Burlington Bike Path, which runs along the beautiful shores of Lake Champlain, I felt another burst of energy and was able to increase my pace. I was told to try to take the first half slower than the second and when I saw the 13 mile marker, I knew it was time to pick it up some. My competitive side was kicking in. I had conquered the challenge of training and now it was time to challenge myself on the course. I saw a couple of people ahead of me who I knew, and I just had to catch up to them!

It was just after this surge of energy that I began to hear the heartbeat of the Taiko Drummers, a local group that traditionally plants themselves at the base of "the hill" of the marathon. The Battery Street hill is about a mile after the halfway point. I had done this hill numerous times on training runs. I just don't think I had ever done it at mile 15; it was always more like mile seven. This hill seems to be the dreaded piece of the race (which every race needs at least one) where participants bond and fret over it together. Fortunately, this marathon only had one major hill. With the aid of the pulsing drums, and the encouraging high fives from spectators lining the street, I was able to cruise right on up and crest that hill with no problem!

The rest of the course wound us through more neighborhoods and side streets, until we reached the other end of the bike path at about mile 20. As soon as my feet hit the paved trail, I knew it was a straight shot home along the wooded path with spectacular views of the lake and mountains. I was tired and sore, but was fortunate to have hooked up with a woman doing the last segment of the relay so I was able to pace myself with her. This woman, who happened to be from out of town, helped keep me going at my desired pace for the last six miles. She was the encouragement that I needed, saying things like, "Jill, you look awesome! You're doing so well, we're almost at the end!" To have been lucky enough to connect with a fresh relay participant was just what I needed.

At mile 25, I knew I had accomplished my goal. As I weaved through the fencing that guided the runners to the finish at Burlington's Waterfront Park, I felt the butterflies in my stomach appear, and sensed my skin being taken over by goose bumps. The spectators behind the fencing were all smiles, shouting "Great job number 2047! You're almost there!" I started seeing familiar faces of friends who had gathered at the end to cheer me in. My last few strides of the marathon felt as if I were floating to the finish. As I coasted under the clock that read a completed time of four hours and six minutes, I experienced a kind of high that only someone who has crossed the finish line of a marathon can appreciate.

I was able to cheer Mary in shortly after I crossed the line. She, too, was grinning ear to ear. I knew exactly what she was thinking—she had done it! Mary had not been so crazy to come up with this idea after all. For the rest of the day, I relaxed at the park where post-race activities took place. Surprisingly, as I left the festivities for the day, there was a slight pang of sadness that the race was actually over. Everything I had worked for was finished. What next? I guess it's the Marathon 201 class and next year's KeyBank Vermont City Marathon. A simple solution, a comforting plan.

Thinking back on my experience with the KeyBank Vermont City Marathon, I can honestly say it is one of the greatest accomplishments of my life. From day one of Marathon 101 class, I knew I couldn't fail with the support and dedication of the RunVermont organization. This marathon is undoubtedly the pride of Burlington. To the staff who masterminded such a wonderful experience, to the hundreds of volunteers who dedicated their time to make sure the course was clear and safe for participants, to the thousands of spectators who offered support and encouragement along the entire course. And to Mary, for her brilliant idea and support through the journey, I thank you for being an integral part of my first marathon experience. I'm hooked!

Jill McManus grew up with parents who were both marathoners and triathletes, so she was bound to get into the event at some point in life! Besides running, Jill loves hiking, cycling, rollerblading, and mostly being outside. She also considers herself an artist, which led her to starting her own jewelry business three years ago. When she's not occupied with her business, she enjoys painting and volunteering for the KeyBank Vermont City Marathon.

Wyoming Marathon

laramie, wyoming

Web site: www.angelfire.com/wy2/marathon
Month: May
USATF Certified: No
Course: Challenging

Author: Tom Conrad
Number of Marathons Completed: 85
Age Group: 65-69

The Wyoming Marathon is the longest continuously run marathon in Wyoming. The first event was held more than 25 years ago. This low-key race is held in the Medicine Bow National Forest mountains — 10 miles east of Laramie. It includes three races in one: the Rocky Mountain — a double marathon; the Wyoming Marathon; and the Medicine Bow Half Marathon. Even with three events, there were fewer than 150 participants, about 35 in the ultra, 70 to 75 in the full marathon, and 35 to 40 in the half marathon.

Exemplifying its low-key approach, the race director, Brent Weigner guarantees nothing; and he delivers. Brent is an adventure runner. He has run more than 120 marathons, completed ultra marathons on all seven continents, ran the North Pole Marathon in April 2003, ran an ultra to the geographic South Pole in January 2002, and raced in the Des Sables Marathon, the 150-mile staged race in the Sahara Desert.

The Wyoming Marathon starts at the Lincoln Monument, the highest point on the first transcontinental highway, now known as I-80. The course is hilly. It runs from an elevation of 8,723 feet to 8,100 feet to 8,500 feet to 8,000 feet and then turns around and returns. Aid stations are located at about four-mile intervals, each with water, bananas, and snacks. In effort to cut down on litter in the national forest, cups were not provided, so everybody had to carry water bottles.

Since the marathon was at elevation and was hilly, my goal was to complete it in six hours, compared to my normal goal of 5:40. When I walked uphill to the start, I found myself breathing hard. That is when I realized that my six-hour goal might be overly ambitious. The first two miles were sub-12 1/2 minutes per mile and no deep breathing, so I thought I might have acclimated to the elevation.

As further demonstration of the low-key nature of the event, about a dozen people arrived late and ran past me during the first mile, including the eventual second place finisher in the half marathon. These were the only people to pass me in the entire marathon. Although miles 2 to 4 1/2 were a gentle downhill, I found I had slowed down—not a good sign. My son, Pat, joined me on his mountain bike along this stretch. After the aid station at mile 4 1/2, the next 2 1/2 miles were uphill, and some sections were fairly steep. I was huffing and puffing on these steep uphills. Miles seven to nine were on a frontage road paralleling I-80—rolling terrain with an overall downhill trend.

At the aid station at mile nine, Pat left his bike and joined me walking. Pat had been training for walking in preparation for this event. He set a very good pace, and I struggled to keep up. Although the course from miles 9 to 13 had a general downhill trend, our times had slowed to about 13 1/4 minutes per mile. In this area, there were spectacular rock formations, called the Vedauwoo Rocks. These rocks were granite that had been eroded by wind and water. There is evidence suggesting that people lived in this part of Wyoming as long as 8,000 years ago, and locals believe that these people felt the rocks were sacred. They looked great for rock climbing.

After passing the 13-mile mark, there was a long, steep downhill, and a significant uphill to the turnaround point—about 1/3 mile. That meant that the course was actually longer than a full marathon. At the turnaround, my time was three hours flat. At that point, I realized that I could not achieve my six-hour goal.

The second half of the marathon backtracked on the same route. Pat walked as far as mile 17, where he retrieved his mountain bike. He biked along with me for another mile, and then he biked back to the start point. The next 3 1/2 miles were gentle to steep downhill. Starting at the mile 22 aid station, the course was gentle to steep uphill. It was not too bad, except for the last mile, which was steep. The last mile took me 16 1/2 minutes; my legs were too tired to walk any faster.

Over the last 4 1/2 miles, many of the runners doing the double marathon were heading out on their second loop. The double marathoners did not have good weather on the second loop. A thunderstorm rolled through at about 4:00 p.m., and few of them had finished by then. The race started at 6:00 a.m. in order to allow 14 hours of daylight for the runners.

My time for the marathon was 6:15, my slowest marathon in four years (when I did the Mosquito Pass Marathon in Leadville, Colorado, at an elevation of 10,000 to 13,600 feet). However, I found a positive spin for my slow time—it was a PR for a marathon at elevation.

There were many other positive aspects of this marathon:

- There was spectacular mountain scenery along the racecourse, with rock formations, pine trees, and wilderness.
- It was fun to do most of the marathon with my son at my side. This was the first marathon we'd done together since the 1980s.
- I knew many of the 75 marathoners. This is one of the traditional marathons for people doing marathons in all 50 states (50 Staters).
- I passed more than a dozen marathoners, and none passed me.
- The weather on race day was ideal. Temperatures were 45 to 60°F and sunny.
- I was greeted at the finish by my family (including grandchildren) and a cooler of beer.

There was an excellent pasta dinner the day before the race. It was held at the Little America Hotel. In addition to good food, I saw many marathoner friends I have come to know over the years. This hotel was also the race headquarters and offered discounts to marathon participants. Packet pick-up was also held at the hotel.

The surrounding area offers many activities if you're looking to vacation before or after the race. Other activities I enjoyed on my three-day weekend were:

- Visiting the Cheyenne Frontier Days Rodeo Grounds. That rodeo is considered the "Daddy of 'Em All"
- Touring the Old West Museum, next to the Cheyenne Frontier Days Rodeo Grounds
- Visiting the Wyoming Territorial Park in Laramie
- Seeing the Ivinson Mansion in Laramie

If you're looking for a PR, this isn't the race for you. If you're looking for a challenging course with a touch of Wild West, and a few unique features to keep you on your toes, literally, as the course runs over some cattle guards. This may be the race for you.

Don't let the Wyoming Marathon race motto: "Where the race director promises you nothing, and he delivers" fool you. This low-key race offers spectacular scenery, friendly people, and a sense of accomplishment!

Tom Conrad began running in 1974 and formed the Reston Runners four years later. He got the marathon bug and continued to run one or two marathons each year through 1989. Tom's first walking marathon was in 1991 and he walked one or two marathons each year until 1996. Since then, he has walked 5 to 13 marathons annually and he completed a round of 50 states in August 2004. Tom also participates in the Reston Triathlon with his three children, has bicycled across the USA, skis, and has climbed Mt. McKinley, Mt. Kilimanjaro, and the Grand Teton. Tom founded SCS Engineers 35 years ago, which has grown to 450 employees in 36 locations. Although born in San Francisco, Tom has decided that Reston, Virginia is a great place to live, and plans to continue living there for the rest of his life.

Deadwood-Mickelson Trail Marathon

deadwood, south dakota

Web site: www.deadwoodmickelsontrailmarathon.com
Month: June
USATF Certified: Yes
Course: Rolling

Author: Jonathan Beverly
Number of Marathons Completed: 25
Age Group: 40-44

One of the best aspects of running is that it doesn't require a special location or terrain. Unlike sports like skiing, climbing, surfing or diving, we don't have to wait to participate until we have vacation time and sufficient funds to travel to an appropriate location. Nevertheless, some places do make for better running; so much better that they would be worth making a special trip.

Imagine designing the perfect running venue: It would be a trail—closed to motor vehicles, of course—with a surface soft enough to be forgiving on joints, but smooth and wide enough to be able to glide along comfortably, looking up at the scenery, not down at every next step. For that scenery, what if we provided dense forests of ponderosa pines interspersed with rolling mountain meadows to provide long views, a few aspen groves with bright white trunks and rustling leaves, and trail-side beds of blue and yellow wildflowers? The trail could run alongside a rocky stream, occasionally crossing it on narrow wooden bridges, descend into deep, shaded canyons, and end on the edge of a historic tourist town.

If we were designing the perfect running venue, one version would certainly look a lot like the George S. Mickelson Trail in the Black Hills of South Dakota. A rails-to-trails conversion, the crushed limestone path winds 114 miles from Edgemont to Deadwood, passing through miles of national forestland and over rolling hills that graced the screen in Kevin Costner's 1990 blockbuster, *Dances with Wolves*. What better way to see a large portion of the trail than to run a marathon on its last 25 miles, finishing on the cobbled main street of Deadwood?

After the completion of the Mickelson Trail in 1998, local runners began saying "we ought to have a marathon here." Terry Smith, a local ultra-runner and director of the Centennial Trail 100, took up the idea in early 2002 but before the first one came off, handed it to Jerry Dunn, who has run with it—long and hard—as is his style. Dunn is known as "America's Marathon Man," for his "marathon of marathons" when he ran Boston on 26 consecutive days, culminating in the 100th Boston, and his record of running 200 certified marathons in 2000. Dunn was drawn to South Dakota by his wife, fellow marathoner and author, Elaine Doll-Dunn (a former Mrs. South Dakota), and the couple live down the road from Deadwood in Spearfish.

I chose Deadwood because I currently live in western Nebraska, 10 miles from town and 4 miles from a paved road. All my training is on dirt roads and trails. This means that it would be very difficult to train well for a road marathon; I tried in 2002 and dropped out of the New York City Marathon with heavily blistered feet. In April 2003, I ran my first trail marathon, the Rockin' K in central Kansas, which is REAL trails: up and down canyons, through sand, with multiple stream crossings, rocky escarpment climbs .... Oh, and more than a mile too long, just for fun. I finished second, although I couldn't compare my time to anything I'd run before. The Mickelson trail appealed to me as a setting for a place that I could run well (relatively fast, closer to a road marathon time than an adventure trail marathon time, but on soft surfaces) and enjoy the beauty of the West.

Jerry Dunn puts on a race with big-city amenities in a small-town setting. Registration, packet pick-up, transportation, finish-line amenities, and results were all top-notch. There was a nice expo for the marathon size, with mostly local exhibitors, and top-level speaker Jeff Galloway and myself (as the Chief Editor of *Running Times* magazine).

The course is a point-to-point with all but the first and last mile on the crushed-limestone rails-to-trails George S. Mickelson Trail. On race day, it was bright, sunny and 92°F—the highest temps recorded for this time of year since 1952. In contrast, there was snow at the higher elevations the year before.

The course climbs gradually for 13 miles then descends for the rest of the run, making it look fast, but "It's not a PR race by any means," warns 2004 winner Scott Walschlager from Sioux Falls, South Dakota. The black Hills may not get as much respect as their towering cousins just to the west, but the mile-high altitude (topping out at 6,200 feet) makes running fast considerably more difficult.

You don't, however, do a trail marathon for a PR, and despite the smooth surface, this is a trail marathon. "I think the silence and serenity of the trail offers something that we don't get at the bigger races," says Walschlager, "and besides, [in] how many marathons will a deer run right in front of you and jump a fence?"

Courtesy of Sally Smith

The trail presents some logistical difficulties in terms of the number of water stops and support, but the support provided well exceeds what is expected at most trail marathons, approaching that provided at much larger urban races. Given the extreme weather when I ran, the number of water stops was inadequate, and not as often as advertised. The race director promises to remedy this, and better weather would make it less drastic.

The race grew from 77 finishers in 2002 to 1,053 finishers from 48 states and provinces in 2004. Most of the race is inaccessible for spectators, but the finish area, in the heart of Deadwood, is a great place for family and friends to pass the time waiting for your arrival.

I stayed at the Holiday Inn Express in the center of Deadwood. Despite its name, it is actually a rather nice historic inn, not a roadside motel. It was a convenient place from which to explore Deadwood, and a short walk from the finish line. The only downside was the revelers in nearby rooms who were in town for the gambling, not the race, but I'm not sure that you could avoid this in any hotel.

Dave Braley, also of Sioux Falls, has run the race each of its three years, winning the first one. "It is the most scenic one I have ever run," he says. He and his family camp each time they come west. "It's great camping out there. No bugs, cool nights."

For some, like Jim Bitgood of Laurel, Maryland, the beauty was so distracting, he said, "I didn't realize it was so hot until I got into town ... running in the woods is just cooler. Or just cool." For others, like 2003 winner Robert Ellerbruch, the heat was debilitating: he was reduced to a walk, and finished 25 minutes slower than last year. As for me, I too suffered. Yet, thinking of the race, the most powerful memories that come to mind are of the quiet beauty of running alone through the woods.

Jonathan Beverly is the Editor in Chief of Running Times *magazine. He has been running competitively since high school cross-country in the late 1970s. He has run 25 marathons since 1980, with a best time of 2:46.*

Grandma's Marathon

duluth, minnesota

Web site: www.grandmasmarathon.com
Month: June
USATF Certified: Yes
Course: Rolling

Author: Jon Carver Carlson
Number of Marathons Completed: 15
Age Group: 50-54

Duluth, Minnesota

When I tell people that I'm training to run Grandma's Marathon, I love to see the reaction on their faces. It's usually one of confusion, and I'm quite sure they're thinking, "But, you're a man! What are you doing running in a race for grandmothers?" I quickly assure them that I'm not sneaking into an all women's race, and explain to them that while Grandma's has many participants who are indeed grandmothers (in fact, there is an award for the first grandma who crosses the finish line), it also consists of thousands of male and female runners from all walks of life.

I've had the pleasure of running 15 marathons — 10 of them at Grandma's, and I have to say that it is hands down my favorite. I may be a little biased since I've lived in the race's host town, Duluth, Minnesota, for the better part of my life, but I can honestly say that I have never been to a race with such beautiful scenery, awesome community support, wonderful volunteers, and a great post-race party. It's not only a marathon, but it's an event, a festival, and an experience that every marathon runner should try at least once in their life.

So, why is it called Grandma's Marathon? The history behind the name is quite interesting and may surprise you a little. It all started in 1977 when a local running group, called the North Shore Striders (for which I later served as president), was bound and determined to host a marathon on their favorite running route that spanned along Lake Superior from Two Harbors, Minnesota to Canal Park in Duluth. The only problem was that the Striders had very little money in their checkbook, and knew that in order to do it right they'd need to find a sponsor. After being turned down by many local businesses, the group approached a new restaurant in Canal Park called Grandma's Saloon and Grill. The owners of the restaurant liked the idea of having hundreds of thirsty and hungry runners finish practically at their doorstep and agreed to give the Striders $600 in return for the title of the race. With money in their pocket and a name for the race to boot, Grandma's Marathon was born on June 25, 1977 with 150 runners toeing the line.

I'm pretty sure the organizers that first year never imagined the race would grow as much as it has. Today, Grandma's Marathon weekend is one of the largest multi-race events in the nation, attracting over 16,000 runners annually for the marathon, Garry Bjorklund Half Marathon, and the William A. Irvin 5K.

I still remember watching the runners during the first Grandma's Marathon as I drove alongside them down London Road (the final six miles of the course) thinking, "What the heck are these people doing?" However, as I continued watching in awe, the "marathon bug" snuck up and bit me, and it wasn't long after the first Grandma's Marathon that I started to prepare to run the race myself.

We all know that marathons are not the most predictable races in the world. A small little bump in the road can upset the apple cart and all of a sudden, you feel like all of your training tumbles to the ground. I knew that if I was going to do this, I was going to do it right or not at all. I trained in softball shorts (who needs running shorts?), read running magazines (or at least looked at the pictures), and ate a lot of healthy foods (Coke and Snickers bars). I put in what I hoped were enough miles, bought a red singlet and running shorts and come race day, I was ready! I had no idea of what to expect, but I knew it was going to be an adventure. Little did I know it would turn into a life long adventure with a race I've grown to love!

A few days before my first Grandma's Marathon, I found myself standing at the finish line, looking up the shore of Lake Superior as far as I could see, and thinking to myself "Boy, that's a heck of a long way, what am I getting myself into?" Then I looked around me at all of the workers preparing the finish line activity area, and felt a great sense of pride that they were working so hard to make the experience enjoyable for me and all of the other runners who would join me for the race.

Living in Duluth, you can literally see the excitement for Grandma's Marathon begin to grow several weeks before race weekend actually rolls around. The community is electrified by this event, and it's often a topic on the nightly news and in everyday conversations. The lampposts lining the streets of downtown Duluth and Canal Park are decorated with colorful Grandma's Marathon Banners, and the local newspaper, as well as the City, hang huge banners that read "Welcome Grandma's Marathon Runners!"

At every race that I've participated in, I always try to attend as many of the pre-race events as possible, and at Grandma's Marathon there are plenty of them. After the first five times that I ran Grandma's, I developed a routine that usually begins with attending one or more of the guest speaking presentations. In past years, Grandma's has brought in some of the most famous running legends in history such as Billy Mills, Lasse Viren, Joan Benoit Samuelson, Bill Rodgers, Gete Waitz, Arthur Lydiard, Garry Bjorklund, and course record holder, Dick Beardsley.

After taking in a presentation, I usually head to the health and fitness expo. The expo features a wide variety of vendors from those that are selling running apparel to the great people who will create a quilt out of your past finisher shirts, and don't forget about the Grandma's Marathon merchandise, energy products, sunglasses, and much more. Right next to the expo is the all-you-can-eat pasta party, where runners (and their family and friends) can load up on as much tasty spaghetti as they want and enough carbohydrates to energize them for all 26.2-miles. In addition to the expo and pasta feed, Grandma's Marathon hosts hospitality suites at three different locations throughout the city that are open to all runners, and truly make you feel welcome, even if you're a local.

I've found all of these pre-race activities and services to be wonderful, and I must confess that many times I go to them just for the chance to be around thousands of runners from all over the world who are just as excited as I am to run, and are eager to swap running stories. There is so much positive energy that you can't help feeling good about the adventure you're about to embark on.

On the morning of the marathon, I am always amazed at the number of buses Grandma's Marathon has rounded up to transport runners to the starting line. There are literally rows and rows of them at various locations throughout the city, and the wait to get on one is never too long.

The course itself is point-to-point; therefore, if you're staying in Duluth, you must travel almost the entire length of the course to get to the starting line. The ride is pleasant and relaxing as I quietly sit there listening to the chatter going on around me about time predictions, training routines, what this person ate and what that person didn't eat.

Stepping off of the bus at the starting line, I always find myself taking in a deep breath of crisp, clean Lake Superior air, and the butterflies always begin to flutter in my stomach.

The starting area itself is an extremely exciting place to be with music pumping out of huge speakers, people discussing more race strategy in the line for the port-a-potties (there are at least one hundred of them, if not more), and participants stretching or jogging up and down to stay warm. The weather at the start is typically between 40°F to 50°F, warming up to the mid to low-60s as the day goes on. The breeze rolling off of Lake Superior acts as a huge air conditioner, so for a marathon in June, the temperature rarely feels too warm.

As the start of the race draws near, everybody begins to place their sweats into the bag they were given at race packet pick-up and deposit them in bins to be transported to the finish line. The race announcers make a few last minute announcements, and in recent years members of Duluth's Air National Guard fly F-16 jets over the crowd of runners right before the National Anthem is performed. It is truly an impressive and honorable way to start a race!

The starting horn sounds, everybody begins cheering, and all of a sudden we're off. We start out with the "starting line shuffle." It's that thing we all do when so many runners are packed around us that we can't take a full stride. In my opinion, it's the best way to savor the experience of starting a marathon.

With the rolling hills on the Grandma's course, it's an amazing site to see the mass of bobbing heads in front and behind you as the race progresses and the field thins out. Over the years, I have had the opportunity to run with some interesting people. One was a local weatherman who decided to not only challenge himself to run 26.2-miles, but also to do the entire race barefoot. The crowds would cheer extremely loud when they would recognize him, which was a great energy boost, so I was very willing to keep pace with him for a few miles.

When the runners become staggered along the course, and you're left alone with the beauty of the great Lake Superior to the left and a green forest on the right, it is easy to "zone out" and really get into your pace. One difficulty that I have found about the race, and it's not something the organizers can control, is that as you make your way down the course you can often catch glimpses of the Ariel Lift Bridge located near the finish line. This, at times, is very deceptive and has made many runners, including myself, think that the finish line is closer than it really is. My advice to future Grandma's Marathon participants is to expect this, stay focused, maintain a manageable pace, and if you get discouraged, rely on the crowds and volunteers lining the streets to keep you motivated — it does work!

As I mentioned earlier, the communities of Duluth and surrounding cities truly embrace Grandma's Marathon, and their pride for the event is extremely evident on race day as over 4,500 volunteers and tens of thousands of spectators come out to support runners along the course and at the finish line. The water stations each span the length of approximately 15 long tables, and are staffed with at least 100 or more volunteers who are ready and waiting with fluids when you need them. In addition, many of the stations are stocked with wet sponges for cooling off, and at least two offer strawberries, oranges, and other food to replenish energy as you get into the final miles of the race.

In addition to the volunteers staffing the aid stations, many people provide entertainment along the way, and let me tell you, this is a treat! My favorite is the group of bagpipers that play at the top of Lemon Drop Hill (the only significant hill on the course, and I promise you it isn't that bad) at approximately the 22-mile mark. Then there is the guy at mile 18 who dresses up as a different character each year, and bounces on a trampoline to taped music, and passes out candy to the runners as they stride by. I have always thought that he is a little crazy or at least crazier than I am, but he is truly a crowd pleaser and something to look forward to as you're running.

Around the 19-mile mark you enter Duluth and this is where, in my mind, the race really starts. I've had many ups and downs during that last seven-mile stretch. In fact, one year I was so tired that I pulled off to the side of the road and had a beer with a frat house that always has a keg in their front yard for us carb-depleted runners. It was just the right thing to help me finish the race or at least forget about how tired I was. In addition to the beer-peddling frat house, the final miles of the course are where the bulk of eager spectators stand to watch and cheer. Depending on how your race is going, and whether you're having an "on" or "off" day, the cheers from the crowds are so loud and motivating that you're more pumped up than ever as you stride down the streets of downtown Duluth, closer and closer to the finish line.

Once you leave downtown Duluth and begin your journey into Canal Park, you begin to hear music and the booming voices of the announcers, Peter Graves and Michael Pinocci, pulling you into the finish line. After winding your way through the final mile of the course, which at times feels like forever, you finally hit the homestretch. It is one of the best sights you'll ever see. Canal Park Drive is decorated with balloons that create an archway to the finish, spectators are cheering their hearts out on both sides of the streets, music is pumping, and the race announcers are welcoming you to the finish line. What an uplifting feeling for a weary runner.

I remember completing my first Grandma's Marathon and seeing my mother in the crowd. It was a great moment in my life. I also remember telling myself that I'd never do that again, which I quickly recanted 15 minutes later as I started to think, "Well if I trained harder, I could cut off X number of minutes on my time…." I'm sure, if you've run a marathon, you know what I'm talking about.

My favorite aspects of finishing Grandma's Marathon are the wonderfully helpful people supporting you as you wobble down the finish chute, the volunteers that go the extra mile (no pun intended) to place a medal around your neck as if you just won the Olympics, being wrapped in a warm "space" blanket, and the best thing of all, the post-race FOOD! Tables upon tables are piled high with boxes full of fruit, bagels, yogurt, cookies, water, and pop. I must admit, however, that I always skip the healthy stuff and head straight to the ice cream — remember I came from a Coke and Snickers background, plus I just ran 26.2 miles!

Sitting down to enjoy Lake Superior after the race is a "must do" even if you're a local. Several runners wade in, but it's also nice to just sit there, relax, and listen to the waves crashing to the shore.

No matter how tired you are after the race, I highly recommend attending the post-race party — it is the best of any race I've ever run. Held all day and into the wee hours of the night under a huge tent that is erected for marathon weekend, runners and spectators are treated to live music, plenty of chairs to kick-back and relax on, dancing (if your legs can handle it), and a plethora of beverages and food. The first round of drinks (beer, pop, or coffee) for finishers of the race are always on the house, as each runner is given a coupon for a complimentary beverage upon crossing the finish line — I've always thought that this is one more way that Grandma's goes above and beyond the call of duty.

It's a little sad when the marathon tents come down and everything is put away after another successful race. What is exciting, however, is the thought of training, one more time, for one of the top marathons in the country, and seeing how you can improve on what you had previously done.

Grandma's Marathon is my favorite, and their old slogan is still as appropriate today as it was when the race started… "A Great Race on a Great Lake!"

Jon Carver Carlson has been running since the early 1970s and has completed 15 marathons, numerous half marathons, and many races of varying lengths (of which he has won two). He served on the Grandma's Marathon Hospitality Committee and Board of Directors prior to his retirement from a local utility company called Minnesota Power where he worked for 23 1/2 years as an Employee Benefit Analyst. Changing careers and fulfilling a longtime dream, Jon is now the Assistant Race Director for Grandma's Marathon.

Kilauea Volcano Wilderness Marathon

hawai'i volcanoes national park, hawaii

Web site: www.volcanoartcenter.org
Month: July
USATF Certified: No
Course: Challenging

Author: Jeff Stone
Number of Marathons Completed: 12
Age Group: 45-49

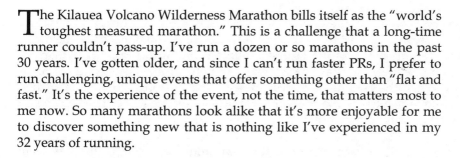

The Kilauea Volcano Wilderness Marathon bills itself as the "world's toughest measured marathon." This is a challenge that a long-time runner couldn't pass-up. I've run a dozen or so marathons in the past 30 years. I've gotten older, and since I can't run faster PRs, I prefer to run challenging, unique events that offer something other than "flat and fast." It's the experience of the event, not the time, that matters most to me now. So many marathons look alike that it's more enjoyable for me to discover something new that is nothing like I've experienced in my 32 years of running.

There are no qualifications to enter this race, but it is a very physically demanding course. Participants should be able to finish the marathon in 7:30 and the field is limited to 225 runners.

The course consists of a very unique and challenging terrain. About 25 percent of the course is on roads and the rest is on trails through lava fields, rain forest, and a crater rim trail. The first half has a net 1,000 feet elevation drop, which is regained primarily over a four-mile long rain forest trail between miles 19-23. It is the lava fields that are the most interesting and challenging aspect of race, as the course has to be marked in this section by flagged rock-piles due to the rough terrain. The biggest transition is going from hot, arid conditions to tropical, humid rainforest within a few moments.

The race headquarters is located at a military R&R facility in Hawai'i Volcanoes National Park on the Big Island of Hawaii. The Quonset-hut setting provides a low-key atmosphere and many repeat marathoners

KILAUEA VOLCANO WILDERNESS MARATHON

and former/current military personnel (with a can-do attitude) ensure a well-organized registration process.

Local volunteers do an excellent job of taking care of registration and solving any problems. Aid stations in the lava fields are brought-in on horseback with aid workers camping out overnight. These volunteers take their jobs very seriously and give the runners both a warm welcome and a lot of attention more akin to manning a base camp than a marathon aid station. There is very little stress in Hawaii in general and problems get resolved.

The course is difficult, as billed, requiring adaptation to many running surfaces — rock, sand, rough road, stony trails, etc. While on course, runners are constantly descending or climbing and there are many climate changes. The aid stations are like an oasis, and the friendliness of the native Hawaiians who come out to the course to provide encouragement and help is genuine and warm (although they seemed amused that people would actually undertake such an activity).

The scenery over the first few miles, with the early morning sunrise over Mauna Loa (with steam coming from the volcano caldera) and the Pacific below, is spectacular. Mauna Loa is the largest mountain on Earth (yes, larger than Mt. Everest — if you measure from the sea floor) and one of the most active volcanoes on earth. When the lava fields appear, descending in front, the view over them to the ocean is inspiring, and the last few miles along the rim of the volcano are unforgettable, although painful.

As with any trail marathon with a few hundred participants, there are long stretches of isolation. My least favorite part of the race was the gradual uphill six mile stretch of road between the lava fields and rain forest, (miles 13-19) as it is the hottest and driest part of the race, and not especially scenic with scrubby vegetation. It is a mentally and physically exhausting race.

The camaraderie of the fellow marathoners is more akin to a group effort, with race veterans lending constant advice and runners helping each other along the way. There were few spectators, save the accidental ones who were visiting the National Park. Where there were spectators, they would do anything they could for you, but they were mostly family/friends of the runners who had run the shorter races that day. Mostly, it was Mother Nature Hawaiian style, and me.

The weather was cool at the 6:00 a.m. start, around 45°F, with dry, sunny conditions throughout the rest of the race. Temperatures at noon were around 80°F, which is typical in Hawaii. However, participants are advised to be prepared for anything from cold and rainy to hot and humid as weather can be very changeable at 4,000 feet on a volcano on an island in the middle of the ocean. Past races have been very windy as well, causing the blowing of fine volcanic sand that can cause breathing and eye problems.

Rooms are adequate but not plentiful in the area. There is a hotel lodge on the crater rim in the National Park, (Volcano House), and B&B accommodations in nearby Volcano Village which is a very eclectic community (it's a different sort of person who chooses to live near an active volcano). Many runners stay in hotels in the city of Hilo, about a 45-minute drive from the start. Local B&Bs are familiar with the event and help runners get an early start and many have very interesting accommodations.

The uniqueness of the course is the key attraction of the race- the opportunity to run through old lava flows and rain forest in the same run, to run on the edge of a volcano crater 10-miles in circumference, and to watch the sun come up over the highest mountain in the world, are the allure of this run. The entire course is breathtaking, literally and figuratively.

The Kilauea Volcano Wilderness Marathon is a very difficult run, which makes it all the more satisfying in just completing it. But, if you have to recover anywhere from the rigors of running a marathon, a beach in Hawaii has to be anybody's top choice!

Jeff Stone works in the European sporting goods industry and ran high school and collegiate cross-country and track in Germany for the Offenbach Leichtathletik Club and in the U.S. with the Charleston Running Club and Reston Runners. An active runner for over 30 years, he now spends most of his spare time at hockey rinks supporting his son's hockey career and acting as off-ice conditioning coach. Jeff's marathon PR is 2:47:06.

Crater Lake Marathon

crater lake national park, oregon

Web site: www.craterlakerimruns.com
Month: August
USATF Certified: No
Course: Challenging

Author: Bob Freirich
Number of Marathons Completed: 13
Age Group: 70-74

Just like clockwork, at 7:30 a.m. in the morning on the second Saturday in August, at the Watchman Overlook high on the rim in Crater Lake National Park, the starting gun sounds. Up to 500 personal adventures begin as the annual Crater Lake Rim Runs and Marathon get underway over distances of 6.7 miles, 13.0 miles, and the marathon. The Rim Runs are open to the first 500 entries on a first come, first serve basis. The footing is good; the first 22 miles are asphalt with the final four in pumice.

It is true that I had run all of the distances at Crater Lake except the marathon and yes, I had run 12 previous marathons. However, all the previous marathons were pretty close to sea level with not much more than a highway overpass to serve as a hill. Crater Lake lies high in Oregon's Cascade Mountains, and I knew full well what was in store for me. No overpasses here, not even hills, just mountains! After all, the marathon runs in, around and on top of a volcano!

My wife Beverly and I have directed the Rim Runs for the past 28 years. Beverly and I even ran, jogged, and walked the entire rim from headquarters to headquarters, which is a distance of 34 miles. Yes, I knew what lay ahead.

So you might rightly ask what would cause me to try this marathon? I could tell you that I felt it was my duty to experience every step of the Rim Runs personally. I could tell you that but that would not be the real reason. The real reason was a challenge made to me by a friend of mine who had run it the year before. Maybe I should say he survived it the year before. So really, I had no choice, the challenge was made.

Wait, I didn't tell you that my friend and I fit pretty well into the Clydesdale division of runners. Heck, my doctor once quipped that for me to weigh in at 190 pounds, I'd probably have to be dead for a couple of weeks. So, now you have the full picture.

The evening before the race there's a get together for runners who are staying in the park. The festivities begin with a video that helps prepare the runners for what's in store for them the next day and there's time to ask questions about the marathon and the park in general.

While the Fahrenheit temperature at the 7:30 a.m. start time is generally cool, in the low 50s with the highs in the low 70s, the high on race day the year I ran was predicted to be in the mid 80s. So the temperature could be a factor. All race personnel were alerted to this possibility, including communications, medical and aid station personnel.

So here I am and the starting shot has just been fired — so we're off!

Over the top of the first little hill during the first half-mile, the glimpse of the lake is all but overpowering. I would say breathtaking, but breathtaking comes later in the run. Head and eyes turn to the right to take in the blue waters of Crater Lake nestled inside the caldera. At some places the lake is 5 1/2 miles across and almost 2,000 feet deep. What must it have been like when this mountain, Mt. Mazama, blew its top so many, many years ago? When the shaking stopped and the dust settled, the foundation for what is now Crater Lake was formed. But that was then and this is now, and I begin to fly down to the North Entrance of the park! No sweat so far!

Almost down to the North Entrance, my eyes look across to the first of the hills, a short one-mile climb to the three-mile aid station. So here we go, bodies start to lean forward, strides shorten and breathing begins in earnest. Some begin to walk. How can one mile be so long? Finally we are at Llao Rock, the three-mile aid station. Feeling better already. Look at them, some are actually drinking and walking! Not me, I know a three-mile downhill is just ahead! Whee! Grab a drink at the 4.8-mile aid station and after a slight up hill it's down to the base of Cleetwood Cove at 6 1/2 miles into the race. I know the 6.7-mile race finish is just around the next corner, but what a finish for a race, two tenths of a mile-up hill! I cast a look to my left to look at the runners sprint into the finish area, all done, finished. Wait, some are already eating watermelon, drinking, and just plain walking or better yet, stopped altogether. Oh, well!

Just past the 6.7-mile finish area is the 6.9-mile aid station, maybe I will walk a bit here, you know, visit and thank the aid station folks. The majority of the 130 to 150 people who work the aid stations and finish areas are from Klamath Falls and live some 60 to 70 miles away from their assignment on the Rim. They get on site as early as 6:30 a.m., which means they leave home no later than 4:00 a.m.! And yes, they even pay to get into the Park like all visitors and runners.

After a bit of up and down and gawking at the lake, I settle in to tackle the 3 1/2 mile climb to the finish of the 13.0 mile run and on to the highest point of the run—Cloudcap at an altitude of 7,850 feet. When I reach Cloudcap, I will have gained 950 feet in altitude from the aid station at Cleetwood. I am beginning to feel a slight tug on my body as the road starts to pitch upward. I know there is an aid station at just under 10 miles, called Wine Glass, I begin to think about it. Cool water, Gatorade, ice, well you get the idea.

I'm gaining on a couple of folks, they are walking, but they have numbers, so they're fair game. The road turns and you are greeted with more of the same, uphill scenery. I pass a Park Ranger who is parked along the road, kind of watching things unfold and trying to be supportive. He says, "Looking good, only 2 miles to the finish of the 13." Have you ever been hit in the solar plexus? Two miles to 13 and I'm going 26.2! Keep chugging.

Looking away from the lake you get a panoramic view of the countryside with snow-capped mountains, and I swear I'm looking down on them! Here comes the aid station at 11 1/2 miles, nestled in tall pines with shade. A couple of gulps, a few thank you's and on to the 13-mile finish and beyond. Finally, to the left of the road there are the directional signs to the finish of the 13 or the route of the marathon. You pass within a handshake of runners who have met their challenge, are telling stories, laughing, eating fruit and drinking water, pop, and Gatorade. It is tempting, all I have to do is lean slightly to the left and it's over. But a challenge is a challenge I say to myself as I pass the 13.0-mile finish and head on up to the 13 1/2-mile aid station. You know that was a good idea, to put the aid station beyond the 13.0-mile finish. It would be just too easy to end your race there.

The 13 1/2 and 15 1/2-mile aid stations are at the same spot and serve the runners going up to the turn around at Cloudcap at 14 1/2 miles and an altitude of almost 8,000 feet. Then, it's back down to the 15 1/2-mile aid station. As you fly by the aid station, you realize that about 75 percent of the runners have finished their races and all of a sudden the "loneliness of the long distance runner," has real meaning. No one is in sight. Not even an occasional spectator as the Rim Drive is closed during the first 2 to 2 1/2 hours of the run and opens by sections as runners pass each finish area. Spectators must get to a spot along the course prior to 7:00 a.m. and stay put until the Park Service opens the road. So running the rim can be lonely and very personal. But it really doesn't matter because the views are spectacular. If you look south as you descend from Cloud Cap, you can see the Klamath Basin, Klamath Lake, and Mt. Shasta in California.

I've been running downhill now for a long, long time. I never thought I would wish for an uphill but…. You know, I'll be real happy to see the folks at the 17 1/2-mile aid station at Castle Rock. In fact, I believe that the people at these late aid stations are really glad to see us. They too know loneliness. It's "Looking good! How's it going? Feeling OK?" All the time giving us the once over to determine if we're fit to continue, or in need of help outside of the usual and making sure we hydrate. You know, just taking care of us.

Finally, the course turns away from the rim at the 19-mile aid station at Kerr Notch and heads down the Pinnacles Road.

More downhill and then the famous aid station at 21 miles. Enough said. You just have to experience it. The course still continues its downhill mode and my legs are questioning just what is going on after all of those hard long climbs earlier. Instead the reverse continues, long downhills all the way to the Lost Creek Campground where the elusive marathon finish is located. As you enter the campground, you pass another well-known aid station located at 22.3 miles (again, I won't spoil the fun, you'll have to see it for yourself). The course meanders past a tiny babbling brook nestled in the forest to the base of Grayback Mountain. Then, the final climb begins, on a pumice service road.

At just over 23 miles there is another aid station, Lonesome Pine I, and finally after switchback after switchback there's the turn around and aid station at Grayback. I am now on the final downhill of the Crater Lake Marathon. It's past the Lonesome Pine II aid station, a turn to the right and there it is, the finish of the Crater Lake Marathon!

Buses are provided for transportation from the Rim Village to the start at the Watchman Overlook and then back from the finish line. There is a parking area at the Rim Village. Lodging is located in the park and in Klamath Falls and in a number of other towns in the vicinity. Campgrounds are also located in and near the park.

As for me, it is all over, except for the great memories, great stories, and friendships that were fashioned on the Rim in Crater Lake National Park. So much for challenges!

Bob Freirich started running road races in 1971. Before that time, he ran to keep fit, being a high school physical education and health teacher. In 1973, Bob organized a running club to promote fitness through running. The club, the Linkville Loper Road Running Club of Klamath Falls, Oregon, ultimately became the sponsor of the Crater Lake Rim Runs and Marathon. The club now reaches out to walkers as well.

Bob continues to coach high school cross-country and track and field and stays involved in long distance running, although he says, "Two hip replacements have made more of a walker out of me than anything else, but I'm still moving."

Grizzly Marathon

choteau, montana

Web site: www.grizzlymarathon.com
Month: August
USATF Certified: Yes
Course: Rolling

Author: Tom Conrad
Number of Marathons Completed: 85
Age Group: 65-69

Montana was the last state to complete my circuit of a marathon in every state. The Grizzly Marathon course was in the foothills of the Front Range of the Rocky Mountains, near Choteau, a town with a population of 1,600; it is 50 miles northwest of Great Falls. My support team consisted of Joan and Bart Conrad. Bart rode his motorcycle to Choteau from Jackson and did the half marathon. Joan and I flew into Great Falls, rented a car, drove to Choteau, then on to Glacier National Park and Jackson Hole, and then flew home.

We stayed at the Race Headquarters hotel, the Stage Stop Inn in Choteau. At the hotel, we saw a number of marathoners who participate in these events regularly. The Choteau volunteers put on a better-than-average pasta dinner at the Recreation Center in the city park. After dinner, Joan and I drove the marathon course. It was a 22-mile loop, plus a two-mile out-and-back. Seven miles were on a paved road, and the rest were gravel roads—some rough, loose gravel and some fairly smooth. Generally, the terrain was rolling grasslands with no trees. There were enough hills that I adjusted my normal 5:40 goal to "less than six hours." I estimated the vertical for the course to be 1,500 to 1,700 feet of uphill.

The marathon had an early start time of 6:30 a.m., to avoid the heat and the wind that kicks up in the afternoon. Bart and I boarded a bus at 5:30 a.m. to ride to the start, 40 minutes from Choteau. Five minutes before the start, a trumpeter played first the Canadian National Anthem and then the Star Spangled Banner. Both races started at 6:30 a.m., with cones separating the full marathoners from the half marathoners. At the 0.1-mile mark, the full marathoners turned to the left onto a gravel road, and the half marathoners turned to the right onto a gravel road for their out-and-back course. The full marathon finished on the half marathoners' course.

A quarter of a mile after the left turn, we crossed the Teton River and then went onto a paved road. At this point, I joined up with Paula from Salt Lake City and Brent from Fairfax, Virginia. They liked my pace, so the three of us walked along the paved road for seven miles at a 12 minute, 36 second pace. It was pleasant and easy walking (1/2 to 1 percent grade downhill) with good companions for conversation. Conditions were ideal because it was overcast and about 50° F.

At mile 7 1/2, we turned onto a rough gravel road and headed due south for five miles. The grade continued to be a gentle 1/2 to 1 percent downhill to the crossing of the Teton River, but the loose gravel slowed us down. Rocks rolled under my feet, which caused me to work harder to maintain a 13-minute pace. At mile 8 1/2, we began climbing a hill that, when driving the course the previous night, seemed like the biggest hill on the course.

At mile eight, Brent started jogging because he wanted to complete the marathon in 5:20. By the time Paula and I got to the hill, Brent was out of sight. While walking up the hill, I got ahead of Paula, although my pace slowed to 14 minutes per mile. The top of the hill was at about mile 11 1/2, which indicated that the hill was about three miles long. While going up, I looked back to find my old friend Don Lang, but he was nowhere to be seen. Either he was out of sight each time I looked, or he had fallen back from the beginning of the race. I estimated the vertical rise to be 600 to 800 feet from the low point of the course at an elevation of 4,100 feet.

As we started down the hill, Paula began jogging, and soon passed me. She caught up with Dror, another walker who also was completing his fiftieth state marathon. The next two miles were a pleasant downhill. At mile 13, I started to chafe under my arms, so I stopped for Vaseline at the water/fruit stop and loaded up with a banana, oranges, and grapes. I reached the half marathon mark in 2:51:34, a 13:05 per mile pace. Not bad considering the significant hill, the gravel road for the past five miles, and spending 1 1/2 minutes at the water/fruit stop.

By this time, I was walking by myself. The next four miles were on a fairly smooth gravel road with an overall one percent rise, but with short ups and downs. I passed both Paula and Dror, who had hooked up and were walking together. Dror started with a fast pace, probably 12 minutes per mile, but he slowed down. During this stretch, I passed a half dozen runners who had dropped back to walking. The gradual uphill continued to about mile 17 1/2, where the route to return to the finish turned off to the right. At this point, there was a first aid station and fruit and water stop.

The next two miles were the out half of the out-and-back route, and they had significant uphills and gentle, short downhills. As I walked on toward the turnaround, which was just short of the 20-mile mark, most of the returning runners looked fairly refreshed, probably due to the general downhill trend for the past two miles. That told me what was coming. The last uphill lived up to its reputation of being a long, steep, hill. By the time that I

Courtesy of Grizzly Marathon

reached the top, I had slowed to a 20-minute-per-mile pace. When I looked ahead at the last hill, I saw my former companion, Brent, laboring up the hill. During the last part of the "out" section, I saw the people that I might be able to pass in the last seven miles of the marathon, and I would pass a number of them.

I was tired enough by the time I got to the turnaround point at the top of the hill that I started down the hill walking slowly, until I realized that I could and should walk notably faster downhill. As I was returning on the out-and-back course, I saw the 10 or so people who were behind me. First was Paula, then Dror, and then a number of others that I had passed since the first hill. Finally, I saw Don Lang, who appeared to be weaving and struggling.

At mile 22, there was an aid station with a water and fruit stop. I grabbed some fruit and decided I was ready to tackle the last four miles. By this time, I had pretty much caught up with Brent, but he would not let me catch him. He did not want a walker like me to finish ahead of him. The last four miles were a struggle. I was tired; the majority of the route was gentle uphill; it was sunny and about 75°F; and we had a 10 mph headwind. I passed a number of other participants along this stretch, including a 50-Stater, who appeared to be in terrible condition. However, those 50-Staters are experienced enough to know what they can do, so I figured he would be okay.

Bart had finished his half marathon at about 8:30 a.m. He hung out at the finish line, took a nap, and then walked out to join me for the last 1 1/2 miles. His support was most helpful. Another highlight in the last section was the water stop at mile 25. The girls there kept up their cheering and dancing, and one of them wore a grizzly bear costume. Although the costume must have been very hot, she kept it on to the end to encourage us all. The 25-mile water stop was the best one on the course because of the entertainment and our need for water.

The last mile was supposed to be downhill, but it didn't feel that way. My pace for the last mile was 14:20. Finally, with about 0.4 miles to go, I could see the finish line, and it looked mighty good, but I was unable to pick up the pace. Nevertheless, I finished in 5:57:50—faster than my goal, and I was excited that I had completed the 50-state circuit. Bart informed everybody within hearing distance of that fact.

Joan walked out about 1 1/4 miles to take photographs, get her daily walk, and give me high fives for completing all 50 states. It didn't take long for Joan to get back to the finish line and bring the cooler, so we could have our post-marathon celebratory beer. We hung around for the awards ceremony. I should have announced that Dror and I had completed our 50-state circuit, but didn't. So there was no special recognition.

Upon returning from the marathon, both Bart and I took a two to three hour recovery nap and then went to a pig roast, which was free. The community couldn't do enough for us, including the greetings in Choteau, the pasta dinner, great support on the course, plenty of water, port-a-potties, fruit, sponsorships on giveaways in the marathon packet, and food at the finish, as well as the pig roast dinner. The pig roast was at JB's Wildlife Sanctuary, which turned out to be a bar in the two-store town of Byner. We were tired, so we drove back to the hotel while it was still light, watched television, and went to bed gratified that the 50th state marathon was such a good one.

Tom Conrad began running in 1974 and formed the Reston Runners four years later. He got the marathon bug and continued to run one or two marathons each year through 1989. Tom's first walking marathon was in 1991 and he walked one or two marathons each year until 1996. Since then, he has walked 5 to 13 marathons annually and he completed a round of 50 states in August of 2004. Tom also participates in the Reston Triathlon with his three children, has bicycled across the USA, skis, and has climbed Mt. McKinley, Mt. Kilimanjaro, and the Grand Teton. Tom founded SCS Engineers 35 years ago, which has grown to 450 employees in 36 locations. Although born in San Francisco, Tom has decided that Reston, Virginia is a great place to live, and plans to continue living there for the rest of his life.

Pikes Peak Marathon®

manitou springs, colorado

Web site: www.pikespeakmarathon.org
Month: August
USATF Certified: No
Course: Challenging

Author: Bill Means
Number of Marathons Completed: 8
Age Group: 40-44

There is a reason that Pikes Peak inspired Katharine Lee Bates to write "America the Beautiful." Pikes Peak is an incredible mountain! There is also a reason that Zebulon Pike uttered the words: "The summit ... which was entirely bare of vegetation and covered with snow ... would have taken a whole day's march to have arrived at its base, when I believe no human being could have ascended to its pinnacle." Pikes Peak is a challenge to walk, let alone run.

I love the mountains. I love the smell, vegetation, wildlife, and rocks — everything about the mountains. I also love to run. I love the solitude, the discipline, and the challenges of running. The Pikes Peak Marathon gives me a chance to enjoy the beauty of the mountains along with an incredible running challenge. Wrap all of this up with a well-run and organized event and you have a near perfect race experience!

The starting line for the Pikes Peak Marathon is on Manitou Avenue in Manitou Springs, approximately six miles west of Colorado Springs, Colorado. The starting elevation is 6,280 feet. After a short flat run on pavement, the course turns onto Ruxton Avenue where the first major climb is encountered. Even though the course is still on a paved road at this point, you will quickly realize that you are in for a difficult run up a very steep mountain!

After the first paved mile, you will pass the first aid station and immediately turn onto Barr Trail on the east face of Pikes Peak where you will start climbing what has become popularly known as the "W's." The "W's" are approximately three miles of steep switchbacks up Manitou

Mountain. At the top of the mountain, you have only completed 4.17 miles and gained 2,500 feet in elevation. You still have 9.15 miles and 5,300 feet of elevation gain to go before reaching the summit.

After reaching the top of Manitou Mountain, you will begin the next 9.15 miles of uphill grade. Keep in mind that the ascent has an elevation gain of 7,815 vertical feet over 13.32 miles before reaching the summit at 14,110 feet. Runners then turn around and go back down the same course (7,815 foot elevation drop over 13 miles) returning to Manitou Springs for a total distance of 26.31 miles. Since the race is so physically demanding, it truly lives up to its description as "America's Ultimate Challenge."

The course is not uniform in grade and varies significantly. Putting aside the detail of the grade in any specific section, the most important point to consider for the ascent leg is that, with only a few exceptions of reasonably flat trail, a slight downhill section roughly 1.25 miles above French Creek and a few other very short downhill segments, the course is a relentless uphill grind! There are no long downhill sections that permit recovery. Combine this with the continuous drop in oxygen as the elevation increases and the demands placed on every runner are significant.

With the exception of a stretch of jagged terrain, roughly 0.7 miles from the summit and common loose gravel, the trail surface is sound (primarily dirt). However, the trail is uneven, has protruding rocks and tree roots, and can be wet and even snowy or icy. In addition, roughly 0.4 miles from the summit you will encounter the 16 Golden Stairs. Fred Barr, the builder of the trail, used the Biblical analogy of the golden stairs leading to Heaven to describe this portion of the trail. Once you finish the stairs you are ever so close (0.35 miles) to the summit. There are actually more than 16 "stairs" (the number varies as to the ways in which they are counted), but the important fact is that most are between 12 and 22 inches high. Do not take the physical demands of the stairs lightly because at this point in the race each stair will be extremely daunting.

Much of the trail is narrow so passing can be difficult or impossible. However, from the top of Manitou Mountain to Barr Camp, there are portions of the trail where it is wide enough to pass. Experienced runners will advise you not to pass frequently as the result is, in most cases, that you will expend too much energy and then slow down only to be passed yourself. On some sections of the trail, and particularly between the spur and the top of Manitou Mountain, the web site advises not to pass if you are in the pack.

Weather is another factor. For example, in 2004 for the Pikes Peak Ascent® (the

Ascent is a separate race held the day before the Pikes Peak Marathon that just entails the "ascent" portion of the marathon), the temperature at the starting line in Manitou Springs was around 40°F. At the top of the mountain, there was approximately six inches of snow and drifts over two feet! The race was delayed due to support personnel not being able to get into position. By the time runners reached the top, it was cold, slushy, and icy and the trail was like a riverbed. In contrast, the weather can be cold at the top and hot at the bottom with no moisture. Or, it can be rainy with hail and thunderstorms. In a word, the weather is unpredictable. Weather is a definite consideration when training for this race!

In general, the condition of the course is excellent. There are no points where the trail is along an edge or steep slope, so you do not need to worry about falling off. The views are spectacular (especially above the tree line), and in the forested section the scenery is beautiful.

Many times, participants underestimate the nature of the course or their own ability. Due to this and for the safety of runners and volunteers, three turn-around points were established. If a runner does not meet a specified cut-off time at each of the turn-around points, they are disqualified from the race and are required to make their way back down the mountain. Tips for training for the race can be found on the Pikes Peak Marathon web site.

How can someone who lives at a lower elevation prepare for the reduced level of oxygen? The effect of "altitude" that accompanies these races will affect each person differently. Keep in mind that those who live and train at higher elevations will have, in most cases, an advantage since their bodies will produce more red blood cells. However, if you train rigorously, try to arrive early to acclimate to the elevation, and do not over-extend yourself early in the race, you may find that you complete the race without much trouble.

Do NOT underestimate the demands of the Marathon! According to the race web site, "for the vast majority of runners it will take more than your average "flatland" marathon (26.2 miles) time PLUS one-half hour to complete just the 13.32 mile ascent." If you think you can take on Pikes Peak without extensive training you are in for a surprise!

As described, the course is exceptionally challenging and runners may encounter extreme weather conditions. The field is limited to 800 participants, and specific qualifications must be met in order to enter the race.

To register for the Pikes Peak Marathon you must be at least 16 years of age and meet one of the following criteria:

- Have completed the Pikes Peak Ascent in under 5:20
- Be a prior finisher in the Pikes Peak Marathon
- Have completed another marathon

- Have completed an ultra distance race or triathlon race with a minimum of a 50K run

I actually "doubled" the marathon and Ascent race last year. Being a "Doubler" means that you run the Ascent on Saturday and then run the Marathon on Sunday. I have run the race several other times, but this was the first year that I can remember looking at the Peak from near the starting line on Ascent day and seeing quite a bit of snow above the tree line. It turns out that there was approximately six inches of new snow and drifts about a foot deep near the top! Needless to say, this made for an interesting experience. Below the tree line was great; it was a crisp, cool morning perfect for running. At the start, the trail was damp, but once you made it close to the tree line (about 10 miles from the start), the trail started getting wet and slick. Above the tree line, the trail was covered with snow — about three to four inches in places. This, mixed with the loose gravel that makes up part of the trail between miles 10 and 12, made it tough going! I'll never forget the literal river the trail was by the time I reached the top! I was lucky to finish the race and get down before any of the real weather came in, but from what I understand a nasty storm carrying sleet, snow, and thunderclouds rolled in about noon. Obviously, at over 14,000 feet of elevation you are very exposed and need to be cautious!

The next day — marathon day — the Peak looked quite a bit different. Most of the snow had melted, however, you could still see from a distance that there was a "dusting" above the tree line. Again, it was a perfect day for running — crisp and cool. Luckily, the trail was damp, but nothing like the river on the day before. In fact, I would have to say that it turned out to be a great day for running the Peak all around!

In a word, the race organization at the Pikes Peak Marathon is excellent. I can't say enough about the hard work and dedication the race organizers and volunteers put into this race. I have run this race for several years now, and every year it never ceases to amaze me how well it is put together. I can't imagine the logistical nightmare it must be to organize aid stations, transportation, and medical care on the mountain. Sure, there are always some problems, but those are to be expected. My experience has always been great. Hats off to the more than 800 volunteers and staff that make this event possible!

To provide aid and other support for the runners, the marathon has seven aid stations on both the ascent and decent plus one at the summit turn-around. Medical support is provided at the finish line and emergency service personnel are located along the trail. Communication is provided between all aid stations and race control. Safety personnel provide the highest level of safety possible.

Providing water and other aid to runners for this race is an incredibly demanding logistical effort. More than 4,000 feet of hose carries water to two of the aid stations (the hose is laid and retrieved each year). Two other stations require all water to be filtered on site by the volunteer race staff personnel who spend the entire weekend on the mountain. Energy bars, energy drink, 22,000 cups, and other materials are backpacked into three of the aid stations. The four other aid stations are accessible by fire roads. Over 400 volunteers are involved in providing critical safety related support for each race.

The race expo is fun. There is free food for registered runners, vendors selling various wares, and lots of people to talk to who are ready to take the challenge!

I live in the area, so I did not use the recommended accommodations. However, there are many wonderful places to stay. In fact, you should go several days early or stay after the races to enjoy many of the fun activities Colorado offers!

This year's Pikes Peak Marathon marked my 8th marathon in less than five years — not including the times I ran the Ascent. I have run the Boston Marathon, and other smaller ones, but I would say that the Pikes Peak Marathon is my favorite. I had only started running a year prior to my first Ascent, and I liked the idea of the challenge of running up a 14,000+ foot mountain. I had hiked several, but never run one! Since that time, I have grown to love the event!

The uniqueness of the Pikes Peak Marathon comes from the relentless grueling uphill 13+-mile climb, its beauty, and how well it is run. There is no other experience quite like running the Pikes Peak Marathon.

Spectators can view the event very easily at the start in Manitou Springs, at the top of the mountain when runners turn around, or at the Marathon finish line in Manitou Springs. Otherwise, it could be a long walk to find a good place along the trail to view the runners. There are a couple of places along the Pikes Peak Tollway that you can park and get to the trail, but it's still a bit of a walk.

It's a mental challenge to run a long race with very few supporters! I enjoy the aid stations where everybody cheers you on and they give you that mental boost you need to continue to the next one. However, part of what makes this race so enjoyable is that there aren't many people — it gives you an opportunity to enjoy the mountain more. I really enjoy the solitude and quiet. It is great just listening to my footsteps along the trail!

Regardless, there is a lot of camaraderie between runners during this race. Most people, although very tired, are certainly having fun!

Five years ago Bill Means would have never imagined running the Pikes Peak Marathon. At the time, he was 50 pounds overweight, with high cholesterol and according to his doctor, was heading toward a heart attack. Since then, Bill has experienced a lifetime of change. He has completed eight marathons and has run the Pikes Peak Marathon four times. His best marathon time is 2:57:35. Bill has also completed the Pikes Peak Ascent and Pikes Peak Marathon on consecutive days and is attempting to conquer all of the 53 "14ers" in Colorado (peaks over 14,000 feet). He has 18 under his belt already! Bill lives in Woodmoor, Colorado with his wife and three children.

Mesa Falls Marathon

ashton, idaho

Web site: www.ashtonidaho.com/marath.htm
Month: August
USATF Certified: Yes
Course: Rolling

Author: Dennis Aslett
Number of Marathons Completed: 60
Age Group: 55-59

Before dawn on a cool, clear morning in August of 1997, seven runners, one race walker, and the first leg of a relay team gathered on a deserted gravel road at a stream crossing in the Targhee National Forest north of Ashton, Idaho. The purpose was to run a marathon distance on a course measured out the day before using a car odometer. The only aid station was a mobile one in the form of the van that had transported the runners to the starting line. In the end, all of the runners finished—in varying degrees of agony and ecstasy and, although no records were set that day, no one died either! I had the good fortune of being one of those runners. After a brief and informal awards ceremony, we all agreed that we should do this again next year—and we did. Thus began the Mesa Falls Marathon.

In time, every race develops a personality—a collection of those special and unique qualities that sets it apart from every other race. Mesa Falls is certainly no different. I suppose that my view of this marathon may be slightly tainted by the fact that I live in the area where the race is held and have been very fortunate to have participated in all eight of the marathons so far. However, I have also had the opportunity to participate in 50 other marathons around the country and for me, Mesa Falls continues to be one of my favorites. Here's why.

Due to the geographic location of the Mesa Falls Marathon course and its proximity to Yellowstone National Park (about 15 miles), a wide variety of wildlife species reside in the area including elk, deer, moose, cougars, bears, and wolves. In the runner information packet handed out at the packet pick-up, runners are reminded of that fact:

"The race committee makes every attempt to clear the race course of unofficial entries prior to the race. However, recognizing that wildlife may not always follow our course rules, there may be four-legged 'bandits' on the course at any point. Runners are reminded to use caution if and when encountering wild animals. Please give elk, deer, and moose, the right of way – they are bigger than you! If a bear, cougar, or wolf is spotted, just remember that you don't want to be the first runner – nor the last!"

Several of these creatures have blessed the race with their presence at various times and locations.

On race morning, runners are bused from Ashton to the starting line before dawn in the comfort of tour buses complete with restrooms! There are also restrooms at the starting area—as well as lots of trees for those who may prefer something a little more primitive—after all we are in the woods! In the predawn light, Fahrenheit temperatures are typically cool and can vary from the high 30s to low 50s at race start – dress warmly. However, as the sun comes up, so do the temperatures. They can be in the 80s and low 90s by afternoon.

After a briefing to cover last minute details, Race Director Dave Jacobson gives the signal and off we go – generally on time. The first 10 miles of the race are on Forest Service gravel roads. This part of the course is relatively flat to slightly downhill and winds in and out of pine and aspen trees into large meadow openings that offer spectacular views of the forest and the Teton Mountain range in Wyoming as the sun is coming up. To me, this is a grand early morning adventure cruise in the wilderness – great soul food!

At about mile six, there is a red cabin in the meadow beside the road that is used by the local range rider (or more commonly known as a cowboy) when herding cattle or mending fences. Runners are cautioned at this point that this is "Cow Country – Watch Your Step!" There has been more than one instance where these domestic bovines have tried to join the race, resulting in a little extra speed work and some rather interesting evasive maneuvers by several lucky runners!

At mile 10, the course joins the paved Mesa Falls Scenic Byway. At mile 11, runners are redirected to a turnout into the Lower Mesa Falls Overlook where they are rewarded with an awesome view of the Lower Mesa Falls on the world famous Henry's Fork of the Snake River – well worth seeing! These falls are the inspiration for the marathon name.

Soon after leaving the falls, the course rejoins the Scenic Byway and at mile 13 goes down a rather steep hill while approaching the half marathon start at Bear Gulch. Many of the marathon runners will arrive at this point before the half marathon starts. Those lucky enough to do so are greeted by a crowd of cheering runners and support crews giving tons of encouragement. After the half marathon starts, many marathoners find themselves with a lot of new folks with whom they can share their adventure.

Immediately after passing Bear Gulch, the course leaves the pavement and drops down a short steep road to the abandoned rail bed of the old Yellowstone Branch of the Union Pacific Railroad. At one time, this was the main route for travelers visiting Yellowstone National Park. This is my favorite part of course. It is a steady, gradual downhill two-track trail that is packed sand and dirt and is easy on the legs — a welcome change from the pavement. It is quite fast and offers incredible scenery as it parallels Warm River for the next three miles — relax and enjoy!

After passing through the Warm River Campground at mile 17, the course reenters the Mesa Falls Scenic Byway. The Henry's Fork, Warm River, and Robison Creek all come together near this point, which is appropriately called Three Rivers. After crossing the bridge, the course leaves the river and proceeds up the steepest and longest hill in the race.

The Warm River grade is 2 1/2 miles long with the first mile being the steepest. It is somewhere in this area that runners who were enjoying a gradual, fast downhill run may find themselves coming back into a touch of reality and slowing down a bit. Once the runners reach the top at about mile 20, they enter rolling farmland in all directions. The volcanic soil here is very productive and is one of the places that grows the famous Idaho Potatoes. In fact, Ashton is known as the Seed Potato Capital of the World! From this point the racecourse makes a gradual decent into the finish line. Runners who are able can once again increase their speed.

Upon crossing the finish line, all runners are awarded finisher medals and directed to the city park where they find shade, ample food and water, and most everything else they need to relax, rest, and reflect on the accomplishment they have just completed.

Aside from the course itself, the Mesa Falls Marathon features a number of unique qualities that make it stand out from other races. Some of these include:

- The race committee strives to keep the race as runner friendly as possible. Race Director Dave Jacobson and his committee go the extra mile to ensure that everyone has a memorable experience. Dave has been the race director since 1998, and his race is well organized.
- The race continues to grow every year, but has retained its small town flavor. In 2004, there were 150 marathon runners in the race and 150 half marathoners.

- Runners ride to the starting line in comfort on tour buses, rather than school buses, complete with restrooms.
- The course is superb from the exceptional scenery to the varied running surfaces. The course is USATF certified as a Boston qualifier. Aid stations are ample and located every two miles.
- The city swimming pool is located near the finish line in the city park. For a small fee runners, their families, and support crews can swim. Showers are also available at the pool for runners for a nominal fee. Towels are provided for free by the race committee.
- The awards ceremony is also located in the city park. Bib prizes are abundant. Included are several runner "baskets" created and donated by one of the local runners. They include some of the local flavor such as Idaho potatoes, Idaho Spud bars, homemade huckleberry jam, and zucchini bread.
- Awards include first place male and female as well as three deep awards in 10-year age groups. The winning runners in 2004 were awarded original paintings from the race artist.
- The race has its own Race Artist. Mr. John Griffith, a gifted artist from Idaho Falls, who is a big supporter of the marathon. He painted two of the original paintings used in the race logo and is an annual guest. Mr. Griffith's artwork is frequently given as prizes and is also available for purchase.
- In future years, age group awards may change to five deep or five year age groups. The goal is to give a lot of awards. Everyone in this race is a winner!
- All finishers are awarded unique finisher's medallions that may range from engraved elk antlers to engraved wood. In 2004, the medallions consisted of the race logo embroidered on cloth and mounted in circular wooden frames. These will not be found anywhere else!
- Finisher's medallions are consecutively numbered so that runners know immediately where they placed overall when they cross the finish line.
- All runners receive a high quality polo shirt with the race logo embroidered on it instead of a t-shirt. These are the best finisher shirts I have received in any race that I have been in—I wear mine frequently.
- All finishers are awarded a complementary huckleberry milkshake from the local drug store. These are the best huckleberry shakes to be found anywhere and are a huge hit with the runners!
- All finishers are awarded a finisher's certificate and the race results.
- Free massages are available to all finishers.
- The Mesa Falls Marathon has been popular with the 50 States and D.C. Club.
- The race is also popular with first-time runners and as many as one third may be first timers.
- Runners from around the U.S. and Canada attend the race. Even though the race is relatively small, 22 states were represented in 2004.
- Although there is no expo, there is a pre-race dinner that is sponsored by the local Running Wild Running Club. The club provides food for the event

including spaghetti and all the trimmings but also locally grown baked potatoes. As a special treat, club members also provide a variety of homemade desserts.

- The race also features a half marathon. The half marathon runners receive all of the benefits and prizes that the marathoners do including finisher's medallions and polo shirts.
- Since Ashton is a small community, crowd support has been sparse in the past except at the finish line, but it is growing. The course, however, is accessible by vehicle in many locations and support crews are welcome on many sections of the course to encourage their runners.
- The race is held annually on the last Saturday of August.
- Entry fees are lower than most anywhere else at only $35.00!

For those seeking a quality marathon race experience, I can highly recommend the Mesa Falls Marathon as a must do!

Dennis Aslett is a wildlife biologist for the Idaho Department of Fish and Game and is currently the manager of Sand Creek Wildlife Management Area near St. Anthony. He has been a recreational runner for many years and began marathon running in 1995. Since then, he has completed over 60 marathons in 15 states and 3 countries, including all 8 of the Mesa Falls Marathons and 4 Boston Marathons. In recent years, Dennis expanded his horizons into the sport of ultra running. He has completed 25 ultra races including nine, 100-mile trail races. In 2004, he completed the Grand Slam of ultras which included running four specific 100-mile trail races in one summer. Dennis plans to continue seeking the grand adventures running has to offer.

Equinox Marathon

fairbanks, alaska

Web site: www.equinoxmarathon.org
Month: September
USATF Certified: No
Course: Challenging

Author: Bill VanAntwerp
Number of Marathons Completed: 20
Age Group: 55-59

The Equinox Marathon was very special to me in more ways than one. To put it in perspective, I need to give you a little history on how I got there. After 9/11 my youngest son Tom enlisted in the Army to do his part. He graduated with honors from boot camp in April. Besides being one of the top guys in Physical Training, he came in first out of 200 in the two-mile run. His first duty post was Fairbanks, Alaska where he ran his first 10K for fun. After the race, some of his buddies were talking about the Fairbanks Marathon and how it was the second toughest marathon in the country right behind Pikes Peak. *Special Point Number 1: Tough course in the middle of nowhere. Now we're talking.*

The following weekend during a telephone conversation with Tom, he asked me how he should train for the marathon. Of course I couldn't let him off that easy with just training advice, so I said if he'd do it I would be there too. He said he had never beaten me in a run, and if I came there he would kick my butt. *Special Point Number 2: The competition begins. I don't care if he is half my age.*

It seemed that with all his other duties he was not able to train in the way we talked about. He got in the short runs but never ran over 12 miles and he only did that a couple of times. As for me, I was distracted since the end of July with training for an Olympic distance triathlon (the Reston Triathlon) and I only did a couple of runs in the 10 to 15 mile range. *Special Point Number 3: To have fun you don't need to train much. You just need attitude.*

After 14 hours on a plane from Virginia with my wife Linda, we got to

Fairbanks and were greeted with snow flurries. Over dinner the next evening as Tom and I were discussing strategy and who would beat whom, Linda decided it was best if she didn't go to the start. In fact, after being around me for 34 years she didn't even feel the need to be at the finish. *Special Point Number 4: Spouse/parent at the finish is not essential. They just get bored, cold, or both. Be considerate. You may have to pay for it later.*

Before the race we both were excited and eager to go. The temperature was 27°F, cloudy with very damp air. We had studied sections of the course from a car the day before. Most of it we could not see since it was on trails. We knew our approaches were different. My strategy was to walk the first uphill and some of the early steep ones, enjoy the scenery as I went up and down on top of the mountain, and then hammer it on the long down sections. With my experience, I should catch Tom while having fun. Tom's strategy was to run easy for most of the uphills and try to stay relaxed and comfortable for most of the first half. Then, he was going to run hard the second half. It was evident we could never run together. *Special Point Number 5: Don't use the other guy's strategy.*

The race started. Up the first hill we went, through a college campus onto a cross-country ski trail, and in and out of the fog. The course then zig- zagged on a snowmobile trail, then onto a dirt road in a cloud, and up a four-mile hill into the sunshine on top of a mountain. Wow, what more could you ask for? Clouds below me and snowy mountain peaks in the distance. Is this a great course or what? *Special Point Number 6: You are rarely disappointed on a course in the mountains.*

I saw Tom at the top of the next ridge. It was not halfway yet. If I passed him too early he could come back on me. (The old fox was worried.) Running up and down the road then onto a trail and through the foliage, I wondered when I would catch him. I eventually caught him on a steep up hill. We discussed how things were going just before I ducked into the bushes (nature call). Tom pulled ahead but I caught him on a dirt road. I gave him some electrolyte pills and Ibuprofen since his stomach was cramping a little and his back was bothering him. *Special Point Number 7: Competition isn't everything.*

I ran hard on the ups and downs of the dirt road thinking I had better keep moving or he would come back on me. I came to a downhill so steep most races would have roped it. As I tried to run this without falling on my face, Tom flew by yelling, "Hey old man it's easier to run it fast than slow." When I got to the bottom, he was well out of sight but I still thought he was mine. I just knew he was going to explode.

We were 12 miles from the finish and I had a lot left. After another eight miles, I saw him about 1/4 mile ahead. He was mine now. He moved out of site over a ridge and around a bend. I picked the pace up and ran harder for a mile or so only to look up and see I hadn't gained an inch. Give me a break! *Special Point Number 8: Experience counts a lot, but don't underestimate the youth in your competition.*

Tom made a right after the railroad track then a left on a trail and up a hill toward the finish. Needless to say, I lost by a couple of minutes in 4:43 — a PW (personal worst) for a marathon but a PB (personal best) on this course. We finished numbers 100 and 101 in the open male category out of 200+ men. As I crossed the finish line, Tom was there smiling and I shook his hand congratulating him on his first marathon finish and the win. This was a real tough course for a marathon and he did it as his first. *Special Point Number 9: It helps to have a course with character as it brings out character on the course.*

From my perspective, this race was so low key you would think it was a neighborhood turkey trot. The running community in Fairbanks is friendly and dedicated. The race encourages participation by having relay teams, so I figure there were about 500 participants total. The people were great and the course was challenging. This event was laid back with no hoopla, no big sponsors, and no race purses for the winners ... and it has been going on for more than 40 years. The mile markers are permanent signs, slightly bigger than a parking sign, and contain the names of families and other individuals who donated each.

There are eight aid stations along the course and showers are available after the race. If you think you'll come back year after year, a lifetime entry fee is also available.

There is a "spaghetti feed" the evening before the race at the bib pick-up for all runners and friends. There is also a dessert potluck at the awards ceremony after the race. A "Spirit of the Equinox" award is given to someone who "has demonstrated sportsmanship, enthusiasm, and the spirit of the running community."

As for Tom and me, we agreed that if he is in Fairbanks next year, there will be a rematch.

Bill VanAntwerp has completed about 20 marathons, most when he was in his 40s. In 2004, he came out of marathon retirement "again" and ran 3:22 at the Flying Pig Marathon in Cincinnati, Ohio. This beat Bill's Boston qualifying time by 25 minutes so he may make a 5th trip there. In addition to running marathons, Bill has completed more than 100 triathlons and has done more than 30 ultras in the past seven years.

Des Moines Marathon

des moines, iowa

Web site: www.desmoinesmarathon.com
Month: September
USATF Certified: Yes
Course: Rolling

Author: Benjamin Allen
Number of Marathons Completed: 7
Age Group: 40-45

I'd lost perspective, again. This past Des Moines Marathon was the third year it was held and it was the second time I ran it. I regret missing the first one now, but it was held four months after my first marathon, and I was still recovering mentally. At the time, I was not ready to run another. However, this time I had five marathons under my belt, and I was familiar with the reactions from friends and coworkers when I said, "I only ran 12 this Saturday. I'm tapering before the marathon." They responded as I, and more experienced runners, have come to expect. "Twelve miles!" they'd say, " I could never run that far!" I appreciated the reminder that from their vantage point, I'd lost perspective on how far "far" actually is. Now that the race is over, I can see that there is one thing I didn't lose perspective on, choosing to run in Des Moines. It was great fun!

My friends' incredulous responses triggered the memory of when running five miles seemed like a lot. Well let's be honest, when running at all seemed like a huge effort. Now, I get a little jittery if I haven't run in three days. I started running about four years ago as physical therapy after injuring ligaments in my ankle playing basketball. At the time, I needed a goal and my first marathon was it. Now, being a runner has become part of who I am and running marathons is part of that. I'm not a fast runner; my goal is usually to finish the marathon. So the policy that there is no qualifying test to get into the Des Moines race is good for me.

With hills in the first 12 miles and then an almost perfectly flat course after that, I had a shot at breaking four hours. Starting just east of the Des Moines River, the first part of the course goes east toward the gilded dome of the capitol. Want to see a great picture of the start? Check it out at the race web site.

The runners then move a bit to the south and then head west through downtown and along Grand Avenue with the occasional loop into neighborhoods with hills. The course runs right by where I work, so I waved at my office knowing full well I wouldn't be as peppy when the course looped back around to pass near this spot again at about mile 22.

The second half of the course is very flat. It loops through The Water Works Park and around Gray's Lake, which has a relatively new biking and jogging path. Both are excellent places to run and are busy year round (even in the bitter cold weather).

Fortunately, race day was pretty good for running this year. Although it started a little cold, it warmed to the mid 50s by the end of the race. Officially, the low was 34°F and the high was 61°F. It was overcast most of the race. I made a small mistake at about mile eight, when I was feeling warm and tossed my gloves to my wife Peg and our friend Janice who were cheering me on at that point. Clouds covered the sun after we ran a bit north on Polk Avenue and as we turned south into the mild wind toward Water Works Park, my hands became painfully cold for the next six miles. Finally, we shifted back toward the east and the day warmed a bit. One of my running friends, Janet, was along Polk to cheer the runners. Polk is a split parkway with towering sycamore trees, houses with deep yards, sidewalks, and plenty of parking on the side streets so it's a perfect place for supporters to gather.

Once entering the park, the course becomes "flat and fast" as running magazines characterize courses. Personally, I don't see a lot of difference in my speed when the course is flat, but I know that if I tell myself the course is flat and therefore easier, I tend to focus less on the various aches and pains that develop later in marathons. The Water Works Park is at times open grass fields where hobbyists fly remote control airplanes and kids fly kites in the summer and at other points it's so wooded that you no longer wonder where all the deer come from that eat the hostas in the surrounding neighborhoods.

The final part of the course runs along the new wide four-lane section of Martin Luther King Jr. Parkway back toward the Des Moines River, which you cross and then finish riverside. There is a lot of interest in future development of walking and cycling paths in the area, so the finish should be even better in the coming years.

Peg and Janice were there at the finish line cheering along with Janice's partner

Lisa who had run the half marathon. Peg and Janice reported that access to the course for fans is pretty easy and they popped up three times to see Lisa run by during the half marathon. The one section not so friendly to fans is in The Water Works Park, so runners experience about a six-mile section with few spectators. Here's a tip though. I learned during my second marathon to write my name in large letters on my shirt so when I run by people can cheer me on by name. Even though I have no idea who they are, at mile 24 it's great to hear someone yell "Go Ben!" It gives me a lift for the next 100 yards. This year, bib numbers weren't numbers at all, but runners' first names, so even with the type being fairly small, all the runners probably got this lift at some point or another.

The crowd at the finish line was a little merrier than usual by the time I came across, because Tom Vilsack, the governor of Iowa, had crossed the finish line a few minutes in front of me and was being interviewed over the loudspeakers. He's not known for being speedy, but fortunately for my pride, I learned the governor had opted to use the early bird start option where runners are given the opportunity of starting an hour early. Apparently, he is the only governor of Iowa to have run a marathon, so he holds the record.

Many of the runners stayed at the hotels downtown just for ease of access. The Embassy Suites is literally a block from the start and finish. The downtown Marriott and the Renaissance Savery Hotel are just a few blocks west of the river, so they are within easy walking distance, even for someone who's just run a marathon. Even if you don't stay right downtown near the start and finish, getting around Des Moines is pretty easy and almost any hotel in the metro area is less than a 20-minute drive from the start. There are plenty of parking spots within a few blocks of the start as well, because of the downtown work force during weekdays.

The race expo in the days prior to the race is held in a large interior atrium of a downtown office building known as Capitol Square. Although not large, it has all the vendors you would expect. This year, I found a great racing cap with no logo on it. (It's a pet peeve of mine. I think I should get paid for advertising a company, so I usually go for the no-logo look if I can.) On the Friday night before the race, the timing chips arrived late, so some runners grumbled that they had to come back for the chips, but I went Saturday morning and everything went smoothly. This year, the race gave out running gloves as an added gift in addition to the ubiquitous shirt—a long sleeve affair that was pretty nice.

The race sometimes uses the tagline, "This ain't no cornfield" to describe itself. Having lived in Des Moines for 14 years, I at first thought the tagline reinforced the stereotypes out-of-staters have of Iowa, but I've come to like it because it's true. The race is an urban race, no doubt about it, so I've come to embrace the tagline as having a little fun and being true to the race. If you want to reinforce any perceptions of Iowa you may have, you can drive out of town and see all the corn and soybeans you want.

The race is well organized, and their web site works well and has all the information you need to find out about the marathon. I registered online months ahead of the race for an early discount. A race day complaint I heard was that some mile markers were not accurately placed. For those of us not trying to qualify for Boston or tracking every mile split, I didn't mind.

In the end, I fell short of breaking four hours by just over five minutes. But at this point in my fairly short running career, I still consider it a major accomplishment to have finished. I couldn't blame my training for not breaking four hours. For the first time, I'd stuck pretty close to the training I'd mapped out months ago. I'd run three, 20 mile runs with a Saturday group of running partners at five, three, and two weeks before the race.

Two of my fellow Saturday runners, Steve and Deb, also ran the race and we kept together for the first 13 miles or so. Then Steve fell a little behind and finished just a few minutes behind me. I fell behind Deb at mile 18. She's run 70+ marathons, so even though I sometimes feel I've lost perspective, I just have to think about Deb, and I realize I'm still new at this and have plenty to learn. She's quite the inspiration. I'll be trying to figure out what I can do better at next year's Des Moines marathon. I'm not sure I can have more fun, but maybe a new personal record would be a worthy goal.

Benjamin Allen manages the creation of gardening and Home Depot-branded books for Meredith Corporation in Des Moines, Iowa. He took up distance running as therapy after injuring ankle ligaments playing basketball. After awhile he needed a goal other than therapy and his first marathon in 2001 was it. The 2004 Des Moines Marathon was his sixth marathon.

Adirondack Marathon
schroon lake, new york

Web site: www.adirondackmarathon.org
Month: September
USATF Certified: Yes
Course: Rolling

Author: Laura Clark
Number of Marathons Completed: 11
Age Group: 55-59

The Adirondack Marathon's race brochure boasts that it is "probably the most beautiful 26 miles, 385 yards you'll ever run." What the advertisement fails to mention, however, is the fact that this road marathon is also a perfect fit for trail runners who prefer contemplating nature rather than the sweaty backs of fellow competitors. Everything about this race reflects the Adirondack experience, from the picture-postcard town of Schroon Lake, New York, to the beckoning mountains arrayed in late September fall glory, to the hand-carved Finishing Bear statues for overall winners. With the full marathon limited to 475 entrants and the half to 400, the size of the field is carefully monitored so that scenery and enjoyment remain paramount. Since the half marathon begins, appropriately, at the 13.1 mile mark, both sections get off to an uncrowded start guaranteeing a hassle-free journey.

It took me about 20 years, however, to get to that start line. While I had run a few marathons in my younger days, family and work obligations gradually whittled my training time. After moving to Saratoga Springs, New York and sampling the local road racing scene for a few years, I decided to spice up my normal routine by entering a few trail races. Anyway, that was my pretend reason. The real reason was a desire to outwit Father Time. I was intrigued by Dr. Bob Arnot's suggestion in his book, *Turning Back the Clock*, that older athletes, suddenly bereft of PRs, could temporarily fool the forces of nature by switching focus and magically wiping the slate clean. The only drawback to my dip into the fountain of youth was the fact that most trail races were fairly far from home. To get more bang for my buck, I shifted to the longer distance options. Gradually, light began to dawn. I realized that if I could complete a 20-mile trail race in August, I was a shoo-in for the fall marathon scene.

There was, however, a looming catch-22. In the time it had taken me to cultivate the level of insanity necessary to actually look forward to such Eastern trail gems as 7 Sisters (up and down seven mountains) and Escarpment (the name says it all), I had become a tree-hugger. Success was measured by how many bears I could spot, how many war wounds I could acquire, and how long it took me to clean the mud off. How could I possibly contemplate a "tame" road race? Still, there was a certain appeal. Tell a non-running friend that you spent the weekend running over mountains and though swamps and he'll move as far away as possible, even if you have already showered. But tell him that you ran a marathon and he'll look at you with new respect.

But where to find a marathon featuring nature, challenging terrain, quiet contemplative moments and a no-hassle, park-and-run frame of mind? New York City, Boston, and other mega-marathons are special, but race day logistics are often more daunting than the actual run. I wanted a Main Street USA race where I would be able to concentrate on performance and enjoyment. After much painstaking research, which basically involved counting ahead four weeks from my last long trail race and investigating local options, I discovered the Adirondack Marathon, formerly known as the Schroon Lake Marathon. It was the only game in town, but serendipitously, it met all my requirements with a few race day surprises left over. So much so, in fact, that I've come back every year since.

The surprises came as soon as I turned off the Northway into the hamlet of Schroon Lake and made a beeline for the local Stewarts convenience store to get my bearings. Before I even opened my mouth, the clerk greeted me with the query, "Are you running or volunteering today?" As if those were the only two choices available! Right away, I knew I was in for a unique experience. It turned out Stewarts was located right by the start. All I had to do was drive around the block, park near the finish, and walk a few hundred meters to the courthouse/library to pick up my race number. It couldn't get any easier. Instead of worrying about corral numbers, drop bags and parking, I was freed to obsess about the important stuff—attire, hydration, and porta-potties.

Although the Adirondack Marathon is billed as "the most beautiful 26 miles, 385 yards," it should also be advertised as the friendliest. For it is truly a town-wide undertaking, involving enthusiastic storekeepers, volunteers, and homeowners. Besides the main event, there is a family-friendly 5K and 10K the day before as well as an expo and a unique swim and pasta party. Director Don Nieradka is justifiably proud of the fact that even lakeside summer residents return to take part in the weekend. When commitments prevent them from making their annual fall pilgrimage, they phone him with profuse apologies.

Even if your idea of a perfect marathon includes a cast of 10,000 runners and streets lined with chanting supporters, the Adirondack Marathon may still be the race for you. And this brings me to the gray area that I have never quite figured out. With an average field of 300 marathoners and an over-the-mountain and around-the-lake course that never doubles back on itself, I have felt neither abandoned nor crowded. If there wasn't someone matching steps beside me, there was always someone up ahead to reel in. The intervals between human contact were perfect for breathing in deep drafts of mountain air, and executing the obligatory body parts check—head up, arms relaxed, feet light, big smile for any curious bears.

While spectators aren't exactly lining the road three deep, Thanksgiving Day Parade-style, their attention is focused directly on you. You feel an obligation to put your best foot forward. Entire generations of family members set up camp in their driveways. They are there for the duration, not just for the frontrunners, with card games, snacks, and reading material to occupy the gaps between runners. And at those places where spectators are few and far between, friendly bears have been known to fill in. Several years ago, while running the half marathon, a woman reported that she spotted a bear on the sidelines, grinning enthusiastically, waving his arms, and stretching taller for a better view. She took note of his efforts, and needless to say, picked up her pace considerably.

Bears and townspeople who were not out there cheering were busy volunteering, especially at the mile-marker water stops, which could easily rival those at any mega-marathon. Volunteers were organized into two groups: pit crew and cheerleaders, including the occasional JHS band, country music trio, and boom box operator. It is not at all unusual to see 15 people lined up to anticipate your every need. I was truly amazed that so many of the volunteers called out, "Thank you for running our race!" They were as much a part of the experience as we were.

Smiling faces, water and assorted colors of Gatorade were in ample supply. The only thing missing was the variety of snack items normally present at longer trail races—gummies, pretzels, bananas, cookies, etc. Granted, road runners subscribe to a more restricted belief system and would scoff at the mere mention of a crème-filled cookie, but this is a challenging marathon and some of us are out there way past any known Boston qualifying time. Nevertheless, the cheerleaders more than made up for the lack of junk food pick-me ups.

At each water stop, there was an advance guard person who would say something like, "Hi, Laura…Way to go!" I have long accepted the fact that brain cells expire in direct proportion to the number of miles run, but I was astonished at how many people seemed to know me. Since I work at the large Saratoga Library and also write for Adirondack Sports & Fitness, I am used to being greeted by people I don't know. But how could I not recognize at least a few of these people? Or did I just look like "a Laura?" As much as I had anticipated each water stop oasis, I began to dread encountering yet more people I had apparently forgotten. Finally, a volunteer jumped out in front of me, noted my race number, consulted a printed list, turned back to the others and shouted, "Her name is Laura!" Mystery solved! I was neither hallucinating nor experiencing a senior moment, but simply the gullible victim of down-home friendliness.

These cheerleaders were all the more welcome due to the challenging nature of the course itself. Someone famous, whose name I have since forgotten, once wrote, "Hills! You ran a marathon with hills? You idiot!" While at certain times during the marathon I might be tempted to agree, I find I do better on hilly courses than on the idealized "flat and fast" venues. The hills add interest, provide motivation, and keep my trail-running legs from cramping up on the less forgiving asphalt. But while the course elevation profile would seem to indicate that the first half is extremely hilly and that the final stretch is little more than an uneventful jaunt around Schroon Lake, don't get suckered in by a casual glance! For my first attempt in 2000, I took advantage of my mountain running skills by charging relentlessly uphill and speeding downhill. I was having a blast! Until mile 14, that is. While the second half appears relatively flat by Adirondack standards, it contains many steady, relentless climbs. Soon I found myself being passed by those I had breezed by earlier. While I did place in my age group, I still felt somehow "beaten" by the experience. Like Hare, I ran impulsively according to the moment, only to be left in the dust by the wiser Tortoises.

Albert Einstein once defined insanity as "doing the same thing over and over again and expecting different results." I ignored his advice, determined to return and conquer the course. No matter how much I craved redemption, a cold, steady rain punctuated by the occasional downpour accompanied my next two attempts. Race day 2004, however, dawned sunny-faced, 50°F, and in considerably better spirits. Thinking that my time had finally come, I latched onto a friend who was slightly slower than I and matched my pace to hers for the first few miles. Besides, I was a bit achy from having run a 5K race the day before. While this normally ranks below stupid on any coach's scale, in this case it kept me reined in and cautious. I curbed my uphill pace, but retained my reckless downhill tumbles. I waved to the cheerleaders at the water stop milestones and filled my mind with slow and steady tortoise thoughts. Even without a bear encounter, I found myself passing people, even some I normally view from the backside only. Apparently, I had cracked the code, earning a first place age group picture of Schroon Lake in the process.

While marathon strategies are, in the end, highly individual affairs, a variation on the above scenario might work for you, too. And as you plan your marathon, be sure and visit the Adirondack Marathon web site, for the blow-by-blow course pictures and accompanying description. And while you are there, be sure to click on the Adventures of a Traveling Bear. Traveling Bear, now real (think Velveteen Rabbit), is one of the huge carved bear awards.

My husband, Jeff, remarked that since I had finally conquered the course, I could now get on with my life. Especially since the Adirondack Marathon usually falls on his birthday weekend. Still … the hills, fall foliage, and smiling faces are a powerful draw, not to mention the long-sleeved windshirts. Then, too, there's always that Bear to set my sights on ….

Laura Clark is a 58 year-old runner who has been pounding the roads and trails for 28 years and counting. Her marathon PR occurred eons ago with a 3:38 time at the Frankfurt Marathon. Her new motto is, "If you can't run fast, run tough." In the winter, she trades in her sneakers for snowshoes and races on the Western Massachusetts Dion Snowshoe circuit. When not running, she records her adventures in Adirondack Sports & Fitness _magazine and other local publications. She and her husband, Jeff, also direct several road races and snowshoe races._

Road Runner Akron Marathon

akron, ohio

Web site: www.akronmarathon.org
Month: October
USATF Certified: Yes
Course: Rolling

Author: Kip Brady
Number of Marathons Completed: 2
Age Group: 30-34

October 2nd was a typical fall day for Akron, Ohio; that is to say it started off cold, dark, and rainy, and then it warmed up a little. While some or maybe most would cite this description of northeast Ohio weather as reason enough to stay away, marathoners are unique in their psyche; to a marathoner, this weather is nearly perfect. Cooler temperatures and light precipitation can mean a faster average race pace and less risk of dehydration. For a marathon runner, Akron, Ohio is a great place to visit in October.

I had come to Akron for the second annual Road Runner Akron Marathon, a race that is also home to the USATF North American Challenge, a marathon relay race between elite teams from the United States, Mexico, and Canada, and an amateur marathon relay race. After running this race (my first marathon) the year before, I was impressed by the overall quality of the event, which offers a challenging, spectator-friendly course that is closed to traffic, exceptionally well organized, and has amazing volunteer support.

My family and I arrived at Akron's John S. Knight Center the previous evening to collect my race packet at the race expo. The packet pick-up process was a snap, and we were through the moderately sized expo, with my race packet in hand, inside of 15 minutes. Since my dad lives just north of Akron, we stayed with him, but there are plenty of nice hotels within a two-block radius of the Knight Center.

Parking before the race was graciously easy. There are several large, inexpensive, and mostly empty parking garages within sight of both the start and finish lines. We parked on the ground floor of a parking garage on South Broadway Street, just two blocks south of the starting line at the National Inventors Hall of Fame and two blocks east of the finish line at Canal Park Stadium.

The starting line was set up on South Broadway Street in front of Inventure Place, a museum dedicated to invention and home to the National Inventors Hall of Fame. There was a slight but steady rain when we first arrived, but this gradually subsided.

In college, my running teammates and I often jokingly proposed that one of the best measures of a well-organized race was the presence of copious numbers of portable toilets. While restroom facilities at many events — both large and small — are often woefully inadequate, the Road Runner Akron Marathon, which rents 150 portables in total, provides a seemingly endless line of them at the start area. By this measure alone, I would rate the Road Runner Akron Marathon an unquestionable Number 1!

The temperature at the start of the race was somewhere in the upper 40s with gray, overcast skies. Racers lined up according to pace, and I found my place among the group gathering next to the sign that read "6:00 to 6:30 per mile." My plan was to run a steady 6:30 pace for the first 20 miles and then try to pick it up for the last 10 kilometers, ultimately running somewhere around 2:45 for the marathon.

The course began in a northward direction, heading first down a long, gradual hill to the north side of the city and then across the All-America Bridge, which spans the Little Cuyahoga River Valley and links the northern suburbs of Akron to the downtown district.

It was a picturesque scene, a long line of runners spread-out across the two north-bound lanes, the river valley 300 feet below, blanketed in trees splashed like paint brushes in pale green with the occasional smattering of yellow, orange, or red. The gray backdrop provided by the overcast skies, combined with the occasional brightness of fall colors to produce a surreal picture, underscoring what I still see as the strange act of running a marathon.

I have always had a problem with pace, and within the first three miles, as the race passed back through the city heading south, I found that I was running at what seemed at the time to be a very comfortable six minutes per mile. Of course, the first mile-and-a-half had been mostly downhill, but the previous year I made the mistake of going out way too hard early and then suffered in the last half of the race. Suffering for the last half of a 10-kilometer race is not such a big problem, but 13 miles is a long way to suffer, so, hoping to avoid my rookie mistake of the year before, I cautiously, if not grudgingly, eased off my pace.

The first relay exchange zone is located at the 10K point of the race. Running in a marathon with a relay component provides an interesting experience in that each time you pass an exchange zone you encounter a whole new set of competitors with fresh legs. This can be both good and bad. If you are anything like me—and if you are  reading this you probably are—when someone runs past you during a race, you tend to try and latch on to that person, to see if you can stay with him. If you can run at his pace, you will most certainly do better than if he had never caught you, and, if you can't stay with him, hopefully you will figure this out pretty quickly and slow again. A marathon is a long way to run in this fashion, but early in the marathon you just feel too good to let anyone get away. This had been part of my problem when I raced at Akron the year before, and this year my enthusiasm was tempered by memories of suffering through the final 10 miles of that race.

In spite of my efforts to slow my pace, when I passed the 10-mile mark, just before entering the campus of the University of Akron, I found that my average pace was still six minutes per mile. I have heard that it takes at least a few marathons before you really know when you are going too fast too early. I suppose this must be true; at 10 miles I felt fine, but then, I had felt fine at 10 miles before.

I crossed the University of Akron Campus, which is mostly downhill, ran past the shimmering façade of the university's Polymer Center, and then around E.J. Thomas Performing Arts Hall where the course swings back across the start line at Inventure Place. My wife, son, and my dad were waiting there amongst the throngs of spectators lining the roads and cheering. Emotionally charged and feeling surprisingly well, I continued down the long hill that drops from there into the Cuyahoga River Valley.

At approximately 11 miles, the course reaches the floor of the Cuyahoga River Valley and turns north onto the Ohio and Erie Canal Towpath trail. This trail has a well-packed, crushed limestone surface. It winds along the Cuyahoga River, following the former Ohio and Erie Canal route, and covers about four miles of the course. It is a quiet section of the race that is shaded for most of its length by a canopy of honey locust, maple, and cottonwood. The presence of a softer running surface is a welcome perk after pounding the pavement for 11 miles. It is in the quiet solitude of this part of the course that you must pass under the giant banner telling you that you have only "13.1 miles to go."

In a marathon, the half-way-point takes on a different feel than it does in shorter events. This is the point where you are hit with the harsh reality of your situation: You have only gone half way! So it was when I passed beneath the large banner, far from the cheers of family and friends and everyone else, that reality struck. I can't imagine that anyone actually feels good at this point in the race. I have heard people say that they do, but I don't believe them. Suddenly, I was feeling pretty bad and the thought of having to run the same distance over again was simply depressing. I consoled myself with the thought that I was surely better off than the year before and pressed onward.

Just past mile 15, the course leaves the solitude of the trail and returns to paved roads and spectators at Portage Path. The course turns south, just briefly, then west onto the Sand Run Parkway.

I consider the Sand Run Parkway to be the most significant section of the race. The road runs through the oldest metro park in Summit County and is shaded along its length by a dense canopy of mature oak and maple trees. After crossing the temporary bridge spanning the ford at Sand Run, a small stream from which, I gather, the Parkway gets its name, the road begins a series of long, gradual climbs that total almost two miles in length and ends somewhere near mile 18.

I knew that this would be the defining point in my race. The previous year I was very tired by this point, and I lost a lot of time in this section, but I felt better this year. If I could finish the Sand Run Parkway feeling strong, then I would certainly have a great race. The hill is never what I would consider steep, just long and steady. I tried to maintain a pace that felt comfortable: as comfortable as one could expect to be when climbing for two miles.

The long climb up Sand Run Parkway gives this race an epic feel. It comes at a point that is late in the race when you are tired, and it challenges you. Like the renowned "Heartbreak Hill" of Boston, Sand Run Parkway is a piece of terrain that sets Akron apart from other marathons. I enjoy races that test my physical and mental limits, and in an age where marathons seem bent on trying to offer the flattest, fastest courses possible, the challenge afforded by the Akron course is a refreshing departure from the norm. The gutsy climb up Sand Run Parkway is just one of the reasons that this race will distinguish itself among the greatest of marathons.

After the big hill, the terrain changes to gently rolling, but even these relatively small, rolling hills present a challenge this late in the race. My pace was dropping off quickly, and there was nothing I could really do about it. I had burned up too much energy in the earlier portions of the course, and now I would have to suffer.

It is a funny thing about marathons, at least from a newbie's point of view, that one can ponder the race beforehand and think of the last 10 kilometers as "only six miles." Of course, the reality is that the last six miles can be far more difficult than the first 15, and, for me, the last six miles were spent in a bonk-induced haze. I can only vaguely recall running across the grounds of Stan Hywet Hall and Gardens, near mile 22, when the course turns down the driveway to the former residence of F.A. Seiberling, co-founder of the Goodyear Tire and Rubber Company. Apparently, the course runs past the manor house, but I don't remember seeing it. It is amazing that one could run past a house large enough to require 23 fireplaces and not notice it, but thus is the status of the bleary-eyed, bonking runner.

Just before mile 24, the course turns east, following West Market Street down a long, gradual descent to South Main Street and the final half-mile of the race. The crowds along South Main are loud and their enthusiasm can carry you like a wave into the finish line at Canal Park Stadium.

The Canal Park Stadium, home to the Cleveland Indians' Class AA Akron Aeros and pride of downtown Akron, is an awesome structure and finishing there adds to the world-class feel of this race. Turning onto the maintenance road that leads into the stadium, I was preparing to relax and savor the final 100 or so meters that would carry me to the finish line when I heard the unmistakable sound of fast-moving feet over my shoulder. It is amazing that you can feel so alone for 26 miles and then find yourself shoulder to shoulder in a sprint for the finish line. My instincts took over, and I suddenly found my running form that had been missing for the past eight miles. I had come too far, and run too hard, to be passed in the final 100 meters. All sound vanished. My eyes locked on the finish line. My legs churned. My feet tapped the ground with a lightness that I could not have expected. The meters clicked by, and then, finally, I was across the line. I bent over, hands on my knees, relishing the sweet comfort of inactivity, enjoying a well-deserved and thoroughly satisfying rest. Volunteers wrapped me in a silver space blanket, draped my finisher's medal around my neck, and helped me up the stadium steps to the complementary massage tents, food, and reunion with my family.

I finished in 6th place with a time of 2:51:16. My time was slower than I had hoped, but, in the end, it really didn't matter. I stood on the balcony of the stadium holding my 4 1/2-month-old son, savoring the feeling of warmth that comes following a good effort, when you have dug down deep inside yourself again and again and each time came back with something more. I had come to the Road Runner Akron Marathon looking for a challenge, and I had found it. What more could I ask of a marathon?

Kip Brady teaches biology and physical science at New Philadelphia High School in New Philadelphia, Ohio. He competed in cross-country running and Nordic skiing at Northern Michigan University and continues to race at the elite level in skiing, triathlon, and cycling. The Road Runner Akron Marathon was his second marathon.

Lakefront Marathon

milwaukee, wisconsin

Web site: www.badgerlandstriders.org/lakefront/default.asp
Month: October
USATF Certified: Yes
Course: Flat

Author: Kristen Adelman
Number of Marathons Completed: 15
Age Group: 30-34

I came across the Lakefront Marathon while searching for fall marathons. I was actually training for my first 50 miler and was running marathons on my "long run" days. It was much more fun running a race than hitting those long runs alone. I was also working on the goal of running a marathon in every state. So as I searched the web and found this run, I realized it could help me with both of my goals. Aside from not yet having run a marathon in Wisconsin I also had some friends there, which added an extra incentive. So with all these things considered, after examining the web site and determining it looked like a really nice event, I decided to give it a try. I am really glad I did, as it was definitely one of my most enjoyable marathons yet.

The Lakefront Marathon is fairly small with about 1,800 runners. The course is a point-to-point and relatively flat. There are no qualifications necessary for entry into this race. The course is USATF certified and is a Boston qualifier, making one eligible for the next two runnings of Boston. Registration may be done easily online. Entries are limited to 2,300, and the entry fee does increase the closer you get to the event.

The race expo was small, but due to the number of runners it was sufficient. There were no lines when I picked up my packet and everything was well organized. There were not a lot of extras to select, however, some necessities were available like gels, bars, gloves, and other minor last minute things.

I was able to stay with some friends in Milwaukee, which was very nice. In fact the race went right past their house, which was an added bonus.

LAKEFRONT MARATHON

However, if you do not know anyone there, the web site offers some choices of hotels, one that even provides transportation to the race start. Some downtown shuttles are also provided by the race, but reservations are needed.

I was able to park at the finish line race day morning (free parking is provided on a grassy area near the finish) and easily catch a shuttle to the start. Again, due to the small number of runners this went quite smoothly.

The race began at 8:00 a.m. from a local high school. The school was open two hours before the race, which was nice because it enabled me to stay warm before the start. The early morning Fahrenheit temperatures were in the 30s so it was a bit chilly starting off, but the race provides gear check bags and allows you to keep them until just before the start of the race. Within a few hours, however, temperatures reached the upper 40s and by the end were in the lower 50s.

I really enjoyed the course. Aside from the benefits of a small field, the course was not pancake flat, which I found quite appealing. I personally enjoy the relief a slightly, and I emphasize the word slightly, rolling course has to offer. The beginning of the race was on country roads. It was a beautiful beginning, and I thoroughly enjoyed the scenery. As I ran the mildly rolling course and witnessed the early morning sun, my breath was taken away—but thankfully not for too long!

The course continued through some beautiful housing developments. There were some spectators along the course cheering us on (the fact that our names were on our numbers made this even better). They were not visible the entire time, but seemed to be there just when you needed them.

Eventually, we ended up running parallel to Lake Michigan. As we ran through one of the developments, I saw glimpses of the beautiful crystal blue lake. I was in awe. In the final stretch of the race there was a clear view of the lake as we approached the finish line downtown. It was a slight decent, which was very welcomed, and the view was spectacular. Aside from the lake, there was a great view of downtown Milwaukee and the new art museum, which in itself was a beautiful sight.

The race was well supported with friendly volunteers, water, Gatorade, and Vaseline at 12 locations approximately every two miles. Other things were also available such as some gels and first aid, if needed. There were also many clocks and mile markers set up throughout the course to help you stay on pace.

The post-race party was really nice. It was in the heart of downtown Milwaukee with a beautiful view of the lake as well as the attractive downtown area. Plus, having my vehicle near the finish line made it very easy to get back to my friends' house at the end.

Prize money was awarded to the top three male and female finishers ($500, $300, $100) respectively. First male and female Masters also received $100. Age-group awards were given (including $100 for male and female 50+ winners), along with awards to the top three relay teams.

All around, the race was excellent, and I am so glad I stumbled upon it. It is a great course and low key so whether your goal is to qualify for Boston, get in some nice long runs, or if you are just looking for a really enjoyable race, I would highly recommend the Lakefront Marathon. It is a truly wonderful event.

Kristen Adelman teaches Algebra, Science, and PE at an elementary school in Elkridge Maryland. She began running in 1997 and has been running ever since, even throughout her three-year battle with cancer. She has completed 15 marathons, several triathlons, as well as eight ultras, one of which was a 100-mile trail run. Her goals include completing a marathon in every state as well as many more ultras.

Twin Cities Marathon

minneapolis/st. paul, minnesota

Web site: www.twincitiesmarathon.org
Month: October
USATF Certified: Yes
Course: Rolling

Author: Brock Foreman
Number of Marathons Completed: 5
Age Group: 25-29

TWIN CITIES
M A R A T H O N

With 10,000 runners, 5,000 volunteers, and 250,000 spectators, the Twin Cities Marathon is the biggest running event in Minnesota. Why is it so popular? Minnesota in early October—who could ask for better weather? Temperatures are usually cool, in the 40s or 50s, but rarely cold. Sunshine is normal. It's perfect for running a marathon.

The scenery is drop-dead gorgeous. Known for clean downtowns, lakes, sweeping views of the Mississippi River, and charming neighborhoods, the Twin Cities Marathon showcases some of the best running routes the area offers. There's a reason the marathon directors trademarked the phrase, "The Most Beautiful Urban Marathon in America™." It's because it's true. I'm probably biased because I live here, but Minneapolis and St. Paul are among the best running cities in the country.

Don't forget the fall colors. I can't tell you how many people, racers and spectators, I've heard say how beautiful the trees are during the Twin Cities Marathon. You would think these people have never seen a tree before. But they're right. The leaves are spectacular.

The relatively flat course is a plus too. I live in St. Paul and run along the River Road section of the marathon course regularly. It's probably the steepest part of race. But it's not that bad. Okay, there's one deceptively long incline, but don't worry, the rest of the course is a pancake and the last mile or so before the finish is a big downhill. Don't worry, you'll run fast.

It's hard to believe the Twin Cities Marathon runs right through my

St. Paul neighborhood! I'm so lucky. Here I am, an avid recreational runner and marathoner, and I've got such a great race like this smack-dab in the middle of my backyard. Surely, I've run 10 or more ....

Actually, last year's Twin Cities Marathon was my first one.

What? Your first one?

I know, I know.

I usually run races in the spring and summer. By the time fall rolls around, long runs are the last thing on my mind. I shift into spectator mode and watching the Twin Cities Marathon has become a sort of tradition.

For years, I've gathered with family and friends near mile marker 24 to cheer on the racers. My wife, Leslie, and I grab sandwiches, a thermos of hot apple cider, and a couple of lawn chairs and hoof it a couple of blocks to meet everybody at our favorite corner on Summit Avenue, St. Paul's historic boulevard most noted for its stately Victorian-era mansions. We arrive at our corner just in time to see the leaders, some of the top runners in the world. Then we settle into our chairs, chat, sip cider, and munch on our sandwiches while we cheer on the rest of the runners, especially the guy that runs in his U.S. Postal uniform every year.

Watching the race is fun. It's relaxing. I look forward to it every fall.

Last spring, however, Leslie wanted to run the race as her first marathon. Although I was somewhat hesitant to give up my lawn chair on race day, I told her I'd run it with her.

Knowing that the race fills up in a couple of weeks through normal mail and online registration, we went to the sign-up party in Minneapolis in May. I'm glad we did. In addition to good snacks, drinks, and mingling with other runners, the sign-up party guaranteed us race numbers.

Leslie and I trained. October finally came.

I picked up my race packet at the huge runner's expo at the Rivercenter in downtown St. Paul the day before the race. The place teemed with runners. Still, even with so many people, I didn't have to wait in line for more than a minute or so before a happy volunteer handed me my packet.

The short wait to get a race packet meant more time to wander around the expo and burn off some pre-race energy with fellow racers. The expo features more than 70 vendors selling shorts, tops, socks, shoes, watches, energy drinks, and anything else you can think of related to running, not to mention official Twin Cities Marathon merchandise. At one booth, I spun a wheel and received a discount coupon at a local athletic store. I was pleased to find several booths offering information about other races throughout the country. I tried on a few pairs of shoes. I ended up buying a pair of shorts and picked up a couple of lemon-lime energy gels (YUM!). I was impressed with the quality of the merchandise at the expo and enjoyed the complimentary cup of java from marathon sponsor Caribou Coffee.

Ready to race!

I'm like a little kid on race-day morning, but this time I had to tone my excitement back a little. A running injury had sidelined Leslie. She had developed trochanteric bursitis with a little stress fracture. That's "runner's hip" in layman's terms. Leslie trained hard all summer, and I knew she was upset about not being able to run. I offered to skip the race and join her in the lawn chairs at mile 24, but I was happy when she insisted that I go ahead and run. Staring across a bowl of pre-race Grapenuts, I told her I'd run extra hard for the both of us. She laughed and drove me to the start.

The Twin Cities Marathon is regarded as a very well-organized race, and the reasons for this were apparent from the moment I arrived at the starting area. Leslie had no trouble dropping me off by car. Despite the huge number of runners and spectators, there was hardly any traffic congestion at the drop off area. Ubiquitous volunteers and police keep things moving.

A helpful hint: Even though traffic is not a problem at the start, I suggest staying at one of the several hotels in downtown Minneapolis if you're coming in from out of town. I met several people who simply walked from their hotel to the starting line. How easy is that?

One of the nicest race features is being able to wait in the nearby HHH Metrodome before the start. Not only is The Dome a great place for 10,000 runners to warm up and stretch, but also the stadium's ample restrooms mean no long lines to use the portables.

I made my way to the starting line.

Race directors recently instituted a two-wave start. A wave start was a new experience for me, and I liked it. Since the Twin Cities Marathon uses ChampionChip Timing, there's no time penalty for starting in the second wave. By putting the faster runners up front and slower runners in back, the wave-start seemed to minimize congestion, especially during the first few miles when the herd is always thickest.

The gun went off, and I quickly settled into my marathon pace alongside a girl wearing a colorful, fuzzy, court-jester hat with bells. A little annoying, but better than a marathon I ran a couple of years ago where I ended up pacing with a guy wearing a t-shirt that said "Go Dave" and someone from the crowd shouted "Go Dave!" every ten seconds.

I ignored the funny jingling hat and kept running.

Aid stations with water and POWERade sport drink, toilets, and medical personnel are available at miles 2 1/2, 5, and approximately every two miles after that. I found the aid stations always well staffed; I never had to wait to get a drink.

At mile 13, I smiled because I clocked my fastest half-marathon time. Certainly, the enthusiasm from the crowd of spectators helped me out a bit. There's one part of the course over by Lake Harriet where the road narrows and a boisterous crowd is a mere arm's reach on either side. At that point, I felt as swift as Lance Armstrong marching through the hordes of screaming fans on L'Alpe d'Huez!

Unfortunately, I am not Lance Armstrong. No amount of cheering in the world would allow me to keep up my blistering pace. I broke the cardinal rule in running: Don't start too fast. Cracked, I struggled for the next several miles.

No worries though. Eventually, I made it to mile 24. Sure enough, Leslie, and several of my family and friends were there to root for me. I thanked them, and gave the thumbs up. Exhaustedly, but with a smile, I pushed toward the finish.

At last, the towering dome of the St. Paul Cathedral came within view, marking the last mile of the race. I embraced the final downhill strides with a deep reverence only an amateur marathoner can understand.

The finish area spreads out over an enormous mall in the shadow of the state's magnificent 100-year-old capitol. The mass of runners and spectators at the finishing chute is immense. But as expected, the finish was as well organized as the rest of the race. Finisher's medallion? Check. Fluids? Check. Post-race snacks? Check? Run bags? Check. Cool long-sleeved race t-shirt? Check. Once again, the huge staff of volunteers made everything flow nicely. "Thank you. We hope you enjoyed your marathon. Please enjoy your time in the Twin Cities and come again next year."

I will.

I enjoyed watching the Twin Cities Marathon for so many years. But I have to admit; running in it is even better. The Twin Cities Marathon has great weather, terrific scenery, and an exuberant crowd. It's a very well organized event to boot. From start to finish, the race runs smoothly. The Twin Cities Marathon is truly one of the best marathons around. Believe me, run it once, and you'll never be satisfied with watching it from your lawn chair again.

See you in October!

St. Paul, Minnesota native and resident Brock Foreman, 29, loves to run and has completed five marathons and a couple of ultras. An attorney, Brock's law office is located on St. Paul's bustling Grand Avenue, only a few blocks from River Road and Summit Avenue, his favorite sections of the Twin Cities Marathon. When not in court or squeezing in a long run, he's lounging in a chair at the end of a dock trying to catch a few fish.

St. George Marathon

st. george, utah

Web site: www.stgeorgemarathon.com
Month: October
USATF Certified: Yes
Course: Rolling

Author: Terry Tucker
Number of Marathons Completed: 35
Age Group: 60-64

I originally chose to run this race the year after I went to the finish line and watched all the runners come across. It was an event that literally changed my life. The first time I ran the St. George Marathon it was my first marathon. Since that time I have run it 19 times. The marathon has a Ten Year Club for those who have run this marathon 10 times or more. Each year they add another 80 or so runners to this club, which says a lot about the quality of this marathon. The last time I ran St. George it was my 35th marathon. My best time at St. George was a 3:11, the worst a 4:01. A lot of things can happen in 26.2 miles.

Entries are accepted either through the mail or online beginning April 1 each year. Entries must be in the St. George Marathon race office by the end of April. Shortly after that date, a lottery is held to fill the remaining 6,400 spots for the marathon. Each year about 2,000 people who apply are not selected to run. The results of the lottery are posted on the marathon web site and both successful and unsuccessful applicants are notified.

A typical race day has temperatures in the mid 40s at the start line (6:00 a.m.) and then slowly warms to the high 70s to low 80s by 10:30 a.m. and hits the mid to high 80s by noon. On one occasion, we had rain for most of the race but that was the only bad weather day in 28 years; pretty good odds for good weather.

Although billed as a downhill course, this marathon has some surprises for those who haven't looked closely. It begins at an elevation of 5,240 feet and ends at 2,680 feet. The first mile is slightly uphill; from mile 2 to 5 1/2 the course drops slowly, with a steep downhill from miles 5 1/2 to 7. From miles 7 to 9, you climb more than 500 feet in elevation then continue a steady climb until about mile 12 1/2. From miles 12 1/2 to 14, there is a steady downhill followed by another big drop from miles 14 to 16. This is also the place where a runner gets a great view of the many colors found in Snow Canyon State Park (named after a person not a weather condition).

From mile 16 through 20, it's mostly rolling hills with a small hill at mile 19 1/2. At mile 20 the drop is steep until mile 21 1/2, then the course is flat until mile 22 1/2. Another steep drop takes you to mile 23 1/2. The last three miles are gently sloping to the finish line. The course runs past several old volcano cones as well as the many differing views of Snow Canyon.

The race expo is small by Boston standards, but about the same as other marathons this size. All of the vendors have running information. I have not seen non-runner oriented merchandise at this expo, something that I personally don't enjoy seeing at some other expos.

Even though I live close to this marathon, I stay at one of the local motels. Most of the motels are very helpful toward the runners. The one I stay in offers a shuttle to the finish line where runners get on buses for the trip to the start. The shuttle runs back and forth as runners show up starting at 4:15 a.m.

I like this race for several reasons. The weather has almost always been pleasant, and for me, fall marathons seem a little easier to prepare for than those run in the spring. The support is excellent, and the crowds are a big help especially from mile 23 until the finish. The food area at the end is the best I have experienced with Gatorade, yogurt, bananas, apples, Great Harvest® bread, cantaloupe, watermelon, grapes, pineapple, Blue Bunny® ice cream treats, and Coke products.

Each finisher gets a beautiful medallion. For those that are a little competitive, they give awards 10 deep in each age division. The overall winners, as well as the Master winners, are given free trips to Japan for a sister marathon during the first part of November.

From a spectator's point of view, the course has both positive and negatives. If you spend some time becoming familiar with the area you can drive the back roads and see the runners at the 7-mile mark, then again at 16, then most anywhere from 23 until the finish line. The negative is that other than those areas, only the local residents can see the runners until they get to the 23-mile mark. There are bleachers set up along the last quarter of a mile before the finish line and the finish area is at a large park making it great for family and friends to enjoy what is usually perfect weather.

The only thing I don't like about this marathon is that it is way too long. I wish they all could be about 16 miles. Actually, the steep downhill from mile 20 to mile 23 is pretty tough on the quads, I find it takes a little longer to completely recover from this marathon than from others I have run.

This race is the best-organized marathon that I have run. It starts on time and the people seem to go out of their way to make sure runners enjoy being there. The only negative I have noticed is the number of runners who would like to enter but cannot. Due to a lack of motel rooms and bus transportation, the race has to put limits on the number of runners. Race organizers have indicated that people in the community have been on waiting lists for up to six years to be able to operate one of the aid stations on the course.

_____

Terry Tucker is a Project Manager for Western Wireless (Cellular One) and oversees special projects in Nevada, Texas, Minnesota, and Kansas. He has been running, or at least participating in marathons, since 1982. He has run St. George 19 times, Boston twice and Big Sur twice, as well as several others for a total of 35.

The LaSalle Bank Chicago Marathon®

chicago, illinois

Web site: www.chicagomarathon.com
Month: October
USATF Certified: Yes
Course: Flat

Author: Anne-Marie Smith
Number of Marathons Completed: 5
Age Group: 40-44

If training for and racing a marathon is analogous to pregnancy and childbirth, then the Chicago Marathon for me was a pink, healthy, eight-pounder with a round head and no baby acne. In other words: perfect.

The dawn lit a cloudless, pure blue sky that Sunday morning in October. The air was fall fresh and still, as it is most years in the Windy City, a nickname earned by 19th century political wind-bags, not its weather trends. It was around 50°F at the 8:00 a.m. start, nearing 70°F by the finish, a little warm for the elite runners, perhaps, but perfect for the pre-race migration of thousands to Grant Park.

The place was ignited by anticipation of the big race. We felt it the day before when we landed at O'Hare, and on the easy "L" subway ride from the airport into town. Runners and their supporters from all 50 states and around the globe filled those train cars with stories of travel, weather, shoes, energy gel, past marathons, or not. We listened mostly, my husband and I, as we rode, and watched the countryside turn to city before de-boarding at "The Loop." The hype was even more intense at the expo that afternoon at the gargantuan McCormick Place convention center where a steady stream of runners rode up and down wide escalators and fanned out into its expansive corridors.

By the morning of the race, the buzz in the city was palpable. Everyone, even the bag checker at the hotel, was pumped.

Chicago is famous for its crowds, both running the race and on the

Courtesy of The LaSalle Bank Chicago Marathon

sidelines. More than 33,000 of the 40,000-plus registered racers started the marathon, although nearly 850 of those wouldn't make it to the end.

I passed more than a million spectators running along the shores of Lake Michigan, turning through the streets of 16 of the city's most charming ethnic neighborhoods, and crossing the finish line in Grant Park, close to where I'd started 3:48:04 earlier. One million people!

Those crowds were my Lamaze partners: coaxing, cheering, and comforting me through the pain. They stood five or six deep in many areas, lined bridge overpasses, balconies, and hillsides. They shouted from the streets of Little Italy, Chinatown, and Greektown. They clapped along to a mariachi band in the Latino neighborhood of Pilsen, danced the polka on the sidewalk, played bagpipes and rock and roll. In Chicago, there was never a dull moment. They inspired me when I hit the, "I'm never doing this again" wall that is my custom around mile 18. It was nowhere near as painful as my four previous marathons.

People stretched across every inch of roadway. In Chicago, it was all about everyone. Chicagoans hooted and hollered more than the baseball-obsessed Boston spectators, who mostly yelled "Sox won!" as I ran by (Okay, so they'd beaten the Yankees that year).

Some running friends have told me they prefer smaller, calmer races than Chicago. I have enough ego that I like attention the whole dang way. After all those 40 to 50 mile training weeks, if I'm going to plod along for almost four hours, someone better watch me do it.

Before the race, runners spilled out of hotels and the subway onto the streets and lawns of Grant Park, which straddles the shore of Lake Michigan. Despite an impressive collection of Port-a-Johns (which looked like a porta-potty city), my friends and I were put off by the lines for the toilets. They make me anxious as gun time approaches, and their smell doesn't help a pre-race nervous stomach.

The herd of racers in Chicago is massive enough to annoy some runners I know who refuse to run there — despite its famously fast course — because of the sheer numbers. Granted, it did take me a full five minutes to get to the start line once the gun sounded, and I thought I was starting close-up. The early miles were clogged with runners. As we headed into the city before crossing the Chicago River and moving out toward the prestigious Lake Shore Drive, runners were funneled into ever-narrowing streets. I found myself slowed to nearly a walk once or twice early on and forced onto the sidewalk other times. But, I now believe that it was, in fact, the unavoidable slow start that enabled me to achieve my goal of a Boston qualifying time (3:50 for women ages 40 to 44). For me, a runner who tends to go out too hard, the sluggish early miles left enough juice in my tank for me to run a strong final 10K. The Boston time had eluded me twice before, once by a mere 12 seconds (and, no, Boston wouldn't let me in!), because of crash-and-burns around mile 24.

The course was flat and fast as promised. In the city, it offered the shade of some of the nation's tallest buildings. When the course twice took us away from downtown, we were treated to spectacular skyline vistas upon our return. I prefer Chicago's zig-zags through neighborhood streets to miles-long straight shots of other marathons. The twists and turns leave open the surprise of what lay around the bend, including the final turn onto Columbus Drive where it was a short quarter or so mile to that glorious balloon arch. The only surprise to me was a wicked, though short, uphill across a small bridge just past mile 25. It was unexpected and made me a little grumpy at the time, but looking back, I was clearly spoiled from having run the bulk of the race at the zero altitude gain.

Despite the demand for hydration, the water and Gatorade stations were well equipped to handle the masses. One friend told me he had to stop and wait for a cup at many water stops at the New York marathon. Not so in Chicago where the numbers of volunteers rivaled that of the participants. There was even a CLIF SHOT stop—and lots of sticky pavement—at mile 18.

Like the waning days of my pregnancies, I ate and slept a lot in the week before making the trip to Chicago. My three kids knew I had Boston-on-the-brain, and seemed to give me more space than usual that week. I allowed myself almost anything I wanted to eat, visited the chiropractor for a tune-up and ultrasound therapy, took a long Jacuzzi bath, and went to bed early. On Saturday, marathon-eve, we met friends for a hearty pasta dinner at an Italian restaurant near the Sears Tower.

We stayed at the Club Quarters Chicago Loop, a great hotel choice recommended to me by an experienced Chicago marathoner. The hotel, in the city's financial district where the "L" tracks form a semi-circle, was a short walk to the start and from the finish line. We even walked to Buddy Guy's Legends club for cold beer, ahhh, and Chicago blues on Sunday night. From the hotel, it was an easy walk to the Sears tower, the harbor and the art museum, all of which we toured on Monday.

Booking a room was a little tricky, as the hotel promotes itself as "members only."

When I "Googled" the name, a university web site link came up and divulged a password for accessing the Club Quarters web site. I helped myself to it and was able to get onto the site and book a room online. To some relief, no one at the hotel ever asked for any "member" credentials when we checked in or out.

We took a cab from the hotel to the expo. McCormick Place was one destination that was a little too far to walk, especially on the eve of the marathon. Shuttle buses ran from points around the city, but once again, on the advice of friends, we avoided them. The few bucks for a cab were well spent; we passed buses bulging with racers, and long lines of people at various points waiting for the next shuttle to come along.

The expo was enormous, alive, well run, and all-around wonderful. Because the place is so huge, it never felt overcrowded. Our friend's three-year-old even found a nice open corner to run around in for a few minutes.

I love expos for their excitement. I love to scan every booth, sample every sports drink and chunk of energy bar. It's satisfying getting my hands on my bib, finally, and the chip, and testing it out. I like stuffing freebies in my bag and spilling them out on the hotel room bed later. Chicago's sling-style goody bag is the best — sturdy and big. I still use mine all the time. The expo experience is like setting up the nursery, a nesting of sorts, in advance of the big day.

So, because of, not in spite of, the crowds, I ran my best. I pushed through my doubts and sore Achilles tendon, to the finish line. Once across, I tried to beat back that heavenly post-marathon delirium/euphoria to "do the math." (I screwed up my watch along the way — pushed stop instead of "split time" — and gave up on timing myself.) I knew my clock finish time and knew how far behind the gun I'd begun. All I had to do was subtract! But, that's a tall order after 26.2 miles!

My clear-headed husband, who finished a minute or so ahead of me, assured me I'd come in under 3:50. I kissed him for that.

A volunteer draped a heavy medal around my neck, another wrapped me in a Mylar® blanket (my favorite part of the whole experience), and a third crouched down to remove my chip from my shoe. We made our way past the food and water, through huge crowds, around the pebbled paths of Grant Park. Our designated meeting spot to hook up with friends seemed lost in the post-race chaos. We stopped where we thought it was and waited for what seemed like an hour, but probably wasn't, until finally I decided I had to sit, which I did, in the midst of the masses.

My husband wandered away to look for friends as I sat plopped on the gravel.

An older woman sitting nearby approached and offered to help take off my shoes. She said she'd been watching me; my poor feet looked so uncomfortable. I smiled, awed by her kindness. She insisted on me at least letting her loosen my laces. The crowd support didn't end at the finish, I guess.

The next day I had my prize: my medal, my Boston qualifying time, my sore legs. They were my baby.

We had fun walking gingerly around town that Monday, passing so many others in their white Chicago long-sleeved shirts hobbling, too.

The legs were my trophy, the achy satisfaction of finishing a marathon. For me, only the birth of my children has compared in the realm of personal accomplishment. During the delivery of each of my children I swore, as I did in Chicago, "I'm never doing this again." Afterward, I'd take my perfect baby home and watch him grow and the memory of the pain of the delivery would recede.

"It wasn't so bad," I'd tell my husband a few days post-partum. He, having held my hand through hours of contractions, would look at me like I was nuts.

The day after Chicago, as memories of the low-points of the race ebbed to the back of my mind, I asked my husband if he wanted to come back next year.

Anne-Marie Smith of Oak Hill, Virginia was 41 when she ran the LaSalle Bank Chicago Marathon. She followed Chicago with a 4:15 Boston Marathon in 2004 which, not to make excuses, happened to be the hottest Boston race in history.

United Technologies Hartford Marathon

hartford, connecticut

Web site: www.hartfordmarathon.com
Month: October
USATF Certified: Yes
Course: Rolling

Author: Mary Anne Chute Lynch
Number of Marathons Completed: 23
Age Group: 50-54

It's mile 16. Runners have thinned out. Conversations are minimal. I'm in my zone (or is it zombie) state of mind. I pass a solo competitor on a long, straight stretch.

"Hi, Mary Anne!" she says. I am jolted hearing my name. Who is this woman? How does she know me? Did I work with her in a former job? Should I recognize her from the neighborhood, PTA, the grocery store? Did I meet her recently and forget already?

It is an unusually hot Columbus Day Weekend in Connecticut. She turns up the heat. "Do you know who I am?" she says.

Is this woman for real? With 10 unknown miles to go, all I'm thinking about is running to the end without a muscle, ligament, or joint popping. I'm wondering why I keep putting my body through this ordeal? Wouldn't a half-marathon be more sane? This stranger's question yanks me out of self-absorption. I frantically flip through the rolodex of faces and names stored in my mind. No results. I'm in a frenzy. I brace to make a fool of myself again, guessing a name that's incorrect.

"Colleen Murphy?" I say.

"Yes," she says. "I recognized you right away."

I hadn't seen or thought about Colleen in 30 years. She was a year ahead of me in elementary school. Her name came to me instantly when I first looked at her, but I thought I must be crazy to imagine

181

it. Yet, here we were suddenly catching up on our lives during the thick of the race.

Welcome to Hartford! The race is like a giant family reunion. The entire day is a community picnic on a New England town green. They serve hot apple strudel with whipped cream after the race, and you can whirl up and down on hand-carved, wooden horses on one of the nation's oldest carousels at the finish.

Scottish dancers, wearing wool kilts, plaid sashes and tasseled socks, jig and reel at miles 7 and 11. Runners impetuously hop off course, swing a partner and do-si-do back on course reeling. No jig experience required. Undeterred by our sticky sweat, body odor, limping gaits, the dancers spin with runners until the last competitor pulls up the pack. I think running the marathon is easier than bouncing and kicking on blacktop for four hours.

During the Revolutionary War, General LaFayette preferred galloping full surge down this country lane to win guinea coins. Along this bucolic heart of the marathon we pass small sheep and goat farms and homesteads built in the 1700s. Corn husks and pumpkins decorate doorways, and residents clap for us in their flannel bathrobes and pajamas. "Good Morning, Connecticut!"

The trees join the party, too, waving red, yellow, orange, and crimson leaves at us, while shading our limbs through most of the marathon course.

But the race is not just a quintessential stroll through the countryside. The marathon takes us through city, town, and country, starting and ending at Bushnell Park in the heart of Connecticut's capitol. The United Technologies Hartford Marathon is a USATF-certified course, utilizing a computerized timing system for the extraordinary number of runners who qualify for the Boston Marathon here.

The secret: Hartford is easy.

- Easy to enter
- Easy to run
- Easy to qualify for Boston

That's where the magic happened for me. I never imagined the Boston Marathon was within my reach, but I qualified for Boston six times in Hartford, and I've made and broken all my personal running records here.

A woman in her 40s sobbed behind me when she crossed the finish line in Hartford in 2004. She gasped for breath while leaning onto another runner. I asked her if this was her first race. "No. I've done 15 marathons trying to get into Boston, and I just qualified," she said. The woman, her friend, and I hugged like long-lost kinfolk, screaming in marathon euphoria!

Who says New Englanders are reserved? Hartford is intimate, friendly, and stress-free.

Start with sign-up. There is no restrictive lottery, qualifying pedigree or deadline to sign up for the races. We're invited to run for free by donating $250 to a sanctioned charity.

I love a race where I can roll out of bed, brush my teeth, throw on my clothes, and walk a few blocks to the 8:00 a.m. start. The official race hotel and several others are a quarter mile from Bushnell Park, where the fun pulsates all day. I drive to Hartford on race day and park my car equally close to the starting line. No freezing in a field with thousands of runners from dawn until midday, waiting for my race to start. No wild weaving through the crowds to reach the racecourse.

Last minute entrants can sign up at Bushnell Park until the 8:00 a.m. start of the marathon, half-marathon, team relay, 5K, and Kids K. More than a few latecomers, including my family members, strip themselves of car keys and sweats at the registration tables and bolt over to the races as they start. No such luck in mega-races.

Elbow room is premium in marathons, and I revel in it in Hartford. I don't spend the first five miles worrying about being trampled by the thicket of competitors rubbing, jabbing, and tripping around me. A mid-to-back of the pack runner, I cross the starting line within a minute of the fast runners up front. Perhaps this luxury is one of the reasons Hartford is ranked the 8th Best Marathon in North America in *Marathon & Beyond*.

Hartford embraces spectators, too. Without leaving Bushnell Park, your fan club can see you at three points in the race: looking buff running half the park's perimeter at the start, resembling road kill when you circle around the other side of the park at mile 21, and shining your blissful, blistered best at the finish line.

I have showered myself in the plentiful water handed out by lines of volunteers at every mile along the way. One man offered me a full pitcher, when I poured two cups of water on my face. Extra porta-potties have been added throughout the course. Phew! That beats the bushes I scouted out when I was desperate in the early years of the race.

We jump and jive through 24 music stations ranging from African drummers to country bands, rock and roll to bagpipers, marching bands to guitarist Geoff

Mateski, who performs in his wheelchair at roadside. Spicing the run with wit between lyrics, Mateski makes us laugh at our fool's mission. His spirit makes me grateful for the privilege of feeling my weary legs pound the pavement.

High school drill teams keep me jazzed through barren stretches, which occur at some point in all marathons. The mid-teen miles, connecting country to city on Main Street in East Hartford, are the most aesthetically challenging part of the journey, as are the teen years, I'm noticing as a mother of four teenagers. But, you never know what gems may be revealed—I had my rendezvous with Colleen on this stretch.

Forget fuel? Hartford has goo galore at mile 18 and a lube station to grease up with Vaseline. Candy Man Chris Childs sports his native Texan cowboy attire and passes out free treats to runners at mile 22. The Candy Man used to compete in this marathon and was so taken with the hospitality that he uses his annual vacation to come up from Texas and volunteer every year.

Which brings me to the hill. We have to climb the only real hill on the marathon course at mile 21 to get our candy reward, but it's no Heartbreak Hill in distance or pitch. A band playing Jimmy Buffett music pumps us up the beginning of the hill even if we do look like we need paramedics reviving us more than melodies.

The last five miles can be spent fantasizing about "being the next millionaire" as we run through mansion row in Hartford's tony neighborhoods—another one of the city's hidden treasures. Here the neighbors sit in lawn chairs and shoot their lawn hoses like fountains to cool us on this last haul.

The crowd cheers as if we are world champions when we cross under the lofty Soldiers and Sailors Memorial Arch at the finish line. The triumphant scene makes me feel like an Olympian. "Mommy, sprint!" my four kids shouted to me on that home stretch in one of my first attempts at the marathon in Hartford.

"I am sprinting!" I yelled back. That's how powerfully uplifting the finale is. The race announcer calls out the names and hometowns of almost every runner as he or she approaches the finish line, a rare thrill in my lifetime. My most cherished running moment was coming through that historic arch, not when I ran my fastest time or heard my name announced, but when my 12-year-old twin daughters ran on either side of me for the last half mile of my race, after running their own 5K race earlier in the morning.

To unwind, I stretch in the park after my run with elite winners from Ethiopia, Kenya, Russia, Gambia, and Mexico, as if they were my next-door neighbors. Hartford at its best!

The Hartford marathon fills a need, a need for human warmth. There's a genuine welcome at the marathon that is all too lacking in our day-to-day exchanges. I feel renewed in Hartford. I am amazed by volunteers who make apple strudel, scrub and bake potatoes, and simmer chili in what is ranked as one of the best post-marathon feasts nationwide. I am soothed by hands that give free massages on the park green, invigorated through face to face conversations with record holders and first-timers, and elevated in a whirl of carefree exultation on the carousel. Ah, sweet welcome!

"If I could run a marathon, anybody can!" says Mary Anne Chute Lynch, who ran her first marathon as a 40th birthday present to herself. She wanted to know what would go through a person's head while putting the body through such an ordeal. After the race, she swore she would never run one again, but she has since run 22 marathons, qualified for and run Boston six times, and shocked herself when she posted her best time after 10 years of marathons. Mother to four teenagers, she never wears a watch when racing and aims simply to run to the end without stopping.

Mount Desert Island Marathon

mount desert island, maine

Web site: www.mdimarathon.org
Month: October
USATF Certified: Yes
Course: Rolling

Author: Matt Woida
Number of Marathons Completed: 1
Age Group: 25-29

I'm not sure where I was when the term "destination event" entered the lexicon of the average runner, but somehow the concept was lost on me. I figure if a place is so wonderful that I'd be willing to pay gobs of money just to travel there, only to then subject myself to even greater gobs of pain, surely it would make more sense (fiscally and physically) to simply move there altogether. So that's exactly what I did, and now I live on Mount Desert Island (MDI), in Downeast Maine. In October, I experienced the thrill of what proved to be the most challenging physical undertaking I'd ever endured, on a course beautiful enough to garner the Mount Desert Island Marathon its well-deserved status as one of America's most scenic running events.

I don't suppose most folks are inclined to pull up stakes and move their entire lives for the benefit of running; some might even consider such behavior irresponsible for a man in the 25-29 age bracket. But in my defense, my decision was motivated in large part by health considerations. Two years ago, while I sat at a hydraulic press in a factory in rural Ohio, my thoughts strayed northward to Maine and neglected to come back. If you've ever been to MDI (or worked in a factory for that matter), then perhaps you might appreciate the danger posed by such a distraction; at least enough to understand that I was in serious peril of losing my mind, if not some limbs, if I didn't quickly convey them to Maine.

My older brother, Mark, moved to MDI with his wife several years ago, and I had occasion to visit them twice prior to my move. Those visits were enough to convince me that MDI was nothing less than a pedestrian's paradise. Home to Acadia National Park, MDI is Maine's largest island, offering more than 120 miles of hiking trails, 45 miles of carriage paths, and plenty of scenic roads. All of these undulate over a 100 square mile landscape punctuated by high rocky hills, colorful foliage, shimmering ponds, lakes, harbors, and bays, including Frenchman's Bay, the only fjord on North America's eastern seaboard. Indeed, "paradise" is an apt descriptor for MDI considering the fact that maps drawn prior to 1918 denote MDI's town of Bar Harbor as "Eden."

Unfortunately, my running career did not prove immediately idyllic upon my relocating to paradise. My first summer and autumn on MDI were confounded by a nagging injury to my left Iliotibial Band. By the following spring, after months of working my way back to health, I was excited to finally have a chance at the sort of racing season I had envisioned for myself. Things started off well enough, but in early June, I contracted a debilitating illness that left me extremely fatigued and unable to run. By the time I was diagnosed with Lyme Disease in July, my red blood cell count had dropped roughly 30 percent, while my resting heart rate had nearly doubled. Needless to say, I was forced to modify my expectations for what remained of the racing season. Through hard work, patience, and heavy doses of antibiotics, I slowly recovered my strength and stamina. By September, thoughts of running a marathon were once again dusting themselves off within my mind.

I had dreamed of running a marathon for years, ever since I had dropped out of college in 1997. (Though I liked to think of it as "dropping in" to reality.) The pain of relinquishing what I had loved most in life: running as a member of my school's cross-country team, had never really abated. The idea of running marathons came to represent a strange sort of personal redemption. I thought if I could achieve my marathon goals, then perhaps I could forgive myself for squandering my once-in-a-lifetime college opportunity. But for over five years, my running all but languished as I bounced along from job to job and town to town. Finally, I owned-up to the fact that I needed to salvage whatever remained of my running potential if I were to ever find peace with myself. To that end, I needed to make some changes in my life, and I needed help to do it.

Help, as I've discovered, comes in all sorts of unexpected forms. When I moved to MDI, I was lucky enough to find a great place to work, as well as a wonderful running club, Crow Athletics. Buoyed-up by the love of my brother and his family, the support of my work environment, the inspiration and encouragement provided by my fellow "Crows," and the sustaining force of MDI itself, I was able to remain afloat when my seas grew stormy. In September, I decided that the time had finally come to take my running to the next level, and begin my career as a marathoner. As a tribute to all my struggles, and to all who helped me surmount them, I chose to make the MDI Marathon my first.

Many have used the marathon as a metaphor for life, but the MDI Marathon lends itself to this purpose only too easily. Provided one's life has had some ups and downs, one will truly appreciate MDI's course profile, as it looks something like a slightly elongated EKG pattern. But if such a sight fails to get one's heart thumping, racing MDI's course most certainly will. This isn't to say that MDI's hills make for a particularly slow course; although the race is relatively young, the winning times at MDI are fairly comparable with those of much flatter courses.

Just about every point along MDI's course offers participants yet another analogy for life: If, in the midst of one's personal struggles, one can find it within themselves to look up and behold the world around them, one will always find beauty. Starting in Bar Harbor, the tree-lined course is a conflagration of color with mid-October's vivid hues setting the world ablaze. Runners tour several picturesque communities, including Otter Creek, Seal Harbor, Asticou, Northeast Harbor, Somesville, and Southwest Harbor. Combined, these communities represent much of what MDI has to offer. High bluffs, roadside beaches, and Sargent Drive provide runners ample views of the Atlantic Ocean and Frenchman's Bay. The entire course is asphalt, and although much of it is open to traffic, roads on MDI are generally afforded wide, paved shoulders. These shoulders also provide spectators plenty of opportunities to pull over along the course, where they can cheer and provide support. In fact, many spectators opt to ride their bikes rather than drive cars, so as to experience MDI's beauty unmitigated.

The logistics of marathon running are further enhanced by MDI's modest size and local tourist industry. Participants find a wealth of options when choosing lodging, restaurants, and entertainment. No matter where one chooses to stay on the island, all options are within convenient proximity to the marathon's start. The furthest one might have to drive is a half hour, though many prefer the prospect of walking to the starting line. As the marathon has matured, more businesses have begun to offer special rates for race participants. If you plan on running MDI, be sure to convey the nature of your trip to the establishments you patronize.

Considering all that MDI has to offer, it isn't a surprise to see running paraphernalia persisting throughout the island well beyond race day. Running shirts and hats can be spied cruising along Acadia's carriage paths, hiking over peaks, kayaking on lakes, and hopping onto whale-watching boats during the weeks surrounding the marathon. Friendly smiles and nods are easy to come by and extol the fellowship of runners.

Mining MDI's trove to create a first-class running event is nothing less than a labor of love (most days) for MDI's Race Director, Gary Allen. Many people are involved in making the marathon a reality, but no one would deny the fact that Gary is the driving force behind the race. His vision imbues every aspect of the event, from the pre-race expo to the post-race party. Gary is determined to provide MDI's participants all the bells-and-whistles offered by much larger events: a modest expo in a beautiful venue, a pre-race dinner with a highly esteemed guest speaker, and a veritable army of enthusiastic volunteers. Additionally, the race provides computer-chip timing, excellent fuel provisions along the race course, post-race showers, massages, refreshments, a party, quality-crafted awards, professional race-photography, and the abiding support of MDI's law-enforcement and medical communities.

Of all these amenities, I was particularly struck by the character of MDI's Guest of Honor, Dick Beardsley. I didn't know much about Dick before the MDI Marathon, though I could recall seeing his photograph in old running books and magazines. Dick is most well known for his epic battle with Alberto Salazar during the 1982 Boston Marathon. In what became known simply as "The Duel," Beardsley and Salazar pushed each other well beyond their limits. Salazar won by two seconds, but both men finished under 2:09; the first time two competitors had ever managed such a feat within the same race. Both men went on to have celebrated running careers, though Dick's was frustrated by several tribulations. After suffering a debilitating Achilles injury, Dick was struck by a car. Then a catastrophic farming accident nearly amputated one of his legs. Over the course of many years, which included more than 20 operations on his legs and back, Dick slowly became addicted to pain-killers. This addiction lead to criminal forgery of medical prescriptions, for which Dick was eventually arrested. After hitting rock bottom, Dick bounced back with the help of friends, family, and running. Nowadays, Dick is a well-respected masters competitor, public speaker, author, and professional angler.

Along with some fellow members of the Crow Athletics Running Club, I had the privilege of running with Dick the morning prior to the race. Although he had already run two marathons within the past four weeks, (each under 2:50) Dick was considering running the MDI marathon as well. We all bantered a bit, and I was taken by Dick's warmth and enthusiasm. Looking at him, one would not imagine they were seeing a world-class athlete. If they did, they would be all the more stunned to discover the depths of this man's humility.

That night, following the pre-race dinner at MDI High School, Dick spoke to a large audience regarding his first marathon, his professional running career, The Duel with Salazar, his tragic farming accident, and his ensuing misfortunes. Everyone was held rapt by Dick's dynamic delivery. His stories and anecdotes provided humor and insight not only in regards to himself, but us as well. As his narrative neared his most painful memories, the cafeteria grew completely silent. Dick stood alone and wept as he recalled his darkest days. Tears fell from many of the eyes that witnessed this powerful lesson in humility, and mine were no exception.

The next morning, when I toed the marathon's starting line on Main Street in Bar Harbor, I knew my life was about to change. From now on, there would be my life as it was before the MDI Marathon, and my life since. As if to underscore the significance of the event, Mother Nature sounded her heralds, and let loose a clamorous squall only an hour before the race was to start. Then, as if having made her point, the sky pulled back its rainy curtain just minutes before the start was sounded. At the gun, more than 380 people leaped toward their destinies.

Long before the race started, I had adopted multi-tiered goals. My first goal was to simply finish the race. My second was to take advantage of MDI's status as a Boston Marathon qualifier, and run a sub-3:10. My third goal was to break three hours, and my fourth goal was a barely acknowledged desire to beat a particular friend's PR. Dick had decided to run the race after all, and indicated he was aiming for three hours, so I tucked in with him and waited to see how things developed. My game plan was to go out easy and determine how I felt at the halfway mark, where I'd have a better sense of which goals were still feasible. At mile 11 my brother, Mark, would join me on his bike to help provide some company and fuel.

Dick and I ran with two other men for the first nine miles of the race. I noticed that Dick started to take fluids at mile two, but I hadn't planned on taking any until mile ten. Stomach cramping was my principle fear going into the race, so I decided to stick to my original plan and not risk the unpredictable. When I checked my splits, I discovered that the pace was already well under the requirements for my first two goals. Still, I felt good, and well within my abilities, so when Dick pushed ahead at mile 10, I went with him. We ran together for the next several miles; our only company my brother, who had since joined us. Mark kept his distance, so as not to interfere, but would hand me a water bottle or some energy goo when I called him. When we hit the halfway mark in 1:26, I began to sense that I might have over-extended myself, but I immediately buried this thought as I ran with Dick along Sargent Drive. At mile 15, my split was 6:40; 12 seconds under a three-hour pace. By mile 16, the pace had dropped another 18 seconds, and I realized I was in trouble. I let Dick go, and tried to re-establish a sustainable rhythm, knowing that mile 18 marked the beginning of a series of progressively bigger hills that rose and fell for the next seven miles. I managed to muster a pair of 6:50 splits for miles 17 and 18, but it was too late. Running up the hill on Route 198, midway through mile 19, I ran out of gas and started to walk.

Mark rode ahead, leaving me with my thoughts. I had heard all the stories about the fabled "Wall," but I hadn't imagined that it would hit me so soon. The prospect of running another seven miles over some pretty big hills, on an empty tank, seemed absurd. As I started to run again, my mind and body buckled under a visceral sense of doom. I thought of all the advice I had been offered by trusted marathon veterans: go out easy, conserve your energy, drink plenty of fluids, and whatever you do, don't stop. When I tallied it all up, it seemed I had managed to do everything wrong. But how could this happen? Why didn't I listen? After 14 years of running, I ought to have known better.

I realized somewhere along Route 102, that the advice of others would be worth nothing were it not born of personal experience. The fact is, people offer advice because they've made mistakes. Now it was my turn. This was my race, my mistakes, my lessons to learn, and I've never learned anything but the hard way. As I trudged along, overwhelmed by exhaustion, I thought of some of the things Dick had spoken of the previous night. Apparently, Dick's first marathon was such a miserable experience, that he declared to himself "never again." But to my own credit, I never doubted I would finish the race, and I genuinely hoped that this marathon would prove to be the first of many. In fact, I was already tabulating what I'd do differently the next time around, which I suppose added to my fatigue.

By mile 23, I was in pretty bad shape. The only goal I cared about now was finishing the race; Boston could have been on another planet for all I cared. There was a fairly steady headwind blowing from the south, and my pace slowed to a death march. I stopped and walked several times, and my brother did all he could to help, which mostly meant staying quiet. He and I were alone but for the brief moments when other racers managed to pass me. They all offered encouragement, but I couldn't heed them, nor could I acknowledge the cheers of friends and fellow club-mates who had stationed themselves at various points along the road. I was somewhere else, and I'm pretty sure it was Total Agony. The echoes of Dick's declaration, "Never again," were gradually drowned out by my own plea: "How? How God? How am I ever going to do this again?"

Amazingly, I still managed to qualify for Boston, crossing the line in 3:06:10. My first marathon was over, and I'd never been so relieved or happy in my life. The more time and space I gain on the experience, the more I realize just how special it was. How many runners can say that one day they stepped out their front door, walked a matter of yards to a spectacularly beautiful racecourse, ran their very first marathon next to one of the world's true marathon heroes, struggled through the pain and despair of The Wall, and ultimately qualified for the Boston Marathon? Well, I can.

I've discovered how I'm going to do it again. The answer to my delirious plea was so immediate and absolute, that I didn't hear it at the time. But it was staring me in the face, moving my legs, running next to me, cheering me on, feeding me, clothing me, massaging me, embracing me, it's no wonder I didn't see it. When Dick spoke the night before the race, he humbled himself not only before me and the rest of the audience, he humbled himself before himself. He forgave himself.

Then he went out there the next day and kicked my butt! Running has taught me that humility and forgiveness are the font of all good things. That's how people get things done, be the tasks great or small, and it's by humility's light that I make my way to Boston.

———————————————————————

Matt Woida is 28 years old and originally from Milwaukee, Wisconsin. He's been a competitive runner for 14 years. Matt ran cross country in high school, where he earned the distinction of finishing dead-last in several races. He also ran cross country and track for two years at Earlham College in Richmond, Indiana. There, he worked his way to the middle of the pack and fell in love with running. Nowadays, Matt wears the black and white jersey for Crow Athletics, on Mount Desert Island, Maine. The Mount Desert Island Marathon was his first marathon.

Columbus Marathon

columbus, ohio

Web site: www.columbusmarathon.com
Month: October
USATF Certified: Yes
Course: Flat

Author: Philip Baetcke
Number of Marathons Completed: 13
Age Group: 30-34

Many runners have a race that's special to them. For me, it's the Columbus Marathon. In 1994, my older sister Anna accepted an offer to work in the corporate office of Abercrombie and Fitch in Columbus, Ohio. At that time, Anna was still living at home in Northern Virginia. With no family or friends in Ohio, she bravely headed out to take on a new job and start a new life for herself. During the fall of her first year there, a colleague was training for the race. After hearing great things about it, Anna suggested I keep it in mind for the following year. I did and in 1995, I signed up for my first Columbus Marathon.

I remember my first race very well. Back then, the marathon was held in early November. At the start, the temperature was in the 20s and there were snow flurries in the air. A lot of runners didn't show up due to the freezing cold. But for me, bailing out on this race was not an option. Having run the Marine Corps Marathon the year before in the rain, heavy rain for some of it, I figured marathons were supposed to be torture-fests. So I just accepted that this was how it was going to be. I trained well for this marathon, and felt I could improve my time despite the conditions. My time did improve, as I finished 20 minutes faster than the year before at the Marine Corps, crossing the finish line in a time of 3:47. This was very encouraging—but I was a little disappointed. I had walked about three miles total, starting around mile 20. In addition to my primary goal of finishing the race, I hoped to finish without walking. This was all the incentive I needed to return the following year.

Thinking back, I have fond memories of my first visits to Columbus. Anna lived in a studio apartment in a revitalized area of town called

German Village. I loved that apartment—one bath, a living room, a small kitchen, and one bedroom. The bedroom was more like a loft with a narrow set of creaky wooden stairs leading to it. The room was drafty and always a little cold, but once I got under a couple of heavy winter blankets, it felt like an old family home. I mention this because my sister, knowing her brother was crazy enough to run a marathon, gave up her bed and slept on the couch. Anna's life seemed so cool to me. You could walk outside the door and be at the coffee house, a bakery or café—all of which we visited. I had a great time hanging out with Anna that weekend.

So it's no surprise that I returned to Columbus to run a second time. Honestly, I remember little about the 1996 race. I do remember that it was again quite cold and there were flurries during parts of it. My time improved by a few minutes from the previous year, to 3:43, so I was happy about that. But I still walked a little. My legs and especially my knees bothered me in the latter part of the race, forcing me to walk/run again between miles 22 to 26. I was not happy about this! It was now three marathons in a row where I failed to run the entire distance (I walked at the Marine Corps as well). Finishing was no longer the goal. I had already accomplished that twice before. When friends asked me how I did, I felt like I needed to tell them that I didn't run the whole thing or else I would be misleading them. I know it's sad. But at that time, marathons were still largely the domain of runners as many of the walk/run groups (which I think are great) were in their infancy. So in my mind, if I was really a runner, I had to do it without stopping. I had to come back next year and try again.

As I started to get familiar with Columbus and its surroundings, it didn't take too long to realize how big football is there. The town is crazy about the Ohio State football team and the marathon takes place right in the middle of the season. The Ohio State University is a member of the Big Ten conference, and I've often wondered how it must be for runners who attended Michigan, Michigan State, or any other Big Ten school for that matter. Part of the course winds through Ohio State, and throughout much of the race the streets are lined with their flags. Houses are decorated with Buckeye banners and everywhere you look, people are wearing Buckeye sweatshirts. During the race, you'll frequently hear "Go Buckeyes!" And if they're undefeated on race day, which isn't uncommon, the town will be buzzing about a possible national championship. Buckeye spirit is definitely a large part of the marathon experience.

Packet pickup (at least during my time there) has always been at the Convention Center in downtown Columbus. It's sometimes difficult to find parking, but with a little persistence, one can generally find a space in the garage. Going early will alleviate this problem. Unfortunately, the race expo has been a little disappointing in recent years, as they haven't had a very good selection of warmer running gear, especially men's. But generally, due to the ample space of the convention center, it's easy to get your race packet and it's a smooth, well-organized process.

I returned the following year, 1997, to resolve the matter of running the race without stopping. Having failed in my first three marathons to accomplish this, I was focused on getting over this hurdle. This year held the promise of being a breakthrough year for me. I started training earlier than ever before, and I was in the best shape of my running life. I participated in the Army 10 miler a few weeks before Columbus as a tune up and managed a time under 70 minutes. From what I had read about extrapolating times from shorter distances to the marathon, I looked to be on target for my best marathon to date. The weather reports called for warmer temperatures so for the first time I was going to have good running conditions.

Soon after the start, I realized I had dressed too warmly. Fortunately, it was still cool enough that it wasn't a big deal. This race would be the first time I benefited from the support of the spectators as the nice weather attracted larger crowds than the previous two years. There were lots of garage bands playing along the course (which sadly, has declined in recent years) as well as some extremely energetic high school bands that were pumping out tunes at deafening decibel levels. For the first time, I really fed off the energy of the crowd. I ran a smart race, tempering my pace more in the first half than I had in the past. I also took in more calories along the course than ever before. It seemed the little experience I had gained from my prior efforts was starting to make a difference. Although I slowed down a little after mile 20, this time I didn't slow to a walk. Around mile 23, in German Village, I got a second wind. I knew I was going to do it! I was actually going to run the entire race. It was a great feeling. A few miles later I crossed the finish line in 3:35. It was a huge feeling of accomplishment. This was my proudest marathon moment to date; even better than the finish of my first marathon at the Marine Corps in D.C.

As it turned out, this year was also to be Anna's last in the apartment in German Village. Earlier that year my sister married John Luehmann, the first person I have ever met who grew up in Minnesota. After the race in 1997, they bought their first home in the neighborhood of Bexley, which is also part of the racecourse. I was sad to think that I wasn't going to hang out in German Village anymore, but was equally excited about John and Anna's new house. Bexley is the same neighborhood that "Family Ties," the 1980s TV show, was supposed to be located. It's Middle America at its finest. Sidewalks and mature trees line the streets and manicured lawns are the norm. Many young families live there, and you frequently see children out on bicycles and babies in strollers. John and Anna have two sons: Noah and Philip (who was named after me). They are now part of my support crew from year to year, coming out with Mom and Dad to see Uncle Philip run.

In terms of the marathon, Bexley used to be in the second half of the race, but the course was reconfigured and now you enter it just past mile four. This is great for the family as John, Anna, and the kids can just walk down the street and cheer for me as I run by. I love seeing them there and can enjoy it because I'm still fresh and energetic at this point of the race. Prior to the course change, Bexley was around mile 18 or 19 and it was where I tended to be a little less coherent, to say the least. I even dropped out of the race there one year due to a sore knee, walking up to John and announcing that I was ready for a Wendy's hamburger. He couldn't believe it and after a few moments finally realized that I wasn't joking. It was a sad moment, but I had to give myself something to be cheerful about!

It's safe to say that I've had a lot of fun running through Bexley, but there are other sections of the course I like as well. Around the 10-mile mark, entering the downtown area, the streets are packed with people and it's arguably the loudest portion of the course, with the exception of the finish line. For about a two-mile stretch, you can really feel the energy of the crowd. Also, the neighborhood of Upper Arlington is well supported and is a welcome change from the open and often windy section on High Street that precedes it. High Street is a long stretch, right around five miles long. It starts off in the downtown area, which is the good part. But as you get further away from downtown, on up to mile 16, you hit a small incline that continues for about a mile until you turn left onto Dodridge. This is my least favorite section of the course. It's usually the point I start to realize I'm running a marathon. With that being said, it's an area of the course where I can tell how I'm going to feel at the finish. So there is a positive aspect to it for me. If I get up the incline at High Street and down Dodridge feeling pretty good, then I'll likely be able to finish the race strong.

The finish line, which was reconfigured for the 2002 race, is a nice downhill stretch on a brick road. It's also packed with screaming fans and is one of my favorite finish areas, much better than the original finish line. It's easy for spectators to get in and out with access to the highway very close by. There's also a nice grassy area outside the finish chute where everyone congregates after the race.

As I mentioned earlier, I dropped out of the race in 1998. Although my knee forced me to quit at around mile 19, it was the result of my body not being properly conditioned to run 26 miles. The DNF was a kick in the pants for me. I took some time off for my knee to heal (and my ego) and started focusing on improving as a runner. For the first time, I ran consistently through the cold winter months and found myself in better shape the following spring. Encouraged by my improved fitness, I participated in some local 10K races and gained more racing experience. My training remained consistent throughout the summer and some hard tempo runs gave me the confidence that I could go back to Columbus and run my best time.

At the start of the race in 1999, I was in the best shape of my life. My goal was to finish in under 3:20. I didn't quite get there, finishing in 3:28, but it was a personal best to date and I was thrilled with the result. The following year I slowed a bit, coming across the finish in 3:45. I can't remember what happened that year, maybe I was a little too comfortable with my success. I recall crossing the finish line and thinking how fast the 3:28 the prior year had been. I thought if I could do it then, I could do it again. I refocused and in 2001, I once again eclipsed my personal best and finished in 3:23. I felt like I was getting closer to reaching my potential as a marathoner. The progression continued as I achieved a time of 3:14 in 2002. After this race, I believed I could qualify for the Boston Marathon, something I would never have guessed was possible when I started in 1995.

I should note that the Columbus Marathon is a very flat course. It's a popular race for this reason and is a good course to run a best time. Like many large marathons, there are organized pacing groups in place to help runners in their respective age groups qualify for the Boston Marathon. They do a great job. The first year I ran with one of those groups was 2002. Although I was unable to maintain the pace until the finish, I got very close to the 3:10 mark — the qualifying standard for males in my age group.

In 2003, the goal was clear. Run under 3:10 and qualify for Boston. I set out to run a smart race and stay with the pace group. As I ran the course that day, I was constantly reminded of my past experiences. Mile 10 was where I used to see Anna on the old course, at Ohio State. I remember telling them once that I'd be there in 80 minutes. On this day, I was there in just over 72 minutes. At the half marathon mark, my time was right on target hitting the mark in 1:35:01. It felt so effortless. At mile 18, where I used to struggle to get to the end of High Street, I turned the corner onto Dodridge and thought to myself "This is how it's supposed to feel!" As I neared the 23-mile mark, I started to feel the effects of my pace. But I had prepared myself mentally for this. I pushed onward knowing that the reward would be so sweet. I struggled mightily after mile 24 to hold on. Finally, as I approached the last turn to head down to the finish, I heard the roar of the crowd. I knew I had made it. It was such a peaceful feeling crossing the line, knowing I had done something great. I crossed the finish in 3:09.35, a mere 25 seconds under the qualifying time for Boston.

Running the Columbus marathon over the past 10 years has been a wonderful journey for me. I'm so thankful for Anna and her family for the support they have given me through the years. I'm also thankful for what the race has been for me personally. I have achieved heights in athletics that I never thought were possible 10 years ago when my goal was to simply finish without walking. To progress this far and qualify for the Boston Marathon is a great feeling of accomplishment. And to share this with Anna and her family makes it even more special. At the race in 2004, I heard the announcer call out the names of the participants who have competed in all 25 Columbus Marathons. I thought to myself, "What about the 10 year veterans?" (We'll overlook the year I dropped out.) It's amazing how much time has passed. I don't know what the future holds, but if I'm healthy and at least in somewhat decent shape, there's a good chance I'll return to Columbus for many years to come.

Philip Baetcke works in the IT department at the Mid Atlantic regional office of Whole Foods Market in Rockville, Maryland. He is a big fan of U.S. Soccer and regularly travels across the country to attend national team games. If the United States qualifies, Philip hopes to visit Germany for the 2006 World Cup.

Detroit Free Press/Flagstar Bank Marathon

detroit, michigan

Web site: www.detroitfreepressmarathon.com
Month: October
USATF Certified: Yes
Course: Flat

DETROIT FREE PRESS/FLAGSTAR BANK
MARATHON
Presented by Greektown Casino

Author: Lisa Harper
Number of Marathons Completed: 5
Age Group: 40-44

Some people were just born to run. I am one of those. As a child growing up in the Detroit area, my primary sport was gymnastics. I did not start running until I was a freshman in college. We were required to run a three-mile field test, which I had never done before. Within six months, I was logging at least 40 miles a week. Many of my friends were on the NCAA Division I Track and Cross Country Team, so I would often train with them for fun. I continued to add the miles each week, and by the fall of 1985, I was running 60-65 miles a week. I loved running twice a day, swimming a mile at lunch three times a week, and doing a little tumbling in the evening for pleasure.

With only three weeks of planning, and only my college field test as a "race" under my belt, I decided to run my first marathon in 1985: The Detroit Free Press/Flagstar Bank Marathon in Detroit, Michigan. My fiancé, Scott Harper, was the real runner out of the two of us, having been an All-American. He graciously ran the 26.2 miles with me. From the start to the finish, I was in "a zone" of my own. I felt like I was on autopilot and finished in a time of 3:09. What a thrill it was to finish my first marathon as the winner of my age group (20 years old then) and the fifth female over all!

My marathon days had just begun. A health instructor at our university heard that there was this crazy girl on campus (yours truly) who ran tons of miles for no competitive reason. He recruited me to train with his wife, who was preparing for the Dallas White Rock Marathon, just six weeks after the Detroit Marathon. Perhaps you have heard of "going the extra mile." Well, I went the extra 26 to encourage my friend.

After two marathons in a six-week span of time, plus the Jenks Half-Marathon in Oklahoma in between those, my body was just a little bit fatigued. I continued to run off and on for the next 17 years, but never experienced the long runs that I loved. My life changed rapidly. I became a dedicated pastor's wife to a devoted man. I also taught school, earned a Master's Degree, instructed gymnastics, became the regular pianist at our church, gave birth to four wonderful children, and even home schooled many of them along the way. My hats were numerous.

Yet what made running even more complicated during those years was the reoccurrence of miscarriages. In the midst of having four priceless children, I also had five painful miscarriages. So, this little gymnast lady/soccer mom/ pastor's wife/educator has been pregnant nine times. How I longed to run more consistently, but after the first few miscarriages, I made the choice to stop running every time I got pregnant. My body stopped and started running more times than you can shake a fist at. I felt like a rubber band for years. It was not until the beginning of 2002 that I was actually able to start jogging a few miles on a regular basis.

In 2002, having only run about five miles a day, five times a week, I had the wild notion to once again lace up my shoes and run my favorite marathon in Detroit. The only catch was that the marathon was six days away when I had the lofty idea to attempt it. I had not completed any type of long run in over 17 years, and I decided to attempt the 26.2 miles with such a base. I told my young children what I was planning on doing by pulling out a map of the inspiring route from Detroit to Canada and back. My son, Jonathan, then asked me, "Mom, are you going to try and win the race?" With a twinkle in my eye I responded, "Well, honey, I don't think so. I don't really know what's going to happen. I might have to walk. I might even have to stop, but I feel like a winner for trying." So after 17 years of no long runs, and 9 monumental pregnancies to my name, I was able to run to mile 22 of my third marathon without stopping. Yes, some people are just born to run. I finished that marathon by walking and jogging to the end. My legs were heavy but my heart was leapin' for joy. I actually felt more satisfaction from this marathon of 4:19 than I did with the 3:09. With God's help I had persevered and returned to the race I loved.

Since then, I have continued to gratefully run the Detroit Marathon every October. In 2003, I felt a deep sense of gratitude and an urgency of purpose to make a difference. Thus, I decided to run the Detroit Free Press/ Flagstar Bank Marathon to raise money for missionaries. I called it my "Marathon Mission." The story was covered in numerous print media, including the Dearborn Press and

Guide, the Detroit Free Press, The Pentecostal Evangel, and the Assemblies of God Internet News. "Pastor's Wife Runs Marathon for Missionaries." It was a catchy and inspiring story. Never did I imagine how contagious it would be.

In 2004, our Marathon Mission became a significant faith- and community-based charity for this heart-warming marathon in Detroit. The purpose of Marathon Mission is for walkers and runners to raise financial support for the plethora of outstanding missionaries and charitable workers, both stateside and abroad. Thus, we had over 75 people join together to run various distances for causes beyond themselves. As a group we concluded that life is not all about us. It is all about God and giving others a hand up.

Many of our 2004 participants were "greenies" to any walking or running distance of any kind, so it was exciting to see them progress on race morning. "Where do we put our numbers? What are these chip things? Where do I go? Where's the bathroom?" I'm surprised that no one actually asked me to run the race for them!

After making sure that my Marathon Mission Team was taken care of, I laced up my well-worn Boston Classics and waved good-bye to them. I was entering the sea of runners once again. Although this 39-year-old soccer mom barely had a moment to herself (due to my newly acquired responsibility as Marathon Mission Founder, Coordinator, Encourager, Trainer, and Facilitator), the adrenaline was ferociously pumping. There was no other place I would have rather been than with my Marathon Mission Team, running on the streets of Detroit that I had loved since I was a little girl. Let me take you to that time and place, and tell you why I so highly recommend this flat, fast, and festive Detroit Marathon to runners all over the world.

First, the pre-race festivities were well organized. The marathon web site kept us all up to date and provided clear maps, training tips, opportunities to Run for a Reason (like Marathon Mission), an invitation to join the official, tasty pasta dinner, and more. Within minutes of registering online, participants received an email of confirmation, welcoming them to this life-changing event. Runners young and old, in shape and out, were readily received into the fold. Two qualifications that I recall were that all participants had to reach the start of the tunnel, near mile eight, no later than two hours after the start. Secondly, the course was to remain open for 6 1/2 hours maximum. After registration, reminder cards were later sent to guide walkers and runners through the process of picking up their race packets at the Health and Fitness Expo at Cobo Hall, in the heart of the city.

When entering the expo, I could sense the anticipation in the air. There were numerous vendors, offering helpful advice on everything from nutrition to running gear, from pacing to picture/certificate framing. I was thankful to have picked up a pair of lightweight, cotton gloves as well as the paper-thin disposable jacket I would wear for the first few miles of the race the next morning. Tasting spoonfuls of the GU gel helped me decide which flavors I didn't want to grab from the volunteers at mile 15 along the marathon route. In addition, the free health food samples were a big hit with the Harper kids!

The accommodations for the race were more than adequate. Several area hotels were reasonably priced and rolled out the red carpet for our participants. Being within walking distance of the start was a definite plus.

My racing experience was just what I expected: exceptional. The temperatures were in the low 40s, and I enjoyed starting outside the well-adorned Comerica Park. In 2003, I was surprised to run a portion of mile two with the Mayor of Detroit. "Who would I meet this year?" I wondered. I was thrilled to high-five the governor of Michigan along the way, as well as Martha Reeves, the woman who graced us with the National Anthem.

From beginning to end, the course provided something for everyone. The one and only major incline of the race was the famous Ambassador Bridge around mile four. It took us across the Detroit River and into our neighboring City of Windsor, Canada. We continued along the Windsor shoreline and returned to the U.S. by running underwater through the tunnel. Hearing the crowds of people cheering on the American side made me proud to be an American. Flags were waving, and spectators were lined quite deep on both sides. I loved smiling at the strangers as if they were my friends. They returned the gesture, which made me feel like both the participants and spectators were one big happy family. All differences of culture, age, religion, ability, and language, just seemed to melt away in this sea of humanity. Everyone wanted everyone to do well. Where else in life can you find such a supportive environment?

The remaining 17 miles were filled with bands, water and gel stations, and great spectators. Detroit is known as Motown for more reasons than motors. We boast being a beacon of great music. Feet were pounding pitter-patter as we passed through Mexican town. We also ran through Greek Town, Belle Isle, and Indian Village.

Finishing inside Ford Field was awesome. The fans had plenty of space to see everyone finish since it was beamed up high onto the turbotron. One aspect that I did not like about the race was the exit off of Ford Field. We had to climb a myriad of steps to get to the main level. Even then, however, one finisher was helping another. My most heart wrenching moment was when I found my brother, Jeff, at the finish line. He had finished walking his 5K (which he called, "Marathon Mission March for Justice") a few hours before me. I hugged him and didn't let go for quite some time. Here were two siblings who had overcome daunting odds. I, with all those miscarriages, and my brother who had three hip replacements and one knee replacement by the time he was only 41. We both embraced each other and gave thanks to a good God for giving us the strength to walk and run for a reason beyond ourselves.

I usually run just one race a year, which is quite rare, I am told. My choice is the Detroit Free Press/Flagstar Bank Marathon. There's no place like home.

Lisa Harper is a 40-year-old pastor's wife and soccer mom who lives with her four children in the Detroit area. She has a Master's Degree in Reading from Eastern Michigan University. In addition to running, her other interests include piano, gymnastics, teaching, writing, and public speaking. Lisa is the Founder of Marathon Mission, a faith- and community-based charity that began at the Detroit Free Press/Flagstar Bank Marathon.

4-H Old Mulkey Classic Marathon

tompkinsville, kentucky

Web site: www.4holdmulkeyclassic.com
Month: October
USATF Certified: Yes
Course: Rolling

Author: David Birse
Number of Marathons Completed: 46
Age Group: 45-49

If the name alone isn't enough to lure the prospective candidate from the sea of mega marathons in Americana today, perhaps the bucolic charm and humble atmosphere of The Blue Grass State will be. It was for me. When I was scanning athletic cyberspace for a 26.2 miler that would distance itself from the rest of the pack, it was a bit like courtship: Lots of candidates but few you'd really consider dating.

Too many were too similar. Been there, done that. I adopted the national motto: e pluribus unum. Out of many choices, a singular marathon would emerge as The One. My finalists included a race in South Carolina, another in its sister state North Carolina, and alas my bride: The 4-H Old Mulkey Classic of Tompkinsville, Kentucky.

Why Old Mulkey? Actually, it was the unique brochure, the history behind the curmudgeonly name, friendly email swapping with its race director, nicely done web page (which cinched my decision), and the fact that I'd never been to Kentucky before. Some events just beckon you. Old Mulkey did just that.

Since I refuse to fly — and haven't in about a dozen years, I was rather looking forward to the millennium of highway miles separating my sleepy domain in Hancock, New Hampshire from the object of my marathoning affections in The Land Of Lincoln's birth.

What better destination than Kentucky, and what better time of year than autumn, to allow my eyes to feast upon the rainbow of nature's colors and permit my feet the liberty of splashing through the fallen leaves in the rural countryside.

No pressure. No chip timing. No porta-johns. No herding the runners into corrals like sheep or sticking them with cattle-prodders before the race. No need to arrive at the starting line light years prior to the race to broil like bacon in the sun. No eye-popping, bank-breaking entry fees, no ultra-elite, and no vendors. Just you, the other competitors, and a challenging course to duel with for a few hours on a late October Saturday morning.

You also don't have to qualify to get there. The entry fee was reasonable for marathons these days, in the $25.00 range. It's also a great place to get your feet wet if you are a marathon virgin. Just hope the weather is anywhere near decent, and you've won half the battle.

On the way to Kentucky and Old Mulkey, a journey of 1,182 miles that included a four-hour stop in a lonely shopping plaza in Eastern Ohio to sleep, I tried to envision Tompkinsville, located in the southernmost part of central Kentucky. Within hours, I was churning through its rolling hills, relishing the splendiferous views, and nearly careening off the interstate as I enjoyed it all maybe a bit too much. The landscape was a delicious blend of New Hampshire and Vermont, but much more spread out.

I made one slight detour en route to the birthplace of Kentucky's most illustrious resident, our sixteenth president. Honest Abe was indeed born in a homemade log cabin in the wilderness. It's a replica of the original though. Abe's family was tight with the Daniel Boone clan. Two legends, one state.

Tompkinsville elicited a midwestern flavor. The Monroe County Extension Center of the University of Kentucky Agricultural School served as Race Headquarters. So it was only fitting that the 4-H gang should sponsor the Old Mulkey Classic. I was beginning to see the light.

I was amazed how mellow things were. Likely, I was the first to pick up my race packet. No waiting. They'd received more entries than anticipated. The Classic actually consists of a 10K, half marathon, and the Full Enchilada. There would be a pre-race pasta dinner at The Joe Carter Elementary School. The UK Extension office simply could not accommodate all those ravenous runners. I just had to inquire if the school was named after the former major league slugger and World Series hero. "No," came the reply. I don't think she'd ever heard of him.

There were about four or five local hotels, and vacancies were hard to come by. I scurried around fruitlessly while visions of another night camping in my car danced in my head. But I did discover one available—perhaps the last—at a little place. Should I mention the gobs of hair in the shower drain? Thankfully, I stayed elsewhere the next night, where sanitation was much better. Several of Thompkinsville's motels revealed words of encouragement for their marathon guests on display boards outside—small town support for their big race.

I was now compelled to research Old Mulkey History and that curious name! John Mulkey was an old Baptist preacher when Kentucky was at the center of the "Great Awakening" of the 1800s, a movement that breathed spiritual life into our nation. It is so named "Old Mulkey" because there was a schism in the Mill Creek Baptist church in 1804 that divided attendees into two camps, and John Mulkey was caught up in the whirlwind. The man was a pioneer in American religion of that era, but was brought up on heresy charges. Oh My! The opposing faction left to start another church, while Mulkey and his devotees remained at The Old Meeting House. You pass Mill Creek Baptist church on the marathon route. I bet Old Mulkey would've made a feisty runner.

The pre-race dinner was a thoughtfully planned, low-key affair with special amenities and earnest hospitality. At the entry to the buffet-style dinner, race officials, scores of amicable 4-Hers and a host of spirited volunteers greeted all. The servers doled out hot bread, pasta, drinkables (tasty iced tea!), and dessert. If you left hungry, it was your own fault. I chatted with a race walker from Ohio, as well as a first time marathoner and her hubby. I may have been the only Yankee present, but that wasn't held against me.

One item worthy of mention is the artwork that plastered the cafeteria walls. Notable because the dear kids of the Joe Carter Elementary School took time to make runners they probably won't ever meet the subjects of their creativity. "Good Luck, Runners!" accompanied expressions of goodwill on a vast array of these imaginative posters. That initiative was exemplary and heartfelt. They went beyond the call. They even had live music in the form of children singing various ballads on a makeshift stage. I was where I wanted to be.

The goody bag had more personal touches including a detail-oriented spiffy orange t-shirt and all manner of stuff. I won't spoil it. If you want one, you'll have to mosey down to Tompkinsville. The most ingenious inclusion was a camouflaged bag of cedar chips designed to offset the pungent odor of your average gym bag. That's all I'll tell you.

I had no alarm clock, and my worst nightmare was that I'd wake up as the lead runners were trudging by my window. I ventured out to purchase one at the local dollar store. Yet upon the return to my motel room, I realized, NO BATTERIES.

What to do. Everything was now closed and the sidewalks were rolled up. Alas, in front of my panic-laden eyes was a battery-operated wall clock. "Please be a double A clock. Pleeaaase!!!!" Hands and fingers shaking like a man being lead to the gallows, I snatched it off the wall, turned over the chintzy timepiece, and BINGO! Whew. Double A! Thank you, Lord! I performed the battery transplant, set the clock and snagged about five hours of shut-eye, waking to the alarm's sweet sound.

Early morning on race day is like no other. The odyssey that started in late spring and which seemed like it would never happen had finally arrived. Every track interval, each race, the nutritional tweaking, minute details—all were geared toward this morning in a locale I'd never visited or heard of half a year earlier.

You'd think that after 45 marathons and 30 plus years of competition, butterflies and jitters would be non-existent. Not so as dawn broke on race day. The big event was slated for 0700 hours. But there was something missing. I couldn't finger it right away. Half an hour before the run, the normal hoopla that envelops most races was conspicuously absent.

It hit me. Running is not a big thing down here. It is simply not a strong part of the regional culture. Hunting, fishing, and farming maybe, but certainly not ectomorphic endeavours like my sport. Locals view it as peculiar.

But that's okay. If this were back home, runners would be doing exaggerated sprints, long jogs, tons of stretching, sweating like it's life or death, and chatting up a storm. I liked this way better. You won't encounter a more laid back group than those assembled here. Next week at this same time these good people may be putting up storm windows, cat fishing in Mill Creek, pheasant hunting, or sleeping in.

A cool, perfect day greeted us. I imagine it was about 50°F with a light wind. There may have been only 130 participants for all three races. For Mulkey it was a mega, record turn out. The 10K-ers would run an out-and-back course. Marathoners would traverse a 13-mile route twice while "The halfers" — lucky dogs — need only endure a single loop. But we all started as one big happy family.

The hallmark of this race was epitomized in the manner in which the event was initiated. Not simply: "Mark, Set, and Go." Not here. Too Dullsville for Tompkinsville. Neither would a bullhorn, predictable whistle or starter's pistol do. So what's left? The good 4-Hers are nothing if not creative.

The signal was, "On your Mark, Get Set, Yeeeeee- Haaaaaaaaaaahh!"

"Hmmm. Time to run," I guess. That'll put you in a jovial mood—Southern style.

In a race where so much can go so wrong, you have nothing but time out there. Each runner has a mindset and a mission, a strategy to now employ. All of it begins (all the games within the game itself) from the moment the stop watch is punched and the first second is recorded, up until the last runner crosses the line maybe a third of a day later.

At 45, this may well be my last shot at a win, which was my chief purpose. It had been a dozen years since I'd captured my last laurel wreath. What a kick it would be to win one at my age, some 27 1/2 years after my inaugural marathon in a February blizzard back in 1977. Only a month after Jimmy Carter had wrestled the reins of presidency from Gerald Ford.

Prior to the race, I hid behind the school, away from the throng, emerging only five minutes before the "yee-hahh" got us all off to a giddy gallop. I socialize like a magpie afterward, but beforehand I didn't want to be seen or bothered. Game face time.

More challenging terrain than Old Mulkey will be hard to find, but none is more gorgeous either. The Junior National Guard was out to monitor traffic, a spiffy police cruiser guided us, and gracious volunteers hung out all day to distribute water, Gatorade and oranges.

The hills were menacing and punishing to the quads. The first step out of bed the ensuing day reminded me of that. No shortage of undulating ups and downs here. You just might get sea sick at Old Mulkey. Do not look for a PR here. You won't find it. Not a chance. It will beat you up big time. And the real hard part is, when you've completed one lap, you get to delight in the agony for grins on Lap two. I can't picture a contest more trying than this baby. My bet is Preacher Mulkey would've prayed hard before, during and after this run. It is feasible Tompkinsville's favorite son might not have been able to stand to sermonize the next day had he even walked the race bearing his name.

There were several times during the race where runners meander a funky loop or approach an apparent dead-end, then turn around and reverse steps. Fortunately, it is well marked and there are course marshals at questionable points to guide you on your journey. It does, however, somewhat break your stride and momentum. The good thing is, you can keep a hawkeye on your competition! I had the benefit of following the flashing blues of the local constabulary, so I didn't have the chance to get lost. Given the opportunity to take a wrong turn, though, I'd have found myself in Nashville.

The route goes into Old Mulkey Park, Tompkinsville City Park, past the most incredible and varied scenery, oodles of farmland, and sprawling, spectacular vistas. I can see why the old timers wanted to conduct camp meetings in these parts.

The elevation begins at 850 feet with a high point of 1,025 feet, and the lowest dip of 750 feet. While that may not seem too bad, don't dismiss this. The whole course is like doing hill repeats for hours on end. It is not as if you hit the high mark of 1025 feet only once, hit the cruise control button, and glide to glory. Oh no. It is relentless. The potpourri of hills and dales, ample bovine mammals, various forms of wildlife, and magnificent splendor will help to take your mind off the torture, however, at least to some extent.

I hoofed the entire distance solitarily and unserenaded, save the first 1 1/2 miles — just the police car, the cows and me. I admired the old fences and pastoral settings, soaking it in. There is one particular stretch, I believe it's at about 23 or 24 miles, when you can see the better part of a mile of Amish-type country ahead of you. It rises, falls, and doglegs right with a gentle, sweeping curve. Take it in and revel in the moment. You'll get to run this section twice. It isn't far from the start and finish at the Monroe County Middle School.

The miles are clearly and cleverly marked. No, they don't have your 5K times recorded for you to peruse later, nor is there a person shouting out your splits every kilometer. Most or all runners today possess wrist stopwatches anyway, so they can record that stuff themselves. Enthusiastic 4-Hers hooted and hollered as runners passed by their aid stations. It is evident the fine people in Monroe Country thrust their whole being into this yearly happening.

I had amassed a lead of perhaps a mile at one point. The second time around is where even the most finely-tuned athlete can run into trouble. I began to labor at 21 miles, not having my "A" game with me that day. Legs were rubbery from the trip down. My fault. Yanking them through this excursion really didn't ameliorate the matter. Fortuitously, there was never anyone in my rear view mirror.

A homespun feature you may appreciate was the posters strewn about the roadside, exhorting the athletes from the various states represented. The drawings and likeness of a particular state and scribbled humorous wording posted at eye level for us Uberlaufers did not go unnoticed.

The home stretch found me virtually crippled, and I'd tightened so badly I wasn't even able to finish with a flashy grin, raise my fists in glorious exultation as planned, blow kisses to the adoring crowd (all 12 of them), or even cross the line with some resemblance of dignity. I was sort of embarrassed. We've all endured the death march. It's how a marathoner earns their stripes. I kept waiting for pursuers to zip past me, break my heart, sadistically smile my way, and claim the laurel wreath. When I broke the tape in a sluggish 3:07, I was thrilled to win, yet surprised by the 4 1/2 minute cushion. Victory was mine, but I was a hurting pup, like the other 50 who would follow suit. I paid for it. Had this been a pancake course, something well under three hours could have resulted. The 1:19 half marathon I negotiated in upstate New York a month earlier indicated a seventh career sub 2:50 was possible. But not here.

The medal they draped over me had only the 4-H emblem on it and the year. Nothing else. But that's okay. That's Mulkey style. And the award ceremony was virtually non-existent. The Race Director just casually handed me a very nice ceramic plate after a foray into the massage tent. No witnesses or applause. No problem. This is Old Mulkey. On the plate it read "CONGRATULATIONS" across the top. Along the bottom: "Monroe County 4-H." Period. No acknowledgment that the award was for being a marathon champion. It could just as well have been for an oxen pull, pie eating contest, or making the best marmalade at the fair. No matter. It will ALWAYS be special to me, for it represents not only the culmination of about 150 days' worth of faithful, diligent physical exertions, but also the entire Old Mulkey experience. When I gaze upon that plate, I smile.

Following the race, I drove the course, savored the whole deal, and retreated to the Ole Cumberland Inn where I made friends with the owners, an affable couple from India. That night I watched my Beloved Red Sox win Game One of The World Series. I had chosen to wear as a race jersey my RED SOX BASEBALL t-shirt. It proved to be a good omen, as I would go on to enter the winner's circle that day while the Sox did likewise that night and proceeded to sweep the Cardinals in four. What a year! Life is good.

The marathon crew and all the support staff were instrumental in Old Mulkey's stellar organization and execution. Though I've probably never struggled through a more agonizing course, I likewise haven't encountered such a high quality race than this one in Tompkinsville, Kentucky.

Give it a try. Some events have a certain aura to them. Old Mulkey has "the aura." Their motto is: "The race where you are a name, not a number." I can attest to the veracity of that credo. I give it five stars. Hmmmm. I also see where the previous year's winner is invited back to compete again for free. Being a frugal Scotsman, that sounds pretty good to me.

David Birse is a three-time marathon champion and a 14-time kilted mile winner (New Hampshire Highland Games and Quechee Scottish Festival, Vermont). He has also run four marathons in full-kilt – twice at Boston, once at Philadelphia, and once at Mount Desert Island. He has won over 100 races and completed 15 sub-three hour marathons (in four different decades). David is the founder and director of the Summer Sizzler Foot Race Series (and a finalist for the 2001 Golden Show Award for Excellence in grassroots running) and the co-founder of the Monadnock Milers. Outside of running, he's a cell biologist, columnist, owner of Per Diem Enterprises, and a descendant of William Diamond, the Drummer Boy in the Revolutionary War.

Marine Corps Marathon

washington, d.c.

Web site: www.marinemarathon.com
Month: October
USATF Certified: Yes
Course: Rolling

As mentioned in the forward, the Reston Runners club of Reston, Virginia (a branch of the Road Runners Club of America) was instrumental in the development of this book. The club avidly supports the Marine Corps Marathon and provides training opportunities for this race to club members each year. The race is known to be particularly friendly to first-time marathoners, and as such, remains dear in the hearts of many Reston Runners who completed their own inaugural marathons there. The number of volunteers we received to author the Marine Corps Marathon section was staggering. Following are accounts by three Reston Runners who were selected to share their first marathon experience at this popular race.

Author: Jessica Torbeck
Number of Marathons Completed: 2
Age Group: 20-24

October 28, 2001 dawned sunny and the temperature crept up to 50°F for a high. I was thrilled by the weather and to run in the Marine Corps Marathon, my first. The Marine Corps Marathon takes place in Washington, D.C. in October each year and is often referred to as "the marathon of the monuments." Besides taking advantage of ideal weather conditions for running 26.2 miles, runners are treated to an up close tour of famous sights in the nation's capital. Having recently moved to the area, it was a great way for me to get out of the house and see some of downtown. Officially coined "The People's Marathon," its patriotic slant and relatively flat course make it a fitting candidate for a first marathon.

Many fellow runners harbor similar feelings. A lottery system is used in the spring to award entries to hopeful candidates. Thousands are turned away, so I felt fortunate to have won a slot. My first indication of this came while balancing my checkbook when I noticed they had cashed my check for $80.00. Then I was committed. That same day, I visited the race web site and printed out a training program for my time goal of four hours. I realized I had better get started in order to get in shape by October.

My longest running distance prior to training for the Marine Corps Marathon was a half marathon, preceded by some casual 5K and 10K races. With the Marine Corps Marathon training program as a general guide, I was confident I would be able to complete the distance of a marathon. Many of my longer training runs were with a club called the Reston Runners in Northern Virginia. Having a group to train with introduced me to some fantastic people, and I gained good advice from seasoned professionals.

Friday, two days before the race, I drove to the marathon expo in Arlington, Virginia. The infectious excitement of hundreds of runners around me took the sting out of paying for parking. Packet pick-up went smoothly. Entertainment included a chin-up bar with Marines to provide a boot camp like setting, and booths selling clothing, nutritional products, and commemorative displays for one's finisher's medal, race number, and even the race t-shirt (although I prefer to actually wear my shirt).

On race day I awoke in the dark to the alarm clock, turned off my two back up alarms, and downed a quick carbohydrate breakfast. The temperature was in the low 30s as I scurried out to the car with my cheering section, my mom. We drove 30 minutes to the closest Metro station (D.C.'s rail transit system), which was open early for the occasion. Already waiting was a motley crew clad in expensive running shoes, holey sweatpants, hats, gloves, and even garbage bags. I had pre-race butterflies in my stomach, but also a sense of calm now that months of preparation were over and there was nothing more to be done. Additionally, I was grateful to be arriving at the start with all training injuries healed and in good health.

After disembarking at the recommended Metro stop, we were unsure where to go but simply followed a snaking line of people all heading in one direction. We joined a growing crowd of runners taking advantage of the early morning light to photograph the spectacular Marine Corps War Memorial (a.k.a. Iwo Jima Memorial). I was taken by its astute placement near the top of a hill and how big it was. This and other area landmarks are just best appreciated in person. Photographers were strategically placed along the course to catch unsuspecting runners in motion. One of the pictures I purchased online after the race was a neat shot of myself running with the Lincoln Memorial in the background.

After shedding extra clothing and a frantic last minute search for the correct starting corral, a cheer arose and the race began promptly on schedule. We stood deadlocked for several minutes and then shuffled toward the start line. The bushes and ground were strewn with discarded warm-up clothes. My mom later described Marines who came with garbage sacks shortly thereafter and picked it all up to give to charity. Some runners returned later to search for their carefully placed items and left baffled.

The field was extremely crowded through much of the race. My race strategy, which I don't necessarily recommend, was to slow my pace to 10 minutes per mile for the first six miles. In theory this would leave me with that much extra energy at the end. A drawback may have been that I ended up spending the next 20.2 miles maneuvering politely past other runners to get on pace again.

There were two scheduled checkpoints for energy gel and one for fruit. I found only one of the gel stations, and all that remained of the fruit were empty boxes and trampled orange peel. Luckily I had brought several gels with me. Water support was fantastic throughout. A long line of Marines in combat fatigues manned each stop with outstretched arms yelling, "Water! Water! Ultima at the rear!" followed by, "Ultima! Ultima!" This created smooth access to beverages and kept us out of each other's way.

The timing of the race, shortly after the events of September 11, meant an out of the ordinary patriotic feel. Each time the course led into a traffic tunnel, runners chanted "U.S.A.! U.S.A.!" The excitement of hearing our voices echo off the cement was replaced by mere breathlessness after the opening 10 miles. Two men behind me started to chant when we entered a subsequent underpass, but trailed off when no one else joined in. "So much for that," they laughed sheepishly. Later I learned that the marathon was nearly cancelled due to security concerns. In addition to approximately 17,000 runners, the marathon drew over three times that number in spectators. While my imagination did produce a few terrorist attack scenarios, I pressed forward with no apprehension and the determination that only comes after six months of preparation.

Indeed the only damage I saw was the self inflicted kind. Several times I heard a nearby runner cry out in pain and saw him or her drop off to the side clutching some body part. The side of my own right knee betrayed a weakening sensation halfway through the race. I kept silently telling it, "No, you have to keep going! You can't give up on me yet!" I felt enough general fatigue throughout the race to be tempted to sit down for a good cry. However, I drew inspiration from the unrelenting runners all around me.

One sight, which I must mention, distracted me from all thoughts of physical discomfort and mile markers. It was the scene of the Pentagon, completely smashed on one side, as we pounded past it on the flanking roads. I was aghast at the gaping hole and ruined structure in contrast with the pristine remainder of the building. Bombarding footage of the damage on the news had not prepared me for the emotional impact of witnessing it first hand. It is a sight I shall not forget.

Nearing the final water stop, I stumbled upon the four hour pace group and ran past them to finish just ahead of my time goal in 3:57. In the final rush up the hill, culminating in a lap around the immortalized figures of the war memorial, I gleefully imagined that, like them, I had completed a grand and noble achievement. Once I crossed the finish line, someone draped a space blanket over my shoulders and a Marine struggled with my double-knotted shoelace to untie my timing chip. As a result of my initial 10-minute mile pacing strategy, my mom got an erroneous prediction of my progression from the folks on hand to help fans keep track of their runners. She got mild eyestrain peering for me at a couple of places that I had already passed. She also had my extra clothing and didn't start to look for me until the 4:30 mark.

The link up area was marked with alphabetical balloons which had blown away earlier. I sat down dejectedly, growing colder by the minute, and hoped the crowd would thin out enough before dark to find my mom. Finally, they reorganized another meeting area and we were reunited.

On the way back to the Metro, we stopped at a concession stand, and I wolfed down the best tasting hot dog of my life. By dinner, at a Mexican restaurant, my knee had rewarded me with stiffness and burning pain that lasted for a week. In following years I have continued to train for marathons and have concluded that my knee pain was a result of under training. This famous marathon stands out as a great experience in my history. It is a wonderful tribute to our free will and fortitude; I would gladly sign up again.

Jessica Torbeck is a pilot for a regional airline based in Washington, Dulles. The Marine Corps Marathon was her first marathon. Since high school, Jessica has participated in various road races, triathlon, and swimming events to make her fitness regime more fun and interesting.

Author: Brad Payne
Number of Marathons Completed: 1
Age Group: 35-39

The Marine Corps Marathon is a well-known and popular race that occurs in late October in our nation's capital, Washington D.C. The race actually starts and finishes in Virginia by the Marine Corps War Memorial (also called the Iwo Jima Memorial as it reenacts the famous photograph of Marines raising the flag on Mount Suribachi during the battle of Iwo Jima in 1945). The course is largely flat, but there are notable exceptions.

Despite the urban landscape, the course is quite scenic and rich in American landmarks: the Pentagon, Georgetown, the Lincoln Memorial, the Washington Monument, and the Capitol are all along the course.

Since the race is so popular, potential entrants need to enter a lottery. However, I did not obtain my entry into the race through the traditional route. Unfortunately, I had signed up for the D.C. Marathon, which was cancelled at the last minute. Marine Corps organizers, sympathetic to our plight, offered up slots to the first 1,000 D.C. "rejects" that contacted them. I moved quickly and as such, found myself on the starting line. I was excited, anxious, and in a strange way, relieved. After a 12-year struggle with injuries and disappointments, I had finally survived the high mileage training and was about to fulfill a lifetime goal of completing a full marathon.

On the Friday before the race, I took a long lunch to pick up my race packet. I ended up taking a taxi since the hotel where the packet pick-up was located was not accessible by local transit (Metro). The expo was packed and run by actual Marines and went very smoothly.

Virginia's October weather is a tricky thing to predict. The temperature can be anywhere from 40 to 80°F on race day, and it can rain or be bone dry. It had been cool on the weekends leading up to the race, but as I stepped out the door on Sunday morning to get to the starting line, I was immediately hit by a wave of humidity that had rolled in overnight. Temperatures were in the 60s, and I heard later that the humidity was over 80 percent at the race start, but decreased as the day progressed.

The Metro opened early to accommodate the thousands of runners converging on the Marine Corps War Memorial. This is the preferred way to get to the race start, as the parking in Arlington is minimal, but be prepared for long train lines after the race. I did not have a lot of time to get nervous before the race as I found I had to hit the porta-potties before the race started and finished that business only five minutes before the race started. The Marine Corps Marathon, in my opinion, is one of the few races I've been to that has an adequate number of bathroom facilities for runners.

I ditched my extra layer, grabbed my fuel belt, and kissed my wife as I made my way to the 9:00 pace corral. My goal was to finish in less than four hours.

As the gun sounded to start the race, thousands of us started and then suddenly stopped. This awkward hop never fails to amuse me in large races where 10 minutes might pass before the runners at the back of the starting corrals reach the actual starting line. With chip timing, however, this is not a cause for worry.

The first couple of miles steer runners toward the Pentagon. This part of the course is primarily flat and straight, and I can see where inexperienced runners might want to take off too fast. I had the opposite problem as I was going slower than I expected. Instead of a 9:00 pace, I was trending 9:30 to 10:00. The first hill at the Navy Annex got my heart rate going a little higher than I wanted it to be in the early stages of the race, which forced me to back off the pace even more.

My slow start frustrated me as I began to reassess my goals. A sub 4:00 marathon was pretty much out of the question, but 4:30 was still possible. The course crossed into D.C. via the Key Bridge, which also passes the starting line. An enormous crowd was still there, and their energy and excitement reinvigorated my spirits. There were thousands of first time runners, just like me, and for a little while I simply forgot about pace and finish time, and just soaked in the moment. I was running a marathon!

After crossing the bridge into D.C., the course takes an out and back run up Rock Creek Parkway. It is pretty and shaded, but persistently and slightly uphill until the turn around two miles later.

The downhill portion of Rock Creek Parkway leads past the Kennedy Center, the Watergate, and the Lincoln Memorial. Crowd support in this stretch was tremendous. My wife had also crossed the bridge and was quite a vocal fan. I could hear her from a block away. Her bright orange Halloween shirt also helped make her visible. As I passed her, we exchanged my empty Gatorade flasks for full ones she had been carrying for me. These flasks, in addition to the water stops, were supposed to carry me to the finish line. However, I was craving my Gatorade and consuming it far faster than I had supply.

I crossed the halfway mark at 2:17. It wasn't as fast as I had hoped, but I was still feeling solid. At this point, the course circumnavigates the National Mall and the Capitol. The first real challenge is Capitol Hill itself. My legs were just beginning to complain as I began the climb. That's when a "Serious Marine" got in my face and barked, "You will climb that hill Mister! Move Move Move!" That was awesome.

Clif Bar had a promotional aid station, but to my aggravation did not have the water necessary to wash their Clif Shots down. Complicating matters was that thousands of runners ahead of us had tossed their remnants on the ground making the asphalt a sticky mess that even the dirtiest cinema floor imaginable could not top. With fatigue beginning to set in, I actually had difficulty picking my legs up since my shoes were sticking to the road.

Around mile 19, we crisscrossed with runners who were at mile 21, and although jealous of their progress, I made my way around Haines Point. Haines Point, on the Potomac River, is a flat four-mile stretch, from which you can see Reagan National Airport, the Jefferson Memorial, and a famous statue called The Awakening, which portrays a giant man climbing out of the ground. This led us to the 14th Street Bridge. By now it was noon, and the sun was high in the sky. This bridge is one of the more notorious choke points in my daily commute into D.C. I joked with my coworkers that I would probably traverse the bridge on foot faster than I can in bumper-to-bumper conditions. Part of me thought it was pretty neat that the bridge was closed to traffic for this race, but the bridge also poses a terminal constraint to a slower runner. You have to cross by 1:00 p.m. (the five hour mark) or you're out of the race as they reopen the bridge to traffic at that time.

Climbing the access ramp to the 14th Street Bridge, my quads seized up and I had to hobble over to the side to stretch them out. After running on asphalt for 21 miles, the concrete of the bridge was most unforgiving. My pace had dropped noticeably. 10:00 to 11:00, and now I was doing 12:00 miles, and I was obsessed with water.

However, a funny thing happened. Eventually the bridge began to angle downhill. After a few more minutes of trudging along, I saw runners turning down an exit ramp and leaving the concrete. Finally, the sight I coveted most, aside from the finish line, "Welcome to Virginia." Hallelujah! Better yet, there were water and cookies waiting for us at the bottom of the ramp!

My morale received a temporary boost from the aid station, but I needed more drill sergeants like the one at the Capitol. "Just a little further" became my mantra as my pace deteriorated to 13:00. At this point, I didn't even think it was possible to finish the race in less than five hours. That realization was what I needed to get moving again, since missing my initial goal by more than an hour was just unacceptable. That gave my inner drill sergeant some good material as I began to pick up the pace and "ignore" the stride shortening effect of cramped quads.

The crowds began to increase in size as I approached mile markers I couldn't believe I was actually seeing: 24 followed by 25. By mile marker 25, my watch read 4:48, and I knew I had to find a 10:00 pace over the final 1.2 miles to break the five-hour mark. Could I feed off the crowd and my determination? It certainly looked like I could as I began to move with "stiff" resolve. As I entered War Memorial Park the path was lined with encouraging fans similar to those seen lining the Tour de France. You only had enough space for your own body as you ascend the last quarter mile.

Finally, there it was, the finish line. Twelve years of frustration and injury now just seconds from satisfaction. Other folks, seeing the light at the end of their own tunnels, became encouraged. I was amazed at how fast we could move those last few meters. I reached down and looked at my watch, 4:59:17. Made it with room to spare.

There were professional photographers doing their best to get finish line shots for each athlete. I was holding my own pretty well as I made my way through the chutes. Dozens of Marines waited on us to remove our chips. I was grateful for their help, but I did not feel right having men and women of uniform bowing down to cut chips off our shoes. I tried to mumble something to that effect, but the young lady just smiled and said it was her pleasure. I thanked her profusely and began a quest for what my body truly craved: pizza, water, and to not move around for a while.

My wife eventually found me and congratulated me with, "So have you finally gotten this out of your system?" I feigned stupid fatigue and mumbled, "Long way ... far." But in the back of my mind I'm thinking, "Next time I know I can do at least a 4:15 if ...."

Brad Payne is a 36-year-old runner who started running at an early age in Richmond, Virginia tagging along on his father's two-mile runs. At Douglas Freeman High School, Mark Harvey coached Brad, where his personal record of 16:21 in the 5000 was set in 1985. Since resuming competitive racing in 2002, Brad has completed eight half marathons with a PR of 1:56, and of course, one Marine Corps Marathon at 4:59.

Author: Tina Carr
Number of Marathons Completed: 3
Age Group: 35-39

The Marine Corps Marathon was my first marathon, and I recommend it for first-timers. Before I started training, I had only run 10 miles and had done so for four months. The Marine Corps Marathon was a local race for me. As a member of the Reston Runners in Virginia, I was able to train with the club and build from that base.

The Marine Corps Marathon is also known as the "marathon of the monuments" and the "People's Marathon." It is run in October in Washington, D.C. and the Virginia suburbs. Although the course changes from time to time, due to construction and security needs, it is relatively flat and picturesque. There is only one significant hill at the Navy Annex, and smaller hills at Capitol Hill and the 14th Street Bridge.

There are no qualifications to enter, however, there is a lottery system for entrance. There are also a number of charity teams that participate in the race, so entry can be gained that way, as well as through local running apparel stores and running clubs. I obtained my entry through the Reston Runners, who receive several slots each year and conduct their own lottery for those slots.

The weather was warmer than normal the year I ran (in the 60s and 70s), although having trained through the muggy Washington D.C. area August, this was not a problem for me. Other runners did have some difficulty with the heat, however, and the humidity in the city can be pretty high, even in the fall.

The race was very well organized. Registration ran smoothly, and I was able to find parking easily at the expo and spend some time there. The expo was held in a busy area of Northern Virginia, and it was very crowded, but if you want to enjoy your time there, the best time to go seemed to be during the day the Friday before the race.

The expo itself seemed much more extensive and of higher quality than others that I have attended. It was fun walking around trying the freebies and treats, although I didn't really purchase anything, and I found it a bit crowded for my taste.

My favorite aspect of the Marine Corps Marathon was the fact that it is so accommodating to first time marathoners. It was great that it was local for me, so I could see several friends in the crowd. It was terrific running with the support of the Reston Runners and having so many of my club members to run with, however, everyone at the race is quite friendly, and people from out of town should have a good experience as well.

It was easy to get to the start and finish. I did not have to take a bus to the start like runners do at some marathons; participants can drive or take the local Metro transit.

The course itself is very nice. One section is on the Rock Creek Parkway, which has lovely forests, a creek, and beautiful old bridges. I love running there. The sections through downtown Washington, D.C. are also quite nice. The course runs right by many museums and monuments. I love the photos taken by MarathonFoto that showed the monuments behind me.

The support on course is great. In the first half, the sport drink was cold, which was nice. They also had oranges, Clif Shot and even cookies to eat. The only bad part was that at the stop where Clif Shots were being handed out, it was a mess with wrappers everywhere, and I feared I might slip on them. Also, at the final water stop, they were out of the sports drink (when I really needed some) and the water was hot.

I thought the course was very spectator friendly, but tended to be concentrated around the National Mall area and Metro stops which is understandable. During the last two miles I got really energized by the crowds, which was nice at the end.

There were also some unique things about the race that I really liked. I saw someone skipping rope, and three women dressed in Uncle Sam costumes. It was also great to see all of the Marines running. My favorite moment, however, was at the finish where a cute, young Marine held my shoulders, looked me in the eyes and said, "Ma'am, are you all right?" How could I respond but, "Feeling Great, Sir!" Then he put the medal around my neck!

Tina Carr works in the IT field in Northern Virginia. Though always active in aerobics, Tina did not begin running until 2001 at age 34. Joining the local running club, the Reston Runners, provided the community she needed for encouragement and motivation. In 2005, Tina finished her third marathon and hopes more are in her future.

ING New York City Marathon

new york, new york

Web site: www.ingnycmarathon.org
Month: November
USATF Certified: Yes
Course: Rolling

ING | NEW YORK CITY **MARATHON**

PREMIER EVENT OF **NEW YORK ROAD RUNNERS**

Author: Steve Smith
Number of Marathons Completed: 3
Age Group: 35-39

The crowds have thinned out for a moment, both the runners and the spectators. In its tour of each of the five boroughs, the ING New York City Marathon delivers me across five bridges. I do not know it yet, but what the soaring, picturesque Verrazano-Narrows Bridge delivers in scenery the rather squat, industrial Queensboro Bridge is about to deliver in emotion.

I climb the soft slope that will bring me to the Queensboro Bridge and then Manhattan and, in the rare moment of solitude, I take stock of my body. Things are going well. It's mile 16, and if things are going to be good at mile 26 they must be good here. After all the hubbub of Brooklyn and the party/mayhem of a start on Staten Island, after all the merging of starting areas and packed streets of smiling kids spilling sports drink … the silence is refreshing.

I enter the shade of the bridge's lower level, and I take in the sights: the East Side lies ahead of me, the East River below me. I peer to the south too, and I do not see the towers of the World Trade Center, wondering, yet again, if that's unusual from this vantage point.

I hear the first muffled roar, a sound that rises from below me, a sound that is filled with pure enthusiasm, with glee. It subsides for a few moments and then it rises again. As I take in the sound I am reminded of my college days, when I would wake up late Saturday morning, shake off Friday night, and wander over to the football game. I lived a mile from the stadium, and on most weekends the 50,000 fans could find something

Courtesy of ING New York City Marathon

worth cheering about. That sound and all that excitement lay in my future, and I savored the quiet approach to the fun.

Running across the Queensboro Bridge, toward First Avenue, is like that. It is like running toward a stadium full of crazy college football fans. The cheers rise and fall as runners come off the bridge and into the mayhem of First Avenue. Fans are lined 6 and 10 people deep and they exude a deep, throaty cheer that bounces off the surrounding buildings. The difference here, of course, is that when I enter the "stadium" the cheers will be for me. As I'm 16 miles into my second-ever marathon, I haven't quite grasped this yet.

I am getting ahead of myself, a full 16 miles ahead. But in order to make sense of the next comment I thought some background was necessary. Don't stop running marathons until you've run the New York City Marathon.

Before I ever ran a marathon, I had two friends tell me, unsolicited and independent of one another, to do the New York City Marathon before I stopped running marathons. If you ask me, this is a strange thing to tell someone training for his first marathon. When pushed for reasons, both women fell back on a few common themes: the crowds, the majesty, and having so much of New York dedicated to us runners. But perhaps it is best summarized with this thought: Any event that shuts down New York City for a day is worth checking out.

As I arrived in New York in November 2001, less than two months after the September 11th disaster, the city was just beginning to exhale. The Yankees had come back from a 0-2 deficit, winning three straight games in New York. With the memory of 9/11 fresh in everyone's mind, the city seemed to take comfort in those things that it also takes pride in: its Yankees, its resilience, its rhythms. While this pride and this resilience are merely one piece of the New York City character, on this weekend it was the most prominent piece visible to me. A gorgeous fall weekend greeted more than 35,000 runners to the city, and the air was filled with a bit of optimism in the face of so much recent confusion.

There are many good reasons to do this race, but there are some things that I believe will make any New York City Marathon experience better. Of course, I've only done the race once, so my opinion is just that, the opinion of someone without too much experience. Then again, I've done the race one more time than most people on the planet, so, for you folks, I'll make a few recommendations.

First, an observation: I think this race hits its potential when the weather is cooperative. There's nothing you can do about the weather, but two things that really make this race—the sights of the city and the throngs of spectators—would suffer in poor weather. More significantly, the logistics of the race requires all runners to be staged on Staten Island for several hours before the race's 10:00 a.m. start. On a pleasant fall day, this can be relaxing, but in a sleety, cold pre-winter day it could be miserable. Thus, my first recommendation: Find other opinions about the race if you run into someone that had terrible weather. My second recommendation, which is true for many mass start marathons and nearly all point-to-point races, would be to bring some throw-away garments that can keep you dry and warm.

The New York City Marathon is a good race to do with friends, especially if you want to take in some of the city's more traditional fares. New York offers just about everything to just about anyone, but that variety comes at a price: hotels can be pricey, getting around town can be pricey, and enjoying the best of New York can be pricey. All that pricey stuff is a little easier if you can go halfsies on the lodging and a few other things. Aside from cost sharing, we've already discussed another reason to show up with a marathon buddy: the Staten Island staging. Lastly, I've always found that training with friends and then traveling with friends to a "vacation" race is one of the most enjoyable experiences in racing.

However, as one of the more popular races in the world, getting your running buddy into the race is not guaranteed. The marathon offers a variety of ways to gain entry. Most people enter via lottery (according to the official web site your chances were nearly one in two in 2004). If you live in the New York area, or visit often, you can qualify by competing in a series of New York Road Runner races. If you're fleet of foot, you can qualify for the race outright by winning your age group in one of these races or with a qualifying marathon or half-marathon time. My advice is this: get four or five people interested in racing and lottery together. Chances are decent that at least two of you will make the cut.

The race web site has the full guidelines to entering the lottery or claiming your guaranteed entry as well as updates on the qualifying times, deadlines for registration, and announcements of lottery winners. As for getting to New York City, there's very little I can add to the enormous store of knowledge dedicated to this subject. I would, however, keep in mind that the shuttle buses leave from Midtown, specifically the New York Public Library at Fifth Avenue and 42nd Street—so that may factor into your choice of lodging.

I arrive in New York City midday Saturday, to the view of an impossibly long line spilling onto the sidewalk outside of the Javits Center. Despite my predictions otherwise, I'm out of the packet pick-up a great deal faster than my predicted finish time. It isn't a fast operation, and midday Saturday is probably the worst time to arrive, but I escape in less than an hour.

After a quick dinner (pasta of course), I retire to my typically small-sized hotel room in Midtown. It's relatively early, about 7:00 p.m., and I wonder if I should get caught up in the World Series. My mild interest in baseball was always directed toward either the Orioles or the Red Sox, but given everything the city of New York has been through in the last few months the Yankees are a sentimental favorite, even for me. A win tonight will give them the series, and New Yorkers something to celebrate. I opt for an early bedtime instead of the local watering hole, and I'm glad — the Yanks are down 12-0 by the third inning, and it doesn't look pretty as I fall in and out of sleep.

On the surface, the New York City Marathon seems to have a civilized start time of 10:00 a.m. But in order to get onto Staten Island before they close all the roads, I'm up at 5:00 a.m., just like any other 7:00 a.m. race start. I have a short walk from my hotel on Third Avenue to the shuttle buses on Fifth Avenue. I head directly cross-town to Fifth Avenue, and I'm stunned to see a line of buses lined down Fifth Avenue. I'm on 51st Street so that makes nearly 11 blocks of buses, lined nose-to-tail all the way down to 42nd Street. In the otherwise quiet morning streets, it's an impressive sight.

It's a beautiful morning. The sun is shining and the city is quiet in the early hours except, of course, for the low hum of some 60 or so idling tour buses and a handful of loud-spoken race volunteers shouting directions to the wandering masses. The final score for Game 6 of the series was 15-2. Ouch. I find the vast majority of New Yorkers taking the drubbing in good stride. Recent events have brought perspective to so many things that seemed terribly important only a year ago.

Once in the staging area, we have about three hours to kill before the race begins. Of course, no trip to the New York City Marathon would be complete without a visit to the World's Longest Urinal. When you have friends like mine, you hear about these things in advance. I'm not sure what I had envisioned originally, but it was more of a shoestring operation than I had anticipated. As the urinal uses gravity to move things along, I would recommend avoiding my rookie mistake and instead position yourself far upstream if you're going to put the thing to use.

I sit on the top of a small hill and marvel at the still-continuous line of tour buses that pour across the Verrazano-Narrows Bridge. All the runners are corralled in one common area before we make our ways to the various start lines. The race start uses three different approaches to the Verrazano-Narrows Bridge, and the first four miles can be quite different for each of the color-coded routes. After mile four the three routes come into much closer alignment until they finally converge at mile eight — but I am again getting ahead of myself.

As I approach the Blue start area, the security that surrounds this race becomes strikingly real. Many of the buses that delivered us here are parked nose-to-tail, so close that I couldn't stick my arm between two of them. Perhaps this is how they always cordon off the runners, but I doubt it. I also doubt the normalcy of the heavily armed men walking along the bus tops. As we come closer and closer to race time, more and more helicopters circle the bridge. The corals pack in tighter and tighter. The entire scene is building to a crescendo. I'm not a particularly worrisome individual; I'm of the belief that the next bad thing will be something completely different, that while the marathon is important to me, terrorists around the world are only vaguely aware of its existence. All this made perfect sense until a few minutes before the race start. But with all these thousands of people crammed into such a dense area, my rational side is a little less confident of itself.

As the entire scene compresses on itself, Mayor Giuliani appears. I cannot make out all the words, but there are some comforting words to the Yankee fans, some somber words about 9/11, and some encouraging words for the runners. Since I'm missing every third word, I don't know exactly how it starts, but I suddenly find myself in a line of thousands of people singing, at the top of our lungs, "New York, New York." People actually start a can-can line. It's just what the tense scene needed and as the grin covers my face from ear-to-ear, the whole mass of people starts moving forward.

I know this is not an event for PRs. The race is so dense in the opening miles that weaving and bobbing through the first few miles can take their toll. My plan is to take it easy, to take in the scenery and then decide how the day will go. Deep down, I know I'm in pretty good running shape, and I purposefully set my absolute best-case scenario at 3:15, outside a Boston qualifying time. I think I may be able to run a bit faster, but I don't want the pressure so I have seeded myself a good ways back from the start.

I'm glad I take the race easy from the start, because the view from the Verrazano-Narrows Bridge is amazing. It is a perfectly clear day. No haze, few clouds, bright sun. I look to the west and I'm struck at how wrong the southern tip of Manhattan looks. For the briefest of moments I even doubt that I am looking at Wall Street; without the towers the skyline seems odd, unbalanced. If I feel this way, I wonder what all the New Yorkers are thinking. I've been in and out of the city maybe a dozen times in the last year, but many people around me have lived most of their lives with that skyline. Where I am confused, I wonder if they are lost.

I look down and we are impossibly high above the water; it's an awesome site and I quickly realize that I was lucky in drawing the top level of the bridge: not only do I get the full affect of the view, but also I don't have to worry about the dozens of idiots that pee off the side of the bridge. For a race so well marshaled by police, I'm a little surprised at this and worry for some of the folks below us.

Once off the bridge we are in Brooklyn, our second borough of the day and where we will run at least 11 of our 26.2 miles. The running crowds, thick all morning long once you get in line for the shuttle bus, are joined by thousands of spectators as soon as we leave the bridge. This is my second marathon, and I'm not prepared for the masses of people (either on or off the course), but it's immensely enjoyable. I will later discover there are nearly two million spectators. There are plenty of people out supporting their loved ones, but to me it seems like many of the people are just out to celebrate the day, to celebrate their particular neighborhood's participation in this grand event, and even to celebrate their hopes, both for the runners, for the Yankees (there are quite a few signs cheering runners and Yanks in the same breathe), and for so much more.

Once the three routes begin to converge at mile four, we are running north on Fourth Avenue. I find that I'm able to pick up the pace if I like. The aid stations are enormous affairs, stocked on both sides with mountains of cups and the road is sticky with their excess for a hundred meters. I enjoy the early parts of Brooklyn, with the kids in their own race, competing to get the most high-fives. Then there are the firemen, raised above the course in their cherry pickers. In an odd reversal of roles, the firemen consistently get cheers from the runners as we pass by. Runners with Yankee hats get some of the biggest grins. Everyone is glad to be alive on such a pretty day.

As I approach mile eight, I decide that I want to race this race, and I shift up a full gear. I had crossed the 10K mark in 50 minutes. Until then, I was there to enjoy myself; I didn't want to fret over the crowds or worry about my splits, but by mile eight the runners have thinned out, and I realize that the crowd support is not a fluke of southern Brooklyn. Now that the miles are going a little faster, the crowds thin here and there but they thicken again and again. I settle into a comfortable pace and make my way through the neighborhoods of Brooklyn. For the most part, the neighborhoods blend from one into the other until I reach the Hassidic Jewish district in Williamsburg. This is the first stretch of road that isn't packed with cheering fans. The sidewalks are occupied by quiet people dressed in traditional Jewish attire. Some watch quietly as we pass by. It was another interesting reversal of roles. Many of these folks stared at us like, well … they stared at us like I may stare at them when they appear in the local grocery store, with curiosity. Much unlike the earlier portions of the course, there are few smiles. This is neither good nor bad in my mind, but it is different from everything I've experienced so far.

The next three miles pass quickly, and I clock in at roughly 1 hour 40 minutes for the half marathon, give or take a few minutes. Passing the half-marathon mark and then over the Pulaski Bridge, I am soon in Queens. This, of course, means I will soon be out of Queens because the race travels only a few miles through this borough. It is fairly quiet with only a handful of the more conscientious spectators who know the course, know its weak points, and are here to lend a helpful cheer in a quiet spot. The party in Brooklyn is behind me and the reality of the distance lay ahead of me.

The Queensboro Bridge delivers me into noise. Cheering crowds, 6 and 10 people deep, it's almost a shock after the quiet of Queens and the high bridge. All of First Avenue is closed for the runners and it's not until I am nearly alone on one of Manhattan's avenues that I realize just how wide they are. I almost expect a snowfall of confetti. Black and white images of astronauts cruising down New York's wide avenues fill my head. It's true, I think: Don't stop running marathons until you've experienced this.

We enter First Avenue around 59th street and the crowds are thick well into the 80s. In the 90s things are back to normal, which is to say thick with cheering spectators but not overwhelmingly so, but then things quickly quiet down again as I approach the 100s, Harlem River, and the Bronx. The crowds of First Avenue carried me through some of the harder miles but as I enter the Bronx I'm on my own. If my stint in Queens was short, the Bronx is the proverbial blink of an eye with just a mile or so of the course. When I finally make the turn south onto Fifth Avenue, around mile 21, I know that I'm in the final stretch. I begin to feel the fatigue, but I don't sense that I'm slowing down. Not yet at least. The kids in Harlem are really into the spirit of the race. Some run along the sidewalks, collecting high-fives, others shout encouragement. Where the other boroughs seemed to cheer for the crowd of runners, the Harlem residents would single out one runner and cheer them on specifically.

Running down Fifth Avenue the towering Empire State building takes control of the skyline. It's strange, when I am in Midtown the Empire State Building doesn't appear so enormous among all its neighbors, but out here, one hundred blocks away, it's the only building I can see. Again, this being my first time in Harlem, I wonder how things should be; I wonder if I should see the towers as well. As the miles wear into me, as I struggle to hold my pace, I am glad to be alive.

Central Park is the beginning of the end. I continue down Fifth Avenue; well, no, I continue toward Downtown, but I'm actually going up Fifth Avenue and its long, slow incline. My pace has adjusted downward slightly for the incline, but it requires substantially more mental effort. Since mile 15 or so, despite my best intentions, I have been eyeing 3:10. Not that my schedule will permit running

Boston next year, but maybe, I think, the following year. Before I started the climb up Fifth Avenue I thought I had a good shot. Once I enter the park, I'm optimistic and I am struggling and I am not slowing down all at once. The crowds line Central Park much like they lined Brooklyn and First Avenue — deep and enthusiastic. When I make the final turn to head back uptown, toward the finish line, I am spent, ready to stop. The clock is in the neighborhood of 3:15, but I'm unsure what my net time will be, but I'm finished, exhausted, and glad. For me, the race is a complete success. I ran the entire race, posted a personal best, and didn't slow down appreciably in the final miles.

In one of the nicest touches in this race, there are greeters lining the finishing chute, each with a badge declaring a language of choice, and each offering the numerous international runners congratulations in their native tongue. I am fairly exhausted and dread the walk to gather my start-line bag of clean clothes and heel-less shoes. After a brief break to drink some water and ease into new clothes, I make my way out of the park to find one of the things I love best about New York City, pizza by the slice. As I walk along the streets, numerous New Yorkers, mostly natives I think, see the finisher's medal and offer congratulations. They do so with a note of pride in their voice, but I don't think they are proud of me.

Steve Smith contracted a serious case of adult-onset athletics at age 28. He has spent the years since avoiding potential cures. He's glad to have a name that Googles poorly, or effectively, depending on the purpose. He spends his days searching the web for results that he can claim.

SunTrust Richmond Marathon

richmond, virginia

Web site: www.richmondmarathon.com
Month: November
USATF Certified: Yes
Course: Rolling

SunTrust
Richmond Marathon

Author: John Loughran
Number of Marathons Completed: 86
Age Group: 60-64

O n one of the first Saturdays each November, just when the trees are showing their brilliant colors, some of the more prominent streets of Richmond, Virginia, are closed and made ready for the running of the city's annual marathon. 2005 marks the 28th year for this event, and with that many years to adjust the planning, the logistics, and the course, this marathon is now a very well managed, top of the charts race. For a beginner or a seasoned veteran, this is a marathon that will not disappoint expectations.

It all started in 1978 when the Richmond Newspapers, in conjunction with its community and outreach objectives, planned the marathon as a way to involve the whole metropolitan area in a fun activity. The newspapers had earlier sponsored a series of international track meets, and the marathon seemed like a natural progression from those indoor running events. In addition, the running boom was in full stride, and many cities throughout the country were experimenting with road races.

The first Richmond Newspapers Marathon, held in late October 1978, was a huge success, and approximately 3,000 runners participated in the five-miler, the half marathon, or the whole 26.2 mile distance. The race director, although a non-runner on the staff of the Richmond Newspapers, put together many excellent planning committees, and the course selection, while challenging, was well received. It was basically a loop course, well marshaled, and took in much of the scenic landscape of the city.

I will never forget the crowds from that first Richmond Marathon. At the start, at the finish, at major intersections, there were so many cheering people. I was not used to spectators actually watching runners do road races. The next year I was pumped for the race, flew up the road when the gun went off, never took the heat into consideration (there was a noon start in the good old days), hit the wall early, and ended up walking portions of the final miles. I had the best tasting cold cola at the end of that death march, and then immediately threw up. Richmond provides great memories.

For the first 19 years not much changed. In fact, the event got a little old and stale. The number of participants started dropping off, especially for the longer race, and the city lost its enthusiastic appetite for "Marathon Sunday." There were fewer and fewer spectators at the major intersections and there was no major drive to attract potential participants. Richmond Newspapers also ran out of steam, and was ready to redirect its resources to other endeavors.

Enter a new coalition. The Richmond Sports Backers, a non-profit sports marketing agency, took over the responsibility for the event. Crestar Bank, as it was then called, was enlisted to provide financial support. In addition, the running community, especially the Richmond Road Runners Club (RRRC), was given a prominent role in improving the marathon. Active members of the RRRC became the race directors, and the Richmond Sports Backers fueled a new direction for the marathon.

The running community had always been unhappy with the noon start, so in 1997 the event was finally moved up to 8:00 a.m. You can't call it "America's Friendliest Marathon" if you alienate runners with excessive heat. The course was also changed to please those who are adverse to hills. Previously, there were major inclines at the first mile, after 10 miles, and a major climb at 17 miles known as Lee's Revenge. The new course runs in the reverse direction, several hills have been eliminated, and Lee's Revenge is now the major downhill portion of the race making the seventh mile the fastest on the course. Also, the half marathon was eliminated from the scheduled events, and the five-miler was changed to the politically correct 8K, which is almost the same distance.

The Richmond Sports Backers, recognizing it was competing with major fall marathons on the East Coast such as New York, Marine Corps, Philadelphia, and now Baltimore, began paying attention to those little amenities that marathoners notice. More attention is given to the race expo and packet pick-up, the Friday pasta dinner, the post-race celebration and food, the on-course refreshments and entertainment, and every runner's can't-do-without long sleeve shirt. There is even a one-mile kids run for ages 6 to 12, which takes the children across the same finish line as the marathon.

Prize money totaling $25,000 for the two races is now advertised, which means a few out-of-area or international runners will show up, run a fast time, collect the cash, and leave. Marine Corps seems to do fine without cash awards, and I question whether the typical runner or spectator appreciates the superior talented runners who can sniff out a paycheck from reviewing a glossy application. But that's just my opinion, and the numbers are certainly up. In 2003 there were 7,600 runners registered for the two races, up from 6,200 the year before. Nearly 2,800 runners finished the marathon in 2003. Although the official cut off is six hours, this being the friendliest marathon, the clock and the next day newspaper listed finishers who took seven hours to negotiate the course.

What amuses me the most about this and all other big city marathons is the rise in application fees. What used to cost $15.00 or $20.00, now is at least three times as much. If you wait until October 1, the SunTrust Richmond Marathon (that's its official name now) will cost you $80.00. At the same time, the 8K is a bargain at $30.00. Of course, there are discounts if you sign up online or if you register early. One reason they have so many unclaimed race packets is that potential competitors will sign up early to save $10.00 or $20.00, then falter in their training, enthusiasm, or commitment, and end up sleeping in on race morning. I guess that running shirt is not incentive enough.

With the rise in entry fees, however, runners get more bang for the buck. The state-of-the-art chip timing and online live splits, the large digital clocks at each mile post, the energy gels at mile 14 and 20, and even junk food stops at mile 16 and 22 all cost money to provide. Also, with so many runners and the logistics involved, race day volunteers are not the only manpower needed anymore. The Richmond Sports Backers have paid staff who are constantly working with marathon planning and paperwork. Also, city workers and police brought in for the Saturday activities are not keen on "volunteer" status. There are so many little extra expenses of which the average runner is not cognizant. Do you think a "certified course" comes without a price?

But the draw of Richmond is the route layout, not the bells and whistles. It does not have the 100-year tradition of Boston or the million-people crowd of New York. What Richmond has is a scenic and varied course with just enough hills, just enough straight-aways, a bit of country, a bit of city, and some history and suburbs to add flavor to a course which has a pit stop every two miles until mile 20, and then every mile thereafter. If you want water or power drink, you don't have to run long to get it.

The course begins downtown on Broad Street within a block of the Marriott Hotel. This hotel, along with the Omni Hotel located six blocks south at the finish line, are excellent overnight accommodations for out-of-town runners. After two miles, the race doglegs left onto Monument Avenue where you will see statutes of Stonewall Jackson and Arthur Ashe. Getting Arthur on that Avenue with Jackson, Lee and Stuart in the old capital of the Confederacy was not done without much political maneuvering. While thinking about this dichotomy, the runners take another dogleg left at the four-mile mark onto Grove Avenue. Then, right after six miles, the long descent down Cary Street to the Huguenot Bridge begins. After taking this bridge across the James River, the race heads east with a view of the river to your left. This section of the marathon has a rural feel to it, and there are very few spectators. At 10 miles the first uphill appears as the runners climb to Forest Hill and Semmes Avenues where there are three miles of small rolling hills.

After mile 14, the race is basically flat with only a minor hill after mile 19. Near mile 15, runners leave Southside, head north on the Lee Bridge and once again cross the James River. This bridge gives the competitors a spectacular view of the tall buildings of downtown Richmond. However, with miles of running completed, this view may not be appreciated. It's a long bridge, though, and you have plenty of time to take in the sights.

A left turn onto Main Street right before mile 17 puts the runners on the campus of Virginia Commonwealth University, but after a mile on Main Street the course takes a big six-mile Northside loop beginning on the Boulevard. Here you get to see the Diamond where the Richmond Braves play Triple A baseball. Approaching the end in the downtown area there is a nice straight downhill to the finish line in trendy Shockoe Slip. You can see the finishing banner, clock, and balloons from a half-mile away, and it really is a glorious feeling to know you have survived long enough to receive that finishing medal. In the Slip, the runners will be treated to enthusiastic crowds and all the food they can eat. The real reward is being able to sit down and be motionless.

It seems like my entire adult life has revolved around this marathon. I ran in high school and college and ran local races around central Virginia for a few years, but by 1978 I was 34 and ready to try a marathon. I never thought at the time that all these years later I would have run every Richmond Marathon. But then, in my 30s, I never thought I would lose my speed either. So now I am 60, have run all the Richmond Marathons, saw my times improve for several years, and now watch, without any power to stop it, my times slip back into the abyss. But this race has provided me with so many memories, and hopefully it will provide many more. In the future, however, most of my observations will be from the back end of the main herd.

A marathon not only humbles you, it can make you smarter. In 1984 we had another hot Sunday (the early years always had the race on Sunday). I went out cautiously, drank tons of water, and had my best place ever—third. That is a sweet memory.

I even had my picture in the paper for that one. There were also those years when the training, the weather, the pacing, and the competition all came together for a fast time. In 1982 I ran a 2:33 and two other years I had times below 2:40. I doubt if I ever had a negative split at Richmond as I tend to go out too fast, but there were one or two years when the final miles seemed almost as easy as the first mile. What a great feeling. I have run 86 marathons but Richmond, my hometown marathon, constantly is the focus point of my year round training.

There are memories involving my whole family. My wife ran her first Richmond in the early 1980s with our two daughters alternating running with her on various portions of the course. Later, our oldest daughter ran the whole thing herself, not once, but several times. But it was not all fun and games. My wife, in one of her later Richmond Marathons, had stomach problems and regurgitated at her mother's feet at the finish line. It was her mother's first venture out to watch the marathon, and I don't think it left a favorable impression.

But it is my younger daughter whom I think about each time I do Richmond. She was a Navy aviator and we were all extremely interested in her accomplishments and marveled at her courage in a male dominated environment. A week before the 1998 marathon, I did an interview for a local television station that wanted the perspective of an "old lion," one who had run all the Richmonds. My daughter was home before a major overseas deployment on an aircraft carrier, and she saw that interview. She took a copy with her to show her fellow aviators. We were so proud of her. We never thought she would be equally excited about what we, her parents, did. A week later her jet crashed while making a night landing on the USS Enterprise, and all four aviators in her plane were instantly killed. We got the interview tape back. We just never got her back. But her spirit lives on especially when I run those final miles towards Shockoe Slip and her favorite nightspots.

With an aging body and much slower times, my excitement now centers on the trappings of the marathon. The expo and conversations with other runners, the training groups and weekend runs, and my volunteer duty as an official guide on tour buses which runners can take to review the course now take on as much meaning as the race itself. The Richmond Sports Backers marathon training team, which helps train and support novice runners to complete the marathon, drew 500 candidates to its program this year. Richmond truly is a running community.

Richmond is my hometown marathon, and I know so many of the main players, so I'm a bit prejudiced. This race has a great course, the size is ideal, the time of year is right, and the history of the city and the tradition of the marathon all come together to make this a marathon you can't do without. For all you four-day, 25 miles per week joggers, you also get a one-year lease on a new Volkswagen if you break the course record for your gender. But there is a maximum of one car per gender, so don't plan on coming in second if you expect to drive this Beetle home.

John Loughran is retired and currently resides in the 60-64 age group where he now runs slower than when he competed in cross country and track in high school (in Arlington County, Virginia), slower than when he competed in college (University of Virginia, Charlottesville, Virginia), and slower than when he finished 86 marathons, five ultras, and multitudes of shorter races over the past 30 years. He would like to complete 100 marathons before the age of 65 or death, whichever comes first.

Valley of Fire Marathon

Web site: www.valleyoffiremarathon.com
Month: November
USATF Certified: No
Course: Challenging

Author: Laena Shiozawa
Number of Marathons Completed: 1
Age Group: 30-34

After weeks of training, I was excited to run my first marathon. The race, the Valley of Fire Marathon, located about 50 miles outside of Las Vegas in the Valley of Fire State Park, is held a mere 20 minutes from my home, so it was an easy sell for me. The other advantages for me, in comparison with other races (i.e., St. George, only an hour's drive from my home), were the time of year (cooler training temperatures and a cooler race day), and the prospect of having fewer runners, and therefore, fewer crowds.

I had previously run the 10K twice at the Valley of Fire, so I was familiar with the terrain and what to expect in terms of organization. I also trained there in preparation for the marathon. Although I had not run a marathon before, I had run two half marathons and a few shorter road races. I like to run about two road races a year. I consider myself a runner, but not a "RUNNER." I don't subscribe to running magazines or anything, but if I plan to run a race, I follow a training guide religiously.

The day of the race was beautiful—temperatures around 60°F, blue skies, and no wind. (Of course, the year before it was blustery, cold, and miserable—about 45°F and windy!)

The race organizers had a baptism by fire, this being their first race to put together, but it turned out well. Registration was easy. There were no qualifications for entry, and the fee was not exorbitant for a marathon. You could either register through Active.com for a small additional fee, or print out the form from the race web site and send it by snail mail.

The race web site was informative and easy to read. The organizers kept it current. I would have liked a more definitive map/description of the course, so that I would have known what to expect over the entire course, but apparently those details were not worked out until almost the last minute (and are now available online). Packet pick-up started at the pasta dinner the night before the race. I did not attend the dinner, but a friend picked up my packet for me, with apparently no hitch. I did not have to stay at a hotel, but the Best Western in Overton, Nevada is the host hotel for the race, and is located about 10-15 minutes from the starting line. It is a nice enough hotel, and reasonable; I would have no qualms about staying there if I had a need.

Because of greater advertising (I'm assuming), there were a larger number of runners than usual. While positive for the race overall, this situation created a new dilemma — having adequate parking. In the past, runners had been able to park near the Valley of Fire State Park entrance and walk to the starting line. However, this year the park authorities had requested that we park at a marina four miles away, and shuttle to the start. This was where problems arose.

Apparently a few of the vans that were scheduled to deliver runners were no-shows, leaving one large van to shuttle dozens of runners to the start line for an 8:00 a.m. start. Around 7:45 a.m., when the line was moving at a snail's pace, many of us started to worry. We were there to run, and wanted to GET GOING! There was a 9:30 a.m. start rumor going around, which added to the tension for some. I was aware of a few angry participants, but after gleaning all the information from others around me, I understood that the race organizers were doing all they could to remedy the situation.

Some runners got creative and started pooling together and shuttling on their own. My group climbed into the cab and back of my running partner's mother's truck and scooted to the start. Not ideal, but we got there! One group even rounded up runners in the back of a cattle truck to shuttle as many people as possible to the starting line. It was apparently not humorous to our race organizer, but it provided comic relief for the rest of us, and was a memorable picture for me. Despite the delay in transportation, the race actually started at about 8:45 a.m., for which we were all grateful.

The start is easy and fast, without too much ado. It is a friendly and fun start as well, another bonus for a smaller race.

The course is tough, with the elevation ranging between 1,640 and 3,040 feet. If you are looking for a PR, this is not the race to run. However, it is beautiful terrain, a nice, low-key race, and a real challenge. You definitely feel that you completed a great accomplishment when you finish this race well.

The course starts with a few small hills in the first mile and a half, and then it rolls slightly upward for the next 6 1/2 or so. I ran into a friend I'd met at a prior race and was able to enjoy running with her for several miles, until she had to turn around at the half-marathon halfway mark. We saw some interesting historical markers and rock formations along the way, as well as a dead tarantula standing stiff in the road.

The slope becomes decidedly steeper between miles 8 and 9 1/2, then there is a big incline, called "the dugway," which appears more threatening than it actually is. The hill that sneaks up on you is actually the 1 1/2 miles before the dugway.

Now, having practiced my long runs out at the Valley of Fire, I assumed that once I had conquered the dugway, I was home free. I was wrong. The next six miles were killers, rolling uphill and down. The turnaround was at the bottom of a downhill. This race can be great fun, if you are realistic about what to expect. I knew what to expect and still started out too fast—I paid for it midway. I only got my steam back as I ran back down the dugway, and was able to finish out the rest of the race strong. The finish was good—almost a mile long downhill to coast in. Support at the finish was plentiful, as was the food and water.

The aid stations were well spaced and volunteers were plentiful. The local HAM radio group was there to help, relaying information to the start and to other stations. It was great to see an American flag flying at each mile marker as well; it kept me going from mile to mile in some areas. Each of the early aid stations had plenty of water and Gatorade, and the later stations (from mile seven on) had bananas, oranges, energy bars, and plenty of other snacks. I was a little disappointed that there were no gels or goo at the stations, but the oranges were a lifesaver. The volunteers were great. They were kind, friendly, supportive and helpful, and gave plenty of encouragement.

The course was set up on a main road, but the road was not closed off. This made it possible for supporters to drive by, pull off the road, and offer encouragement to runners. One runner's husband rode his bicycle out and waited along the route with snacks and drinks for her. My husband drove out and stopped along the way for me as well. My only complaint with this set-up was that some drivers got too close to the runners. I was brushed closely by a woman in a green minivan several times, which was disconcerting, not to mention annoying. It is easy to view the race from the road, with a car, of course, and there is plenty of shoulder on which to pull off and wait.

The terrain is broad, open desert, with large red rock formations (which gave the valley its name) and vast blue sky. There is no shortage of interesting things to see. I heard a few comments from people, running the race for the first time, saying

241

that it would also be their last time at this particular race. Unfortunately, they were not prepared for how hard the course would be. I believe the biggest challenge in this race is to not underestimate the toughness of the course, not overestimate your ability, and not start out too fast.

There is a definite small-town feel to the Valley of Fire Marathon, but it is a professionally organized race. It is adequate for any level of runner, however, if you want to run the Valley of Fire, be sure to train on hills!

Laena Shiozawa has been running off and on for 18 years. Her first races were in New Zealand when she was an exchange student. There, she ran a three-mile leg of a team triathlon and a 9K race. In addition to the Valley of Fire Marathon, Laena has completed two half marathons and various small road races. A native of Washington state, she now lives in Nevada with her husband and two children. Laena is elated that she finally did a marathon and she doesn't plan for it to be her last. She also enjoys bicycling, aerobics, tennis, and just about anything she can do outside.

Oklahoma Marathon

tulsa, oklahoma

Web site: www.oklahomamarathon.org
Month: November
USATF Certified: Yes
Course: Flat

Author: Tom Conrad
Number of Marathons Completed: 85
Age Group: 65-69

The Oklahoma Marathon was one of my most enjoyable marathons, possibly number three overall, right behind the Pikes Peak Marathon and my first marathon (Marine Corps Marathon) 20 years ago. I may return to do this marathon again. It is a low-key, friendly, small, and fun event. The festivities included an outstanding pasta dinner and motivational program, the marathon itself, and a post-marathon party. About 1/3 of the participants were members of the 50 State Marathon Club, the 50 State and DC Marathon Club, and/or the 100 Marathon Club. In other words, many marathon crazies participated.

The marathon course is on a pathway along the Arkansas River. It is two loops of a "flat and fast" out-and-back course. The course was pretty, being along the banks of the Arkansas, and the entire six-mile strip is parkland. The weather was great—sunny, 45°F at the start to 65°F at the finish, and minimal wind.

My time was my fastest this year, 5:34. My pace for the first half was 12:31 per mile, and the second half was 12:57 per mile. I attribute my faster time to a brilliant discovery—taking quicker steps caused me to walk faster!

Another interesting aspect of the marathon is that there were no police on the course. The course does not cross any streets. Tulsa Boys Home residents and their friends staff the water stops. There is music in a half dozen places, and we passed each group four times. Several of the water stops have food, including bagels, pretzels, bananas, and, of course, Gatorade. Best of all, there was a beer wagon at the finish!

OKLAHOMA MARATHON

There are several other unique features of this race. Each of the 286 finishers received a shirt with the names and times of all finishers; that was sent after the race. The finishers' medallion is also a unique design and plaques are awarded to the first 50 finishers. In addition to the National Anthem at the start of the race, there is a festive balloon release that seems to be famous now. Another thing that is fun about this race, is that each runner who is the first to enter from their state, receives a special shirt to wear during the race with their state name printed on it.

The host hotel was the nearby Hilton Southern Hills, which offers discounts to race participants. The pre-race pasta dinner was the best I have ever attended. About half of the marathon participants were at the dinner, which was a sit-down affair at the host Hilton. The pasta was excellent—far better than most pre-race pasta dinners.

Following the dinner, there was an hour-long program with two entertaining MCs. During this program, the impetus for the Oklahoma Marathon was explained. In 1998, Bob Lehew, who lives in Tulsa and is the president of the 50 State Marathon Club, wanted to help marathoner Rick Worley (who raised funds for the Cal Farley's Boys Ranch and Girls Town USA in Texas) complete a goal of running 50 marathons in 50 states in one year. This goal included the continuation of a continuous weekend marathon streak (for which he broke a world record with 75). When the Tulsa Marathon, scheduled in the fall of 1998, was cancelled, Lehew knew that Worley would be short a state. So he planned the marathon in just three weeks.

Now, there are two beneficiaries: Cal Farley's Boys Ranch and Girls Town USA, and the Tulsa Boys Home. Proceeds from the marathon provide scholarships to these facilities. About eight young men and one girl from Cal Farley's Boys Ranch and Girls Town were there to do the marathon, along with the director of the Cal Farley facility. One of these young men gave an inspiring talk about how he started living at the Ranch when he was nine years old and was into drugs. He has since turned his life around; he graduated from college, and the race was his fourth Oklahoma Marathon. It was a great testimonial for the environment created by the Cal Farley facility.

The craziest of the marathoners were recognized at the dinner. Norm Frank, who was about to do his 799th marathon, Ray Schwagerman, who had completed marathons in all 50 states 7 times, Ed Burnham, an 82-year-old who had completed more than 110 marathons and Rick Worley, the 71-year-old, whose streak ended with 200 marathons in 156 consecutive weekends. That streak included three full-rounds of marathons in all 50 states. In addition, all 53 first-time marathoners were introduced and asked to come forward to be cheered.

The festivities finished with a post-race party at Race Director Bob Lehew's home, which was in a very nice neighborhood of Tulsa (although now the post-race party is held at the finish area). Bob's wife made chili and cookies, and there were lots of other goodies. All in all, it was a great marathon festival, and one that I heartily recommend. I will probably return to do this again. In fact, I got so excited about this marathon that I joined the 50 State Marathon Club.

Tom Conrad began running in 1974 and formed the Reston Runners four years later. He got the marathon bug and continued to run one or two marathons each year through 1989. Tom's first walking marathon was in 1991 and he walked one or two marathons each year until 1996. Since then, he has walked 5 to 13 marathons annually and he completed a round of 50 states in August 2004. Tom also participates in the Reston Triathlon with his three children, has bicycled across the USA, skis, and has climbed Mt. McKinley, Mt. Kilimanjaro, and the Grand Teton. Tom founded SCS Engineers 35 years ago, which has grown to 450 employees in 36 locations. Although born in San Francisco, Tom has decided that Reston, Virginia is a great place to live, and plans to continue living there for the rest of his life.

Philadelphia Marathon

philadelphia, pennsylvania

Web site: www.philadelphiamarathon.com
Month: November
USATF Certified: Yes
Course: Rolling

Author: Bob Mina
Number of Marathons Completed: 20
Age Group: 30-34

There might not be such a thing as an easy marathon, but Philadelphia is far from the hardest out there. It's very comparable to New York City in that there are no major hills past halfway, but you certainly feel like there are. It's easier than Marine Corps, and Boston beats it to death (but doesn't Boston beat everything?). The late November date usually will bring you a cool, crisp day to run, but there have been exceptions.

I first ran the Philadelphia Marathon in 1997, and have run it each year since. At the time, it was marathon number three for me, and I still didn't know how to run a good marathon. Seventeen marathons later, I still don't, but I know how to enjoy the bad ones a little more.

I've set my personal best at the Philadelphia Marathon three times (3:56 in 1998, 3:54 in 2000, and 3:53 in 2002), and train on many parts of the course on a weekly basis. It is my "hometown" race, and one I look forward to running every year as a season-ending journey. One of the great things about this marathon is that it is run three days before a major holiday that centers on food.

The race organization is top notch. I've never experienced any problems with registration, packet pickup, directions to the expo, the expo layout, or race day logistics.

The race starts and finishes on the Eakins Oval in front of the Philadelphia Museum of Art, the course tours all the landmarks of the City of Brotherly Love.

A Quick Overview of the Course:

It is flat for the first 6 miles, hilly from mile 6 to 12, and then gently (but persistently) rolling from mile 14 to the finish. The big hills are all concentrated in the middle, but the ups and downs from Manayunk and along Kelly Drive between miles 20 and 26 feel much larger than they look to be.

Now, Details for the Anal Retentive:

You'll start at Eakins Oval, headed down the Benjamin Franklin Parkway. From there it's a flat to slightly downhill run towards the Delaware River, and the waterfront. You'll turn parallel to the river, and get a view of the Battleship USS New Jersey as you run along Columbus Boulevard on a new loop added in 2003, which cleared up a lot of worries and turned ankles resulting from a brief cobblestone section around mile four in Society Hill.

You'll then turn back toward Center City, and make your way through Old City, following the narrow streets that were laid down in the 1700s. A quick right-left rumba brings you onto South Street—Philadelphia's equivalent of New York's SoHo District. You'll pass the bars and shops, still not really headed uphill or downhill just yet. A left turn onto Chestnut Street just before the 10K mark brings the first gentle upslope of the day.

You'll run nearly two miles on Chestnut Street, including your probable fastest mile of the day as you descend toward the Schuylkill River at mile seven. From there, you'll pass through University City—Drexel and the University of Pennsylvania—and then turn right onto 34th street to begin the serious climbing of the day starting at mile 7.5.

From University City you'll climb in steps up toward Fairmount Park. The climbing basically goes on from mile 7.5 to mile 10 in three steps—headed to the Philadelphia Zoo, headed to Girard Avenue, and then cresting at mile 10 in front of Memorial Hall. Patience is key through this section as these hills are coming when you're still fresh, and you might be tempted to run up them a little too briskly. With 16 miles yet to run— patience, patience, patience.

You'll pass Memorial Hall (built for the 1876 Centennial Exposition), and then descend through the Japanese Gardens and Arboretum run by the Philadelphia Fairmount Park Commission. The gardens are spectacular if you get a moment to look around, but I'll understand if you don't.

From mile 11, you'll descend steeply to West River Drive, now parallel to the Schuylkill River, where you'll spend essentially the rest of the race. West River Drive is flat and winding, and at this time of the morning is shaded for the most part. You can see Center City as you run toward it, and soon the Art Museum will come into view— you're halfway home.

You'll pass 13.1 miles before you get to the Museum, and soon the crowds will start to appear. There isn't very much crowd support along this course, but along the Art Museum (and again in Manayunk) is where it's at its best. You'll run uphill to the Museum just before mile 14, and then descend down Kelly Drive, leaving the finish line behind you with 12 miles to go.

Make a note of how good you feel at miles 14 to 15. This is because you're descending a grade that you'll meet again at the very end of the day (sorry!). Once you find yourself on Kelly Drive, this is where the mental toughness portion of the race begins. Kelly Drive runs parallel to the river, and is devoid of spectators. By now it'll be very quiet around you, and it will take some concentration to maintain your pace if you've been having a good day to this point.

From the Museum to Ridge Avenue is four miles. Focus on those four miles as you head toward Manayunk, for there will be big-time crowd support when you get there. You'll see the elite runners coming back—gain strength from them. Look at their form; remind yourself to relax your shoulders, your arms, and stay loose. Stay smooth. Stay strong.

Once you've left Kelly Drive and made the left onto Ridge, work your way into Manayunk. You'll feel the rise of the road all the way into town—stay strong through here. Listen for the cheers as you crest the rise and descend into Main Street, you'll feel great! The turnaround point at 20 miles is just ahead of you in front of the massive, concrete railroad bridge (the Pencoyd Viaduct, if you're interested in such things). When you make the turnaround, you'll see why you felt so good—you ran downhill all the way there. Rats!

You'll climb out of Manayunk, and then rejoin Ridge Avenue once more. On the way to mile 22, you'll meet "The Ramp." The Ramp is just that, a highway entrance ramp, all of 20 vertical feet in elevation gain. You'll run it backward (I mean, you'll be facing forward when you run it, but you run it against the way people normally drive it). It stings big time. Just persevere over the ramp, and you'll be back on Kelly Drive, headed for home.

As you hang on through Kelly Drive one more time, focus on getting to Boathouse Row. Boathouse Row is a strip of crew boathouses that marks the home of the famous "Schuylkill Navy" of Philadelphia. All of the established rowing clubs have a house there, as well as the universities. Does that matter to you as a runner? Maybe, maybe not. What SHOULD matter to you is that when you see Boathouse Row you've got half of a mile to go.

You'll run past the boathouses and start climbing that little grade to the Art Museum. By now, it'll feel like an Alpine Pass (don't worry, it does for everyone).

Just hang in there, you're almost home. By the time you crest the climb and turn the last corner in front of the Art Museum and the thousands of spectators waiting there, you won't remember how much it hurt to get up there.

One last note, before the race, everyone looks at the Art Museum steps (the steps made famous by Sylvester Stallone's run up them in Rocky), and jokes, "I'll run up those for a great picture post-race!" Key Statistic: Since 1997 do you know how many people I've actually seen run up those steps after the finish? Zero.

There are no entry qualifications for this race. Elites are not given appearance money, but may be eligible for hotel rooms courtesy of the race based on times run in the past two years. See the race web site under the "Elite Athletes" page for more information.

The years I've run this race, the weather has officially been all over the map. In 1997 it was cool and overcast; 1998 saw starting temperatures in the 30s with finish line temperatures around 50°F. 1999 was a "hot" year with highs in the mid-70s. It was back to cold in 2000 (31°F at the start, 33°F at the finish), 2001 was another "hot" year (mid-60s), 2002 was cold, and 2003 was mild (mid 50s to low 60s), etc. At the risk of jinxing the next running, it has not rained or snowed on any of the past Philadelphia Marathon's that I've known about.

This year will bring a change in the expo location for the first time. It moves from Memorial Hall (at the 10-mile mark of the route), to the start/finish line on Eakins Oval. It is to be determined if this is an improvement or not, but I can see the immediate benefits of bringing all the athletes to the same place they'll return to for race day, that familiarity will certainly help race morning.

The expo has always been one of moderate size. Boston, New York City, and Chicago might have larger expos, but with two to three times the field size, that's to be expected.

The start/finish line is located on Ben Franklin Parkway, right in front of the Art Museum. This is a gorgeous starting venue for a race, it couldn't be placed any more perfectly. The wide lanes of Eakins Oval allow for a very quick lineup and start (I've never waited more than 45 seconds to cross the line, even as a 9-minute miler), and the Parkway allows plenty of room to spread out and find space instantly, even as the field has grown to over 7,000 runners.

There is a runner baggage check within 100 yards of the start line, and that makes it a very short stagger post-finish as well to get to your dry clothes.

The only drawback to running a large race in a metropolitan location is parking, or the lack thereof. There are several lots within a 1/2 mile walk of the start/finish line, but there's a strict no parking zone within the blocks surrounding the course. It's best to plan ahead and do a drive-around the day before to see where you might want to park on race day. Finding a space on the street is all but impossible unless you plan on arriving and parking before sunrise.

Aid stations are every mile, or so it seems. According to the race web site, they're actually every 2 - 2.5 miles. "Water will be supplied at race start and miles: 2.5, 5, 7.5, 10, 12.2, 14, 15.5, 18, 19.5, 20.5, 22, 24, and race finish. Replacement fluid (Gatorade) will start at mile five water stops and continue to the finish line." With the cooler temperatures of late November (with 1999, 2001, and 2003 bearing exception), it's a very acceptable layout.

There are plenty of hotels within walking distance of the start line, but they book up quickly. It's best to check the race web site for deals, or head to the Philadelphia tourist web site, www.gophila.com for the latest deals and package offers. I've been living in Philadelphia since 1995, so I've never actually stayed in a hotel before this marathon, just in my own bed.

What do I like about the Philadelphia Marathon? Cool weather (most of the time). Great sights along the way that give you a fantastic tour of what Philly has to offer. The small field (compared to New York City, Boston, Marine Corps, or Chicago) makes it feel like a local race, even as the race has continued to grow. Lastly, if you're going to have a Philly Cheesesteak, running the marathon allows you to have TWO without guilt.

The Philadelphia Marathon is very spectator friendly. If a spectator is at the start/ finish, they can walk a short distance (five blocks) to catch the field coming through at mile six on Chestnut Street, then head back to the start/finish for the 14 mile mark. Once the runners head out to Manayunk, however, that's the end of any coordination or meeting until the finish. If you head down Kelly Drive to see a runner coming back, you won't be able to get back to the finish line unless your runner is moving very slowly (or you have a bike).

Boston has Wellesley. New York City has First Avenue. Philadelphia doesn't have a signature spectator section as such, but the Art Museum and the setting of the start line, halfway point, and finish line are hard to beat. You couldn't have a race in Philly in a better place!

Bob Mina is a triathlete, author, and techie-geek (in that order). He works for Wyeth in Malvern, Pennsylvania. After a high-school existence as the fat kid in the band, he changed his ways at college and discovered the joys of racing by walking onto and joining the swim team. He has since completed 20 marathons, 6 Ironman triathlons, and 35 shorter distance triathlons. Philadelphia continues to be his favorite race, mainly because of the closeness to good food at the finish.

St. Jude Memphis Marathon

memphis, tennessee

Web site: www.stjudemarathon.org
Month: December
USATF Certified: Yes
Course: Flat

Author: Rich Brown
Number of Marathons Completed: 8
Age Group: 40-44

Every marathon offers a different experience. Before I traveled to Memphis for the St. Jude Memphis Marathon, I had run only in small races on mostly rural courses. Memphis was my first big-city marathon, but the experience went far beyond moving up in size and venue – and it all has to do with St. Jude, an amazing institution and the inspiration for hundreds of runners who are official St. Jude Heroes.

The official name of the institution is St. Jude Children's Research Hospital, founded by the late entertainer Danny Thomas. It exists to treat children with cancer and to find cures for childhood cancer. No child ever pays for care at St. Jude.

Yes, it takes an effort to run 26.2 miles, but don't mention "hard" to someone who has learned about what goes on at St. Jude. *Hard* is being a kid fighting cancer and hoping to be a grownup. *Hard* is being a parent; hoping and praying your child will make it. *Hard* is being a doctor or nurse who sees many victories over cancer, but also many defeats.

I have run in all three St. Jude Memphis Marathons and been more inspired each time. The race is run on the first Saturday in December. On this day, downtown Memphis, and a big part of the rest of the city, focuses and works around runners. Streets are closed, sidewalks are densely populated, and signs with messages of encouragement are painted and waved. People from all walks of life come out to see runners do something most of the spectators don't understand. Some, I suspect, secretly wish they were on the course themselves. If they were, I guarantee they would enjoy it.

What all the spectators have in common is the knowledge that many of the runners are out there to help St. Jude, and many are running because of help received at St. Jude. The people of Memphis are proud of the work being done at St. Jude and proud that it is in their city. On this day, they are proud of the runners in the race that bears its name. They don't mind waiting in their cars to let the runners go past. They don't mind getting up early to be sloshed on as they hand out POWERade to people dripping sweat and made clumsy by fatigue.

They love the hospital, the kids and parents who have to go there, and the people running to help them. This race is great because you sense the love people have for the place it is named after.

The marathon is run on a flat and fast course, starting at 250 feet above sea level and finishing 24 feet higher. There are only two real hills, the first at about two miles and the second ending at the beginning of mile 15.

At the highest point in the race you are 380 feet above and at the lowest 237 feet above sea level. The race starts downtown and soon has participants running by the banks of the Mississippi River heading past Mud Island, where the whole river, from Minnesota to the Gulf of Mexico, is replicated in concrete. In sight is the Pyramid arena, which seems small from a mile downstream but huge as you run past it a few minutes later.

Leaving the river, you turn onto Beale Street going past W. C. Handy Park and four historic blocks of blues clubs, restaurants, and shops. Beale Street has welcomed celebrities and entertainers for years. On the first Saturday of December, the stars of Beale Street, cheered by a huge crowd of supporters, are the runners gliding past easily after just two miles and with settled determination again halfway through the race.

Leaving the downtown area, the course heads near the Pyramid before turning to pass in front of the St. Jude complex. As you pass the edifice, it is easy to be thankful for the ability to run—free from need for what St. Jude provides. Not quite five miles into the race, there are still many steps to take, and the reality of the marathon begins to set in. Seeing the hospital, and the people coming and going from it, you realize that running a marathon is easy compared to what goes on inside it.

The course offers many of Memphis's best sights: the Gibson Guitar Factory; the Orpheum Theatre; the Lorraine Motel where Dr. Martin Luther King Jr. was assassinated (it is now the National Civil Rights Museum); Humes High School, Elvis Presley's alma mater; Sun Studios, where Elvis made his first records; and the Hunt-Phelan Mansion, where General Ulysses Grant planned the campaign that led to the capture of Vicksburg. The course also features the lovely campuses of two small colleges in the Memphis Midtown area, Rhodes College and Christian Brothers University. You also get a runner's-eye view of the Memphis Zoo in Overton Park (a huge area with virgin forest). Back downtown there is the brand-new FedEx Forum, the new home of the Memphis Grizzlies, and the Rock and Soul Museum.

The course also takes you through picturesque neighborhoods: Victorian Village, with three and four-story homes dating to the 1800s; the Central Garden District and Peabody Avenue, built by Memphis aristocracy in the early 1900s and added to the National Registry of Historic Places in 1983; and the Cooper Young Community, a revitalized area now made up of an eclectic collection of homes and unique shops and restaurants.

I keep coming back to the St. Jude Marathon in part because when I'm running I'm always in sight of something worth seeing.

Qualifying to run the St. Jude Memphis Marathon is easy. All you have to do is enter, which you can do from their web site. Lately, the race has attracted a stronger and stronger field, but you don't have to have a shot at the $30,000 in prize money to belong and enjoy running in it.

Downtown Memphis has plenty of hotel rooms, all within walking distance of the start and finish lines of the race. Many offer discounts to race participants. The race web site makes it easy to find your favorite chain and style of hotel.

Everything about the race is done right; the people in charge are well organized and know what they are doing. Registration is easy, traffic is well controlled, the pre-race expo is interesting, packet pick-up goes smoothly, water and POWERade stops are well manned, stocked and plentiful, and the finish in AutoZone Park (where Memphis's AAA minor-league team, the Redbirds, play) is a blast. On race day, all you have to worry about is running. The race organizers have taken care of everything else, including logistics, support, safety, and location.

As previously mentioned, I have run this race three times. Each time it has been a better experience. The first year I ran just for myself, because it was near where I live, and I had always wanted to run a big-city marathon. It's cool to run in a race where you are always in sight of civilization, spectators and other runners.

Only people who run in a race this size can understand and value the temporary friends you make between miles 22 and 23 as runners in various conditions pass and speak to each other with perhaps nothing in common other than the distance done and yet to go. I discovered this the first time I ran this race.

The second and third times I ran the St. Jude Memphis Marathon, I ran it for the kids at the hospital. I joined the St. Jude Heroes fund-raising team. This is one of the most rewarding things I have done in a life that I am pretty well satisfied with. In 2003, I raised more than $6,000, and it was easy. I just went to people and businesses and told them I was running a marathon to raise money for kids at St. Jude. There is something almost magically effective about asking good people to give to a cause they love because you are doing something they are afraid of or wish they could do.

I am a marketing professor at Freed-Hardeman University, a small Christian school in west Tennessee. This year, several students and a couple of faculty members joined me as St. Jude Heroes. We raised more than $13,000. While I chose to run the full marathon, the others ran the half-marathon. Next year, some of these students will run the full marathon and others will run the half and they will raise money for a worthy cause.

The best part of the St. Jude Memphis Marathon for me is the pasta dinner the night before the race. It takes place on the St. Jude property and is only for St. Jude Heroes. Also attending the dinner are people who have benefited from what St. Jude does.

Two years ago, I heard a dad tell the horrific story of the diagnosis and treatment of his little boy in another institution, and then at St. Jude. It was gripping to hear this father describe his feelings and what the treatments were like. At the end of the story, you could imagine what it was like to be the parent of a really sick little boy, and you knew that he loved St. Jude for what had been done. What you did not know was whether the little boy had made it. There was not a dry eye in the room when little Max ran up the aisle and jumped into his daddy's arms. This year, his mom and dad both ran in the race, and I bumped into the three of them while waiting for a post-race massage. I don't need to say again that this race is great.

Running any marathon north of Houston in December can be iffy with respect to the weather. The last three years in Memphis, the weather has been good, and in 2004 it was perfect race weather. The temperature was in the high 30s at start time and did not ever get above 55°F. There was practically no wind and the sun was out. It was one of those days you are glad to be a runner and to be outside. The average temperature in Memphis this time of year is ideal for running a marathon. There are no guarantees, of course, but odds are you won't freeze or melt in the St. Jude Memphis Marathon.

When people find out I run marathons their response is often an incredulous, "Why?" They often follow up with, "You must be crazy." When people find out

I am running a marathon for St. Jude, their response is different, by far the most common one is "That's cool."

This race continues to grow because it helps a great place do great things, gives would-be runners a reason to become real runners, gives real runners a reason to become marathoners and marathoners a way to help other people. Hope to see you in Memphis eating pasta in the near future!

Rich Brown has been running for 30 years. He's run too many races to count, from distances as short as 400 yards to the marathon. To celebrate turning 40, he ran 40 miles in less than seven hours. It took Rich seven weeks to get over that. A 50-miler is in his future, but he doesn't think he'll wait to turn 50 to do it. This year in the St. Jude Memphis Marathon, he ran his best race ever, finishing in 3:17:33, good enough to qualify him to run in Boston this year, his first. He had dreamt about it for 30 years since he was a 13-year-old just realizing he could run. He hopes to see you in Memphis eating pasta in the near future!

Kiawah Island Marathon

kiawah island, south carolina

Web site: http://recreation.kiawahresort.com/marathon.html
Month: December
USATF Certified: Yes
Course: Flat

Author: Veronica Crandall
Number of Marathons Completed: 18
Age Group: 40-44

The Kiawah Island Marathon has been held the first or second Saturday in December every year since its inception in 1977. The marathon is held at the Kiawah Island Golf Resort in South Carolina, which is 21 miles south of Charleston.

There are no entry requirements for this marathon, and the race begins at 8:00 a.m. Participants have eight hours to complete the race. Although the roads remain open to traffic on the racecourse, this time of year is the "off-season" in the Kiawah Island Golf Resort, so traffic is virtually nonexistent.

I have never heard of this race closing early, like many others, but the registration closes when the entrants reach 3,000. The Kiawah Island Marathon is a USATF-sanctioned race and is listed as a qualifier for the Boston Marathon. The weather can vary greatly in the Kiawah Island area during the December timeframe, averaging from 40 to 60°F. When I ran, it was very misty and rainy during most of the race, but warmed up considerably and became quite humid. The course is generally flat and fast and has two scenic loops, with the half marathon racers stopping after one loop. This could be difficult for many folks, as it is easy to get caught up in a pace much quicker than you planned by going along with the half marathon racers. One thing that I found to be a bit of a let down was that the course emptied out quite a bit on the second loop, since the shorter distance racers were finished. Just knowing that many people were already getting to eat all the good post-race goodies did get into my head. However, the way the course is laid out, nearly every section is an out and back section, so you can keep busy and motivated watching the other competitors or checking out your competition.

The course has some very scenic forest and marsh views and is tree lined, which helps block much of the wind. It even goes through a secure private community of beautiful grand homes, where the homeowners come out to cheer on the runners in robes and slippers with coffee in hand. However, because much of the course does go through this private gated community, you cannot preview this part of the race beforehand by vehicle. If you are the type of person who thrives on the crowds to get through a marathon, then this one may not be for you, as there are many sections where there is no one out there except for your fellow competitors and the only sounds you hear are your footsteps and your own heavy breathing.

There are mile markers every mile and "refreshment" stations and port-a-lets every two miles. This is definitely a low-key race, and one of the last races of the year to qualify for Boston. Qualifying for Boston with this race will actually qualify you for the next two Boston Marathons.

There are some great race packages available to the athletes and their families, and if golf is one of your other hobbies, then this is a great race for you. I stayed in one of the condos within walking distance to the start line, and it was beautiful. I traveled to the race with some fellow athletes from Virginia Beach, and a group of them rented a beach house. The Kiawah Island Golf Resort is the only official owner and operator of resort amenities on the island. If you want to partake in something other than golf, such as shopping or trying out some great restaurants, you have to drive into Charleston, 21 miles north, to enjoy these and other activities.

The Kiawah Island Marathon does provide some race festivities before and after the race. The packet pick-up begins on the Thursday evening before the race, and there is a small expo along with the packet pickup on the Friday before the race. There is a pre-race banquet dinner provided to the athletes, and reservations are required for this. There is also a great buffet provided for the competitors immediately following the race, along with the awards ceremony and a post-race party Saturday night. The year I ran, there was no post race evening party yet, so the Virginia Beach group went into Charleston for the partying and dancing, yes, dancing! The dancing actually kept the post race soreness to a minimum, so I highly recommend dancing after a marathon!

This was marathon number seven for me, as I had just completed the Marine Corps Marathon two months before. At the time of this writing, I have completed 16 marathons, with a 3:30 PR, and two additional marathons at the end of Ironman Triathlon races. This is a fast course, as the course records reflect, 2:21 in 1983 for the men, and 2:51 in 1999 for the women.

Some significant changes to the Kiawah Island Marathon were made since my trek to Kiawah with my Virginia Beach buddies. The addition of shuttle buses and bike rentals are now available to spectators, making it much more spectator friendly. Although this is a beach resort, this time of year is generally not the best for sunbathing on the beaches, and the evenings can get pretty chilly, so sweaters and jackets are definitely needed. Weekend packages are available through the Kiawah Island Resort and are listed on the race web site.

I believe this is a great marathon vacation to take with a family or a group of friends because of the beautiful location, the wonderful amenities, and the low-key race atmosphere.

Veronica Crandall started running after watching the 1972 Olympics. Growing up, she watched her father run marathons (he ran track in Germany and was on the official "travel team"). Veronica ran track and cross-country in high school and in college at Virginia Tech. After taking a few years off from racing after college, she ran her first marathon at age 26 and got "hooked." Veronica also learned to swim in 2000 and took up triathlon. Since then she has run 18 marathons, including two that were part of Iron-distance triathlons.

Honolulu Marathon®

honolulu, hawaii

Web site: www.honolulumarathon.org
Month: December
USATF Certified: Yes
Course: Rolling

HONOLULU MARATHON®

Author: Hope Hall
Number of Marathons Completed: 7
Age Group: 35-39

Turn back the clock to the year 1992. I am a young Naval officer stationed in sunny, warm Jacksonville, Florida. I have one marathon experience under my belt and am itching to try my hand at a second. When it comes time for me to "select" my next duty station (keep in mind the needs of the military far outweigh personal preference), I am offered two very different locations: Keflavik, Iceland and Pearl Harbor, Hawaii. While I feel certain Iceland has more than its fair share of admirable qualities, I am not a cold weather person. I shiver through the mid-40 degree Florida winters. Keflavik? Who are they kidding? I envision blinding snowstorms and endless darkness, a rather difficult training environment for someone with a newly found running obsession. Hawaii, on the other hand, conjures images of tropical breezes, lush vegetation, and Zen-like running experiences. Without a second's hesitation, I opt for Hawaii and a few months later, find myself on a plane to the island paradise.

I arrive in Hawaii in early September. To say that the weather is perfect is a tremendous understatement. That's like calling Beethoven pretty good on the ivories. The moment I step off the plane, I realize I have found a place on this planet tucked away for runners just like me. It isn't long before I find my way to Kapiolani Park on the edge of Wakiki. This park is a mecca for runners and triathletes of all abilities and experiences. I very quickly meet and befriend like-minded athletes and learn all of the popular running routes, local hangouts, cool bike shops, and awesome running stores. I also learn some VERY important lessons that are absolutely essential to fitting in with the Hawaiian lifestyle, regardless of your length of stay on the island. Hawaii is the 50th state, but they play by different rules. Learn these rules and you will save yourself from a few potentially embarrassing situations:

- The Hawaiian language is comprised of only 12 letters. Limited letter combinations make for really, really long street names. This being the case, never ask for directions from a local. You will have no idea what is being said. Always consult a map.
- Mahalo: This word is written on every trashcan in the state of Hawaii. One would logically conclude that Mahalo means "trash." It doesn't. It means "thank you." So, don't be offended when a local says "Mahalo" to you.
- Wahine and Kine: Don't be confused when you see these words on a public bathroom door. Wahine = Woman. Kine = Man. Enough said.
- Geckos are good luck. They like to live indoors, just like people. So, if they find their way into your abode, leave them alone. Harm to a gecko angers the Good Luck Gods and you may find yourself in a scary Brady Bunch-like storyline. (For any reader under the age of 35, ask your parents about the Brady Bunch reference. Or watch TV Land.)
- Bra: When used in Hawaiian context, this word is not a feminine undergarment. Rather, it is short for "brother" or "man" and is used as a term of masculine endearment. For example, "Hey, bra. You surfing da Pipe today?"
- Never, ever order a dish at a Thai restaurant "Thai Hot." Stick with Three Chili Pepper Hot if you like your food spicy. The chef is typically from Thailand and will take it as a personal challenge for a non-Thai person to assume they can tolerate food as spicy as a Thai person. The unindoctrinated will suffer the aftershocks of "Thai Hot" for many, many days. Trust me.

By mid-October, I am beginning to understand the culture and learn my way around the island. Most importantly, I learn that Honolulu plays host to one of the largest marathons in the world. The race is held the second Sunday in December. What better way to get involved in the local scene than to try my hand at their marathon event?

Unlike my first marathon experience, there is nothing low-key about this race. Like I said, this race is HUGE. Honolulu now ranks third in runner participation in the U.S. behind New York City and Chicago, boasting over 25,000 runners. There are no required qualifying times and no participation cap. Over 15,000 of the runners come to the island from Japan just for an opportunity to participate in this well-orchestrated event.

Hawaii is no stranger to the demands of tourists, so the city of Honolulu truly opens its arms and embraces this event. The hotels are plentiful, plush, and provide easy access to the race route. The countless restaurants range from authentic Thai to Japanese to Italian to traditional American. There is something for every palate from every corner of the world.

The race expo is an event in and of itself. If you want to see the latest product lines from your favorite vendors, the expo provides excellent one-stop shopping for the marathon enthusiast. All of these factors combine to make the Honolulu Marathon a true destination event and one of the foremost races in the world.

I ran in the Honolulu Marathon three times during my three-year tour in Hawaii. Each year, the race begins in downtown Honolulu well before sunrise. In fact, the shuttle bus drops runners off at the starting line at 4:30 a.m. I seriously considered curling up at the feet of my 25,000 fellow participants for an hour-long nap before the gun time. There are several reasons this race begins so early. First, because of the large number of runners, the racecourse is closed to traffic. Closing roads on an island can be disruptive to both residents and tourists. (Imagine shutting down the Lincoln Tunnel and you get the order of magnitude.) The sooner the race starts, the sooner the runners are off the streets. Also, the temperatures in Honolulu creep into the 80s even in December. The best way to ensure a safe running of the event is to start it as early as possible. The truth is most runners are early birds. Who can sleep the night before a marathon anyway?

The starting line crowd buzzes with excitement and anticipation. The marathon organizers really know how to get a crowd motivated. Music plays over loud speakers and the race directors provide instructions. Due to the number of Japanese participants, all of the race instructions are given in both English and Japanese. So, if you don't understand the first round of instructions, just sit tight for the next version.

As advertised, the starting gun fires at 5:30 a.m. and an enormous herd of athletes begin their 26.2 mile personal journeys. The racecourse winds its way through the downtown area of Honolulu, past the Aloha Tower, and the Ala Moana Beach Park before looping back towards Kapiolani Park, the eventual finish area.

At about the eight-mile mark, runners encounter the first hill of significance in the racecourse, Diamond Head. Upon reaching the summit of Diamond Head, participants are treated to a truly spectacular view as the sun rises over the Pacific. Then it's a speedy downhill and out to Kalanianaole Highway for the longest out and back stretch of the racecourse. The really cool thing about this portion of the race is that it provides the first opportunity to see all of the other participants both ahead and behind you. You will be absolutely awed at the sheer size of this race. The course then makes a left hand turn out to the Hawaii Kai neighborhood. This area provides the turn around point in the racecourse. So, it's back up Kalanianaole and toward Diamond Head in the reverse direction. One of my favorite memories of the course involves the last aid station before heading back up Diamond Head. This aid station appears to be official. It is actually manned by some fun-loving members of the community who every year pass out beer to unsuspecting runners. The first year I ran the marathon, I, too, fell victim to their prank. I wised up the next two years and simply smiled as the unindoctrinated greedily slurped down a Bud. Seeing someone throw back a beer when they think they're getting water at the 22-mile mark of a marathon can provide some amusing reactions ... and oftentimes surprised gratitude. Perhaps this tradition has faded with the passing of the years, but it will always remain a fond memory of mine. After the beer "aid station," runners again summit Diamond Head, and the rest of the course is literally downhill.

As good as the starting line celebration is, it pales in comparison to the finish line party at Kapiolani Park. The music is cranked and the spectators are rowdy. The race announcers make a concerted effort to herald the crossing of each and every marathoner. There is enough finish line food to feed an army. Even the weariest runner appreciates the festivities.

Since my participation in the early 1990s, certain aspects of the race have surely changed. Like the shifting of the Hawaiian sands, traditions are created, broken and resurrected. But, I am confident that any runner who selects this event today will be treated to an unforgettable racing and life experience. The Aloha Spirit, the lifeblood of the island, is a palpable force sweeping through the racecourse. Climb onboard, let the Spirit guide your footsteps and enjoy the journey.

Hope Hall is a 38-year-old Construction Manager for Nextel Communications in Reston, Virginia. She was a competitive gymnast at the United States Naval Academy in Annapolis, Maryland. She discovered her passion for long-distance running and triathlon in the early 1990s and plans to continue competing until they run out of age groups. She has completed seven marathons and seven Iron-distance Triathlons.

Ultra Distance Races

Aaron Schwartzbard

Once upon a time, the marathon was considered the "ultimate" distance for distance runners. Covering 26 miles, 385 yards on foot is certainly no mean feat. But with so many people running the distance, it seems inevitable that some runners would ask, "What lies beyond?" If marathons are a shining castle on a hill that only a small portion of the general population will ever reach, then ultra distance races (a.k.a. "ultras," "ultramarathons," and "endurance races") are the dark forest beyond that castle where fewer still will venture.

Ultras can be any distance longer than a standard marathon. One of the most common distances is 50 kilometers — at 31 miles, these are only 5 miles longer than a marathon. Other standard distances are 50 miles, 100 kilometers, and 100 miles. Of course, there are races at all distances in between, and even longer. However, even at a 50 kilometer race, an observer would notice striking differences between ultra distance races and marathons. Most obvious is that most (but not all) marathons are run on roads, and ultras tend to be on natural surface trails. Within the course of a single race, an ultra might traverse gentle bridle paths, dirt and gravel roads, and rocky, hilly single-track trails. An observer would also notice that the largest ultras have as many racers as the smallest marathons. Whereas marathons often count their racers in the thousands or tens of thousands, ultras count their racers in the tens or hundreds.

Together, those differences distinguish ultras from standard marathons. Running in a 50K race is not "like running a marathon, just longer." It's a different sort of event. Whether you run in one of the older and better known ultras, like the Western States Endurance Run or the JFK 50 Mile, or you run in a smaller race with only a few dozen other competitors, you'll find that the joy of running and the satisfaction of finishing are commensurate with the challenge.

Ultra Distance Races

Rio Del Lago 100 Mile Endurance Run

JFK 50 Mile

Bull Run Run 50 Miler

Mountain Masochist Trail Run

Western States Endurance Run

Sunmart Texas Trail Endurance Run

Bull Run Run 50 Miler

clifton, virginia

Web site: www.vhtrc.org/brr
Month: April

Author: Aaron Schwartzbard
Number of Marathons Completed: 13
Number of Ultra Distance Races Completed: 15
Age Group: 25-29

In the midst of the sprawling suburbs of Washington, D.C., is one of the largest ultra marathons in the country. What's more, the race is on isolated dirt trails that someone might be surprised to find just 30 miles west of a large city. The race is The Bull Run Run 50 Miler.

The Bull Run Run 50 Miler is mostly on the Bull Run Trail, which parallels Bull Run, a large stream. The race starts and ends at Hemlock Overlook Regional Park, in Clifton, Virginia. Clifton and the surrounding areas are part of the Occoquan River watershed—an area protected by the Fairfax County government with five-acre lot zoning regulations. Due to the restrictive zoning of the area, the trails of Bull Run retain a nice rural feel that is lost just a few miles outside of the watershed.

Bull Run Run was my first 50 miler. I had completed shorter ultras and long triathlons, but never a 50-mile race. Some of the racers stayed in the bunkhouses at the park the night before the race, but I slept in my own bed, which is close enough to the race site that I could drive there the morning of the race. I arrived at the race site well before sunrise on Saturday morning. Volunteers guided me to a parking spot in a grassy field, and then I made my way to the main buildings of Hemlock Overlook Park.

I was unable to attend the Friday night race dinner, which meant that I had not yet picked up my race packet. I easily found the pre-race packet pick-up, got my race packet, and then found a seat in the cafeteria of the park's main building, where most of the 350 other racers were loitering. Digging through the race packet, I found a nice, technical (non-cotton) t-shirt with the race graphic and a pair of technical socks, also with the race graphic.

Ultra distance races—even large ultra distance races—are smaller than most marathons, and before a race, the atmosphere seems to be less tense than at shorter races. Bull Run is no exception. Everyone knows that a long day is ahead, so even the most competitive racers are more focused on enjoying the day than on sizing up the competition.

A few minutes before the start of the race, we began to file out of the building, toward the starting line. Mid-April in Virginia offers comfortable running weather during the day, but the early morning, before sunrise, can be chilly. We stood at the starting line, listening to the last of the pre-race announcements. The morning was calm, but the temperature was in the upper 40s. I had dressed for temperatures in the upper 60s, since those were the temperatures expected for most of the day.

The race started. We began by running through a small parking area, and then looped around through the grassy field where I had parked my car, through a short section of single-track trail, and back to the starting line again. After running through the small parking area a second time, we turned away from the loop, and started down the single-track trail we would be following for the remaining 49 miles of the race.

The first mile loop in Hemlock Overlook Park served a purpose—to allow the racers to spread out. By the time we reached the single-track, where passing other racers became more challenging, most people were among other racers who would be running at a similar pace.

From Hemlock Overlook Park, the course went downhill to the Bull Run Trail, which parallels Bull Run, a large stream that flows into the Occoquan River. The Bull Run Trail is marked with permanent, concrete mile markers for the 18 miles between Fountainhead Park and Bull Run Regional Park. The first part of the race heads upstream toward Bull Run Park. Although there are a few hills between Hemlock Overlook Park and Bull Run Park, this is generally the flattest section of the race. After heavy rain, it can also be the muddiest section of the race.

Six miles upriver is Bull Run Park, and the first aid station and crew access point. I knew I was getting close to the turn around at Bull Run Park when I started seeing race leaders coming toward me. I popped out of a trailhead to an open area with eager race volunteers and runners' crews waiting. There were fruit, candy, bars, and small sandwiches. Seven miles into the race, I didn't need anything. Since it was still cool outside, the water bottles I was carrying were still mostly full. I stopped for a moment only to assess whether I was sticking with my race strategy, which was to run at a pace that felt ridiculously easy. I decided that all was good, and that I just needed to continue doing what I had been doing.

One of the pleasures of doing The Bull Run Run is that the course is generally an out and back upstream, followed by an out and back (with a small loop at the bottom) downstream. There are nine aid stations, with sections between aid stations anywhere from three to six miles. Between aid stations, racers only see trails, trees, and each other. Near the turnarounds, racers going in opposite directions act as spectators for each other. From the first racer to the last, competitors offer each other encouragement and cheers.

Heading back downstream to Hemlock Overlook, I felt a boost from the good words exchanged with people heading in the opposite direction. It was only after passing the last racer when I realized that in my enthusiasm, I had picked up the pace. I settled back into my easy, easy pace, and thought that the hills were starting to seem just a little higher. After a small stream crossing and a big hill, I found myself crossing the start line for the third time. Thirteen miles into the race, I was passing through Hemlock Overlook again, and I felt that I had reached the first milestone of the race: I had completed the upstream section of the course. Again, I stopped at the aid station to assess how I was doing, and again, I decided that I was doing fine.

From the park, the racecourse continues back down to the Bull Run Trail, and follows the trail downstream. Downstream of Hemlock Overlook, the Bull Run Trail is almost a continuous series of hills. The longest hills might be a quarter of a mile. Most hills are shorter, but steep enough that all but the strongest runners spend time walking.

Four and a half miles after Hemlock Overlook, I passed through the aid station at Bull Run Marina. Four and a half miles after that, I passed through the next aid station, at Wolf Run Shoals. I knew I was getting close to the aid station at Wolf Run Shoals when I started seeing plastic pink flamingos on the trail, and inflatable monkeys hanging from trees. The theme for the aid station—the Wolf Run Shoals aid station has a different theme each year—was a tropical party.

After Wolf Run Shoals, I was looking forward to reaching the aid station at Fountainhead Park. In my mind, that would be my next major milestone of the race. I knew that the 18 miles of the Bull Run Trail were marked with permanent mileposts that counted up in either direction. As I passed each milepost, I was yet one more mile closer to milepost 18, and Fountainhead Park. I had forgotten that before reaching the park, the racecourse strays from the Bull Run Trail to follow the two-mile "White Loop" (so called because of the white blazes on the trees).

The end of the White Loop dumped me out in Fountainhead Park. I refilled my water bottles at the aid station and began the next section of trail, satisfied that I had reached another milestone in the race.

After the aid station at Fountainhead, the course follows some trails that are normally reserved for mountain bikers. This section of the course is a lollipop—follow the trails straight into the woods for 2 1/2 miles, continue around a three-mile loop, then follow the trail back out to Fountainhead Park. If every racecourse has one infamous section, the "Do Loop," as the three-mile loop is known, is Bull Run Run's. Forty-seven miles of the course of the Bull Run Run is on well-marked trails with few turns. In addition to the yellow ribbons that mark the racecourse, racers can follow the blue blazes of the Bull Run Trail or the white blazes of the White Loop.

For 47 miles, a racer would only go off course if he or she really wanted to go off course. The remaining three miles, the Do Loop, are not so kind. The course is still marked with yellow ribbons, but the trail is almost non-existent. If you look closely, you might find the faded remnants of orange blazes on some of the trees, but it seems like any trail that might have been there was abandoned years ago. There is no bushwhacking, but every racer does need to pay close attention to avoid getting lost.

The strategy that I followed was the ribbon-to-ribbon strategy. That is, I ran to the first yellow ribbon, and then took a moment to sight the next ribbon. If I looked closely, in many places I could see how the "trail" weaved between the trees and around any obstacles (but otherwise seemed to ignore the contours of the land). Eventually, I came across a person sitting in a chair in the middle of the woods. I was confused until I saw runners coming toward the person (who turned out to be a volunteer) from a different direction. My sense of direction is usually keen. I would normally expect to know instinctively when I was coming to the end of a loop. But the trail had me so turned around, that had it not been for the volunteer, I would have started a second loop. I probably would not have realized I was retracing my steps until halfway through the second loop, when I would have passed the old, rusted-out body of a Nash Rambler that sits incongruously by the side of the trail, among dense brush.

The reward for finishing the Do Loop is the satisfaction of knowing that for the rest of the race, you will be heading closer to, rather than farther from, the finish line. The course heads back out to Fountainhead Park, around the White Loop in the opposite direction and along the Bull Run Trail. Beyond milepost 11 on the Bull Run Trail, the racecourse takes a right turn up a long, rocky hill. After 49.5 miles, this is the last challenge of the day. Run, walk, or crawl up the hill. Make your way across a field. There's one final turn, and then the finish line.

The race director greeted me as I crossed the finish line. He shook my hand and congratulated me on my first 50-mile finish. The finisher award was a nice long-sleeve, fleece pullover, embroidered with the Bull Run Run logo. The next task was retrieving a towel from my car to take a shower. Ironically, the couple of hundred meters from the finish line to my car and then to the showers and back to the finish line (to enjoy the post-race pizza, and to cheer for other finishers) felt like as much of a challenge as anything I had done during the day.

Aaron Schwartzbard is a 2:37 marathoner who has competed in ultras as long as 100 miles and triathlons up to the double Iron distance. He finished his first race in 1999. When not on the roads or trails, he does software development. He has run the Bull Run Run three times.

Western States Endurance Run

squaw valley, california to auburn, california

Web site: www.ws100.com
Month: June

Author: John Chappel
Number of Marathons Completed: 104
Number of Ultras Completed: 72
Age Group: 70-74

The Western States Endurance Run (100 mile trail run) starts in Squaw Valley, California. The finish is across the Sierra Nevada Mountains westward in Auburn, California. The race takes place in June, usually the last weekend, beginning at 5:00 a.m. on Saturday and ending 30 hours later at 11:00 a.m. Sunday.

When I turned 50 in 1982, I thought I should do something to mark the event. The Western States Endurance Run began in 1977 and seemed like a good choice as a "marker" for my age 50 milestone.

I completed the Western States Endurance Run that year and again in 1987 at age 55. Both times I finished in 28 hours and 45 minutes. I tried it again in 1996 (age 64), 2001 (age 69), and 2002 (age 70) and had a DNF (did not finish) each time for different reasons. The weather was good each year. Rain was rare and in only 2 years was there snow at Emigrant Pass and along Red Rock Ridge. Heat in the canyons was the main weather problem.

This is a challenging course. It begins under the Olympic sign at Squaw Valley at 6,200 feet elevation and climbs beside the ski runs to Emigrant Pass at 8,700 feet, the highest point on the trail. A long downhill leads to Red Star Ridge with spectacular views to Duncan Canyon. The climb to Robinson Flat completes 30 percent of the course and is the first place where family and friends have relatively easy access.

The canyons between Robinson Flat and Foresthill (62 mile point) are run by most of us during the heat of the day with temperatures often reaching 100°F. The 1,565 foot climb to Devil's Thumb accentuates the problems of dehydration and heat exhaustion to the point where the aid station looks more like a MASH unit.

Courtesy of John Chappel

If you leave Foresthill before the 11:45 p.m. cutoff, there is an excellent chance of finishing the race. The 16 miles to Rucky Chucky river crossing are mostly downhill but require a good flashlight since it is usually run in the dark. The crossing of the American River is safely done with a sturdy rope, but feet and legs get very wet. It is wise to have a towel, socks and shoes in a drop bag on the other side. The rest of the trail is relatively easy, finishing at the high school track in Auburn.

In the year prior to the race year runners wish to enter, each applicant must have completed an official 100-mile trail race in the allotted time, or three 50-mile runs in not more than 12 hours. If you are faster, one 50-mile run will qualify, with different times for different age groups. The times must be certified by an official race result, newspaper article, or listing in *UltraRunning* magazine.

This run has become so popular that the National Forest Service has limited the number of runners to 400. For this reason, a lottery is held every November since over 1,000 entries are received each year.

This is one of the best organized races in the country. Once you get in, you receive a lot of information. It is worth planning to be at Squaw Valley early on Friday to register, weigh in, and visit the expo.

The Western States expo is smaller than those of big city marathons. The focus is on memorabilia, which are great as gifts for your crew and family, and ultrarunning equipment such as fanny packs, liquid packs, gaiters, clothing, etc.

The towns of Truckee and Tahoe City are closest to Squaw Valley, but lower prices for accommodations can be found in Reno. You will have the most flexibility if you drive—either your own car or a rental if you fly into Reno. Since this is a point to point run across the Sierras, you will probably want accommodations at Auburn or in nearby Sacramento which is an easy drive to Auburn. I live in Reno, which makes it easy for this race. When I travel, I start with Motel 6 and Enterprise car rental, moving up to the recommendations of the race organizers; depending on the time and money I have available.

The one thing I dislike about this race is that in many ways it is a glamour run. The focus is on the fastest runners. There is no allowance made for age and it is rare to have anyone over 65 complete the race. When I requested a pacer from the start in 2002 when I was 70, I was turned down. One of the Board of Directors, in his 50s, wrote to me explaining that we older runners had so much running experience that a pacer would be superfluous and hamper our early efforts! It is not an older age friendly run.

This is not a spectator friendly course. The easiest places to see the runners are at Foresthill (62 miles) and at the finish in Auburn. Crew with determination and dedication can get to Duncan Canyon, Robinson Flat, Dusty Corners, Michigan Bluff, and Highway 49, but parking is limited and contact with the runner is brief, unless he/she decides to stop and visit.

There is a lot of history and tradition in this run. It is not the toughest of the 100-mile endurance runs, but it is one of the best known. Even non-runners have heard about it. The trails are good and well marked. The aid stations are excellent and well stocked. Everyone is friendly as long as you are ahead of the sweeps and cut off times!

If you like mountain trail running that is not as punishing as Hardrock, Wasatch or Leadville, this is a great choice. It is harder to get in, due to the number limitation and lottery, but you are guaranteed acceptance if you are turned down two years in a row. This feature will help you maintain an ultrarunning life style which can contribute greatly to your health and well-being.

John Chappel's wife sparked his running career in 1975 when he was 43. She gave him a copy of Ken Cooper's Aerobics, *and John began running to earn aerobics points. The next year, John ran his first marathon in 4:22:15, but the last five miles were agony. His immediate reaction was, "Never again." However, the reaction faded, and his marathon PR was set at Lake Tahoe in 3:35:30 at age 48.*

To mark his 50th birthday, John completed the Western States 100 Mile Endurance Run in 28:45:10. In the 28+ years since his introduction to marathon and ultra distance running, John has run 104 marathons and 72 ultras. At 73, he has slowed so much that he cannot complete 100 milers or 50 milers in the time allotted. He is, however, enjoying his 50Ks, his memories, and very good health.

Rio Del Lago 100 Mile Endurance Run

granite bay, california

Web site: www.ultrarunner.net/rdl100main.html
Month: September

Author: John Chappel
Number of Marathons Completed: 104
Number of Ultra Distance Races Completed: 72
Age Group: 70-74

The Rio Del Lago 100 Mile Run course (the best kept secret in ultra running) represents the ultra trail running wisdom and genius of Norm and Helen Klein. Norm and Helen were the race directors of the Western States Endurance Run from 1986 to 1999, when it rose to prominence as one of, if not the most popular, 100-mile trail run in North America. During this time, Helen won the 60-year-old plus age group for women four times, including the age group record of 29:25:03 in 1989.

The qualifications for entering the race are similar to the Western States Endurance Run with the completion of one or more 50 mile or longer trail runs. The big difference is that there is no lottery and the race director is willing to consider special cases, particularly younger runners who are starting their trail running careers and us older runners who are near the end of theirs.

I ran this run in 2001 and 2002. The weather each year was excellent, warm and dry during the day and cool at night.

The Rio Del Lago, while smaller than the Western States, is at least as well organized. There is no expo yet, but the goodies bags are well-stocked and commemorative shirts and jackets are available for you and your crew. The aid stations are excellent with friendly, knowledgeable, and supportive staff. The majority of the aid stations are accessible to crew and several have good parking.

The layout of this race is outstanding in two respects. First, it is challenging and rewarding. The challenge comes in the first part of the course, which follows beautiful trails into the foothills of the Sierra Nevadas, followed by the late afternoon or night run along the American River horse trails. The reward comes in the latter third of the run, which follows relatively flat trails around the lakes and Folsom dam. If you can make the cutoff (1:30 a.m.) at Cavitt School (67 miles) you are almost certain to be able to finish the run with all the sense of accomplishment.

The problems of older runners are well recognized and all entrants 60 or more years of age can have a pacer throughout the entire run.

Crew access to so many aid stations makes this race more relational than most. Photo opportunities are excellent and runners can enjoy the cheering support of family and friends often.

The course starts and finishes at the Cavitt School gymnasium at Granite Bay. The toughest part of the trail is run early and in daylight. The dawn finds us running west up the best section of the American River 50-Mile Endurance Run course to Auburn Dam Overlook (22.74 miles). Instead of taking the road up from the river, we climb Cardiac Hill, which is reminiscent of Devil's Thumb in the Western States Endurance Run, but shorter. The course then links to the end of the Western States trail to No Hands Bridge (26.68 miles). This point is also the turnaround for the Sierra Nevada Endurance Run, a popular double marathon and alternative for those who do not wish to run the Rio Del Lago 100.

Shortly after leaving the aid station at No Hands Bridge, runners climb the second challenging Hill named K-2. Norm describes this as "essentially a firebreak with seven false summits." He also points out that at 1 1/4 miles, it is not nearly as long as hills on the Western States, Angeles Crest, or Leadville 100-mile trail runs. The aid station at Cool marks the start/finish of the popular Way Too Cool 50K race. The remainder of the run is less physically challenging, but heat exhaustion and dehydration require attention throughout the afternoon.

The return from Cool bypasses K-2 and follows the Western States trail over No Hands Bridge then up the hill trails back to Auburn Dam Overlook where you should pick up a good flashlight from your drop bag. Going down Cardiac Hill (approximately 47 miles) in the daylight is more fun than the uphill climb. A good flashlight is essential for the mostly downhill run from Maidu to Twin Rocks (62.88 miles). The last third of the run is both easy and beautiful, skirting the shore of Folsom Lake and almost circling Lake Natoma. Norm guarantees that any runner making the final cutoff (8:35 a.m.) at Hazel Bluff (89.93 miles) will be an official finisher even if they arrive at the finish line "a little late."

Most ultras are not designed for spectators unless they are run on a track or on city streets. However, if only trail ultras are considered, the Rio Del Lago is among the most spectator and crew friendly 100-mile trail runs in existence. Cavitt School has good parking and is a good rallying point. Aid stations along the American River are accessible and scenic, but the runners pass through fairly quickly. The Auburn Dam Overlook, No Hands Bridge, and the Cool Fire Station are very scenic, have good parking, and have good views of the course. The return to Cavitt School is usually in the dark, but the last third of the race on Sunday morning is easily accessible and scenic around Folsom Lake and the park area that extends around Lake Natoma, both of which are created by two dams across the American River.

The initial choice for me to run this race came in 2001 at age 69 after I had been pulled from the Western States while running with a slower runner and not recognizing what it meant when we were passed by the sweep. At the time, I had completed over 50 ultras. Completing the Rio Del Lago after that frustrating experience qualified me for the next Western States. Fortunately my name was drawn. Unfortunately, I injured my right tibialis anterior (shin splint) tendon at its attachment in my foot in the next Western States (2002). This injury required surgery with a transplant of the tendon lifting my big toe into the middle of my foot. 2003 was a year of rehabilitation, ending with the Helen Klein 50K, which runs the first weekend each November (and also has a 30K race). Rehabilitation continued in 2004 with six 50K races, one marathon, and one 50 miler. My next, and probably last 100-mile trail goal is to complete the Rio Del Lago again.

At age 69 I loved this race as the first 100-mile trail run I completed in my 60s. Now, in my 70s, the only complaint I have is the cut-off times which get harder to make each year, but seemed easy in my 60s. My tendon avulsion which occurred in 2002 is described in Campbell's textbook of orthopedic surgery as an "attritional injury" when it occurs in older runners. This means that I am clearly on the downhill slope of ultra running. However, it has been a very healthy lifestyle, my rehabilitation has gone better than expected, and many trail marathons are waiting when ultras are no longer available.

The host hotel is the Oxford Suites in Roseville, California. We have stayed there each of the times I entered the run and have enjoyed the pool, Jacuzzi, and breakfast.

The most unique and unusual feature of the Rio Del Lago is the design of the course. Helen and Norm Klein have used their rich and varied experiences as ultra race directors and runners to design a course that is challenging, picturesque, and crew friendly. This is an ideal course for runners who love rivers, lakes, forests, and mountain foothills. It is also ideal for those who have begun ultra running and wonder what a 100-mile trail run is like. This run can also provide great memories and possibilities for older runners who can no longer complete Hard

Rock, Leadville, Wasatch, or Angles Crest 100-mile trail runs. Come give it a try.

John Chappel's wife sparked his running career in 1975 when he was 43. She gave him a copy of Ken Cooper's Aerobics, *and John began running to earn aerobics points. The next year, John ran his first marathon in 4:22:15, but the last five miles were agony. His immediate reaction was, "Never again." However, the reaction faded, and his marathon PR was set at Lake Tahoe in 3:35:30 at age 48.*

To mark his 50th birthday, John completed the Western States 100 Mile Endurance Run in 28:45:10. In the 28+ years since his introduction to marathon and ultra distance running, John has run 104 marathons and 72 ultras. At 73, he has slowed so much that he cannot complete 100-milers or 50-milers in the time allotted. He is, however, enjoying his 50Ks, his memories, and very good health.

Mountain Masochist Trail Run

lynchburg, virginia

Web site: www.extremeultrarunning.com/mmtr.htm
Month: October

Author: Bill Turrentine
Number of Marathons Completed: 45
Number of Ultras Completed: 100
Age Group: 55-59

Some people take fall bus tours to see the colors on the trees, but I enjoy the fall colors on a different type of annual trip to the Blue Ridge Mountains of Virginia. Depending on the year, the colors have been visible on the trees covering the mountainsides or visible in the fallen leaves covering the course. In 1985, I ran the Mountain Masochist Trail Run (MMTR) 50 miler for the first time. There was some fascination with the name of the run. Why was it considered masochistic? I found it to be a spectacularly scenic run along forest service roads and mountainous trails. Since then, I have returned whenever possible for a total of 15 finishes.

The MMTR is located near Lynchburg, Virginia and takes place in October. The briefings before the run and the awards afterward are held at a school in Lynchburg. There are plenty of accommodations in motels around the city, but lodging can be more difficult if it is homecoming weekend at Liberty University.

The MMTR is not an easy course. It is probably not the best choice for a first 50-mile run, but many people have run it as their first 50-mile ultra distance race. Most of the people who have run it agree that the appellation of a 50-mile run underestimates the total distance by between two and four miles. The overall time limit of 12 hours means that the runner must average around 4 1/2 miles/hour to finish in time.

There are 16 well-run and well-stocked aid stations, which provide excellent support for the runners. Many of the aid station workers have been supporting the run for many years. Each aid station has a cut-off time, which is based on historic times of runners who went on to finish the course in the 12-hour time limit. There are several long climbs on the course and a runner must not strictly follow the maxim of walking the up hills and running the level and down hills. It is easy to go too slowly on the up hills and to run into trouble with the cut-offs. When you average walking speed and time spent at aid stations with the running, you have to keep up a brisk pace to finish.

The MMTR starts in the early morning before dawn at 6:30 a.m. Since the start at the James River Visitor's Center on the Blue Ridge Parkway is far away from any city lights, the view of the stars and, occasionally, the moon is often spectacular.

As I start down the smooth pavement of the parkway, there is always the mental debate regarding whether or not to carry a flashlight. Usually, there are enough other runners with flashlights to make it optional in this first out-and-back section. I start in the morning cold with a long sleeve t-shirt, gloves, and shorts. I travel down the road with the sound of many running feet and a few conversations. The course follows the parkway for a short out-and-back segment before crossing the James River. After what seems like a long time, I begin to see runners coming the other way in the darkness and then see the turn around defined by a car with emergency blinkers flashing at the 1 1/2-mile point. As I draw near to the start again, I begin to remove gloves and push up my long sleeves as I settle into my pace. I pass the start with the cheering crowd of people who accompany the runners and plan to provide support during the day.

I then pass the first aid station with a quick drink, circle around under the river bridge, and begin following the river up the valley on the highway. Here another choice is presented as the hills become gently rolling. How much walking should I do in this first segment? I know that a downhill and level section will soon follow the uphill to the second aid station. The road is nearly deserted at this early hour, but the occasional car and truck require vigilance. After we pass the second aid station, we enter the first trail of the day (which begins a series of climbs and descents on dirt roads all the way to the sixth aid station at mile 18).

After a few climbs past the third aid station, the trail makes a hard left turn and starts down a rocky road. Because of the rocks, I try to balance caution with a bit more speed as I gradually descend to the stream at the bottom. The stream crossing has enough rocks to keep my feet dry, as do most of the crossings on the run. After a run through a tunnel under the parkway, I begin a climb to the next aid station using a mixture of running and walking. This aid station is followed by a short steep downhill dirt road and the first of the longer climbs. This is another section that can be covered using walks interspersed with runs. By the time runners reach aid station number six, the course has climbed from about 600 feet at the start to around 2,000 feet.

The next segment is one of my favorite sections of the course. After some slow climbs and loosening up during the first 18 miles, the next four miles have quite a bit of gentle downhill and level sections that can be covered at a comfortable running pace. Of course, this is just a prelude for the sections to come. After aid station number eight (around 22 miles), what I consider to be the steepest long climb on the course begins.

The course goes up with few breaks until about a mile before the well-stocked aid station at highway 60, which is located at about 27 miles. An aid station in the middle of the climb provides a welcome oasis. By the top of the climb, the course has gained back most of the altitude lost after mile 18. There, it levels out to a dirt road following rolling green fields to the right and woods on the left with a view of the mountains to come. It is here that some of the best views of the fall colors have been visible in the past. The contrast of the green of the field and the brilliant oranges, yellows, and reds of the trees on the mountains is spectacular. The race briefing always states that doubling your time to that point can give you a good indication of your potential finishing time.

It is in this section that I pick up the pace and let gravity carry me down the long hills. I run down the gravel road eventually passing another aid station and continue on the roads around the Lynchburg Reservoir. There are occasional glimpses of the water between the trees. By this time, the temperature has warmed enough to make me cautious about pushing the pace too much. I also know how many hills are left.

After I pass the end of the reservoir, I start up a valley with a very gradual climb until the next aid station. I stop long enough to refill my water bottles, drink some soda or sports drink, and grab a bunch of food to take with me as I turn across the bridge and begin the climb up the ridge on the other side of the stream. I like to minimize the time stopped for aid and take advantage of walks on uphill sections to eat food. It is during this section that I begin to have a good idea of how the day is going. If my time is particularly slow or my legs are feeling really tired during this climb, I know the rest of the run is going to be tough.

After cresting the hill, I look up the road and finally see a point, beyond which, nothing but sky shows, the mostly level section preceding the next aid station. Again, the comfort level or difficulty of running this part gives an indication of what to expect later. The aid station has a wide variety of food available. It is also a point where runners can access their drop bags from a bus or meet their crew. This is where runners will need to get a jacket or other warm clothing, if their finish time will be toward the end of the run at 6:30 p.m. After about 5:00 p.m. on the last part of the course, the temperature often drops dramatically.

The course again begins to climb, up to the top of Buck Mountain, though not as steeply as the preceding climb. This is one of the stretches of the run that provides beautiful views of the mountains and valley to the left of the course as you make your way to the next aid station at the top. Often, this aid station has music playing with the theme from *Rocky*. You hear the music and are inspired, thinking that it cannot be far to the top. It is only after a while that you realize that the sound is echoing off of the other side of the valley and that the forest service road curving to the right ahead of you looks like it has a long way before it reaches the top. Finally, the sound comes from straight ahead, and an apparent end of the valley is visible. Then, you finally reach aid. The following section is another pleasant mostly downhill segment that provides a chance to stretch out your legs. After the aid station at 31 miles, a short steep climb takes you to the beginning of what is referred to as the "Loop."

The next aid station is another one that allows me to grab a handful of food and start the climb while eating it. I try to mix walks and runs on the less steep parts of the climb. The miles pass relatively quickly as I enjoy the fall colors on the mountains off to the left and trees that I pass beneath. It is warm, but the pace is slow enough to not become overheated. After having drinks and salty food at the top, I try to run as much as possible of the mostly downhill course to the next aid station. I know that station is followed by a steep climb and that I will be walking most of it.

The loop has changed slightly over the years. But the start of the loop is one of my favorite sections of trail. As you leave the aid station to enter the loop, the trail is mostly level and quickly turns into a segment with what appears to be a green carpet. The entire width of the trail is covered in moss. This unfortunately passes after less than a half mile and the trail turns up the mountain to ascend to the high point on the course — Mount Pompeii. This is a section of single-track trail with a very rocky surface, which limits my speed through the loop. Of course, by this time my legs are feeling all of the uphill climbs. The trail climbs gradually to the top of the next ridge (where I meet hikers who have climbed the peak) and it is here that I begin to question how much energy I have left. But finally, the top is reached followed by a steep downhill. The next up and down, which complete the loop section, are not too bad.

After exiting the loop, the next few miles are on dirt roads that allow quite a bit of running. There is a gradual climb to an aid station followed by a steep 1.5 mile uphill, which takes you to another aid station known as Forest Valley. This is the only point on the course that has an absolute cutoff time (4:35 p.m.). This section is about four miles and covers the miles from 43 to 47, according to the race materials. However, the runners generally agree that it is probably longer. This is the section that takes mental toughness to keep up the pace and not slow to a really slow walk. There have been several times that I have attempted to calculate a finish time while doing this section and found myself continually increasing the estimated time.

The single-track trail after the Forest Valley aid is mentally the toughest and is a seemingly never-ending section of single-track trail. Just after leaving the aid station, the trail takes a sharp left and begins to climb. It is here that I find that my legs either are feeling pretty good or have no energy left. I struggle up the climb and enjoy the next downhill. The next two noticeable climbs don't seem as bad. I try to run as much of the rest of the trail, continuing to look for familiar landmarks identifying the approach to the last aid station before the finish.

It is always a relief to reach that final aid station (#16) before the finish. Changes in the course over the years have made the final few miles a long gentle downhill interspersed with a few steep downhill sections. The road surface at the beginning of the section is mostly grass-covered forest service road with some rocks. You cannot let your mind wander too much or you will find yourself flat on the ground as I did one year. If your quads are not totally shot, you can really pick up the pace after reaching the gravel road a couple of miles from the finish. The "1-Mile to Go" sign finally appears and the course follows a gravel road past a fish hatchery to the last part of the mile on asphalt. The finish line is still out of sight around the curve as you turn on the final road but it soon becomes visible with about 500 yards to go. It is here that the sound of the crowd surrounding the finish is finally heard. That provides a final motivation to pick up your pace as you complete the course.

The fall weather can range from pleasant to hot and can even approach winter conditions. The runners at MMTR must be prepared for possible changes in the conditions during the day. I had an experience of nearly succumbing to hypothermia on the course during my fifth 50 miler when the starting conditions of mid 50s and clear turned to rain and low 40s on the mountain tops after the loop. I started the run wearing shorts and a singlet and was relying on aid stations alone without a water bottle. I was faced with a dilemma of dropping out at an aid station and freezing or continuing as fast as possible to keep generating as much body heat as I could. That run ended up being my fastest on the course. Since that time, I always carry a pack for water and include a windbreaker to provide additional protection in case of a change in the weather. Some years there have been snow flurries at the higher elevations.

The run is one of the best-organized 50-mile runs around. There is a dinner in Lynchburg, Virginia the night before the run with a trail briefing. After the run there is another dinner available before the awards ceremony. The awards are always worth it and the race shirts have had original art designs over the years.

The race provides bus transportation to the start and buses from the finish back to the school where the awards dinner is held. The bus leaves the school early Saturday morning to drive to the start. Some runners hate the bus ride back. The ride winds down the roads from the finish at Montebello back to Rt. 29 in the valley and then on to Lynchburg. After a grueling run, it is probably not the best choice for a person susceptible to motion sickness to sit in the back of the bus. An alternative choice to the bus is to bring crew along or to ride with friends in a car.

Crews for runners are permitted at half of the aid stations. This is mostly determined by the availability of parking and the difficulty of getting a car to the aid station. There is usually a good size crowd at the aid stations, especially those with crew access.

Bill Turrentine started running during his active duty tour in the Navy when there was a physical fitness push. At the time, he was stationed in Hawaii and the runs at work were through pineapple fields. In 1974, he moved to California and began running road races. In December 1975, he did his first marathon and began running a variety of other distances. His wife's Navy career took them to Naples, Italy and they enjoyed many local Italian races as well as various marathons in Europe. One of his best runs was a win at the Stra Ischia in May 1982, a run of 33k finishing in 2:34. Bill and his wife moved back to Monterey, California in 1982 where his wife ran a 50-mile run. Inspired by her, Bill ran his first 50-mile run in April 1983 at the American River 50 miler and has been doing ultras ever since. Bill currently has 45 marathon finishes and 100 ultra finishes.

John F. Kennedy 50 Mile

hagerstown, maryland

Web site: www.jfk50mile.org
Month: November

Author: Jim Ashworth
Number of Marathons Completed: 15
Number of Ultras Completed: 5
Age Group: 40-44

The John F. Kennedy 50 Mile race (JFK 50), affectionately known to many as "America's Ultramarathon," is a challenging, wonderful, and unique event, which provides an emotional and rewarding experience, especially for first time ultra distance runners. This race, coordinated by the Cumberland Valley Athletic Club and traditionally run on the Saturday before Thanksgiving, is a well-planned, coordinated, and supported event. While the inaugural running of the JFK 50 (1963) had 11 participants, approximately 1,000 runners now come from around the country and even other parts of the world to participate each year. The registration process is simple and effective, download an application from the official JFK web site and mail it to the race organizers along with your check. There are no specific qualification requirements, although several people have commented to me, "you must be crazy" to want to run 50 miles!

This race has a 12-hour time limit for those choosing the traditional 7:00 a.m. start. Runners anticipating a finish between 12 and 14 hours can coordinate with the race organizers and participate in the optional 5:00 a.m. start. Race organizers provide all 5:00 a.m. starters with reflective vests and strongly suggest they bring a flashlight or headlamp that can be dropped off at one of the early aid stations. In addition to the time limit for completion, there are time cut-off standards at miles 15.5, 27.1, 34.4, and 41.8.

The race organizers offer packet pick-up and a very small race expo the day before the race, in the lobby of a hotel in Hagerstown, Maryland. Hotel accommodations are available for runners at the "host" hotel or numerous others in and around Hagerstown. The expo offers specific JFK merchandise, such as hats, t-shirts, sweatshirts, and usually some special bargain prices on leftovers from previous years' events. Those opting for the 5:00 a.m. start must pick up their packet on Friday or make special arrangements with the race organizers. Other runners have the option of a Saturday morning packet pick-up before the start. Race organizers conduct a mandatory pre-race participant briefing on race morning in the Boonsboro (Maryland) High School Gymnasium at 4:30 a.m. for those using the 5:00 a.m. start and at 6:30 a.m. for the 7:00 a.m. starters. This includes some important safety information and a reminder of the importance of respecting the Appalachian Trail. For example, the race director reminds everyone to get off of and away from the trail if "nature calls" between aid stations.

The JFK 50 race organizers do a great job of providing support to the runners through fully stocked aid stations. There are 14 scheduled fully stocked aid stations on the course, tentatively at miles 4, 10, 16, 20, 22, 25, 27, 30, 34, 38, 42, 44, 46, and 48. The provisions provided vary somewhat between the stations, but typically include Coke, POWERade, water, sandwiches, salty items, sweet items such as cookies and candy, and basic first aid supplies. This is of course a much wider variety than you will find at a standard marathon, but ultra runners tend to have a serious need for sugar! It surprised me the first time I tried it, but that Coke sure does taste good late in the race. Some later aid stations may have hot drinks and you might even find some hot soup, a favorite of many runners. The aid stations are staffed by volunteer groups from throughout the local area and often feature a special theme, uplifting music and a great deal of enthusiasm and support for the runners.

In addition to the course support provided by race officials, many runners choose to have a crew (race organizers call them "personal handlers") support them while on the course. While this is permitted, the organizers offer a request to leave the support to the officials due to concerns from the National Park Service concerning congestion and traffic safety along the route. If you do opt for (and are lucky enough to have a great friend or family member willing to spend the day leap-frogging you in a car) a crew, they should only go to the official race-designated points along the course and yield right-of-way at all times to Park Service personnel, officials, volunteers, participants, vehicles, and pedestrians on the course. Race officials do not permit crewmembers in automobiles or on bicycles on the final 8.4-mile section of the JFK 50 Mile course. Violators are subject to having their runners disqualified and risk fines and/or arrest.

This is a point-to-point race, which begins in Boonsboro, Maryland, traverses three distinctive sections (Appalachian Trail, C&O Canal towpath, paved/country roads), and finishes at the Springfield Middle School in Williamsport, Maryland.

The route is horseshoe shaped and is actually only about 12 miles driving distance from the finish back to the start point. A shuttle service is available after the race, running approximately every half-hour, to take runners back to the starting area.

Starting on U.S. Alternate Route 40, the main street through Boonsboro, runners stay on paved roads for the first 2 1/2 miles, climbing up approximately 510 feet and joining the Appalachian Trail (AT). This AT section provides approximately 13 miles of mostly trail running on the famous North-South footpath. The trail is often rocky and narrow, forcing runners into a single file line in many places. "Passing on your left" is heard often as the trail widens or clear areas are present along the

Courtesy of John F. Kennedy 50 Mile

sides of the trail. The leaf covered rocks and roots can be especially challenging, resulting in some precarious footing. It is not uncommon to see runners take a fall and get bruised and bloodied on the AT. Of course, other runners are very quick to assist the fallen. There is truly a shared bond of respect for each other and the course, which is one of the many aspects about this race that make it so special. The trail takes runners up a mountain, traverses a ridgeline across the top, and runs down the other side at a place called "Weaverton Cliffs" at 15.4 miles. I must admit this is the only race I have done with a section described as "Cliffs." That should tell you something about this event! This is a short but at times very steep section consisting of a series of switch-backs taking runners down the mountain to complete phase I of the journey. On this portion, runners sometimes grab trees for stability and to keep their speed down to prevent a tumble down the mountain.

The aid station at 15.7 miles serves as the transition point onto the C&O Canal towpath. After running the trails, dodging loose rocks, jumping over roots, and traversing the steep switchbacks to get down Weaverton Cliffs, runners need to make mental and physical adjustments for the second phase of the journey. This second section of the course covers 26.3 almost totally flat miles on an unpaved, packed dirt surface along the C&O Canal. This towpath section, which some runners refer to as a "marathon within a marathon," is in many ways a welcome relief from the mental energy required to negotiate the AT. The towpath provides an even, consistent running surface, beautiful views of the Potomac River, and more frequent aid stations and access points for crews. Like the AT section, runners have no automotive traffic to contend with on the towpath. While many runners find this section a welcome change from the more challenging AT, some find the towpath to be monotonous and very much look forward to hitting the final road section.

Runners exit the C&O Canal towpath at Dam #4 (41.9 miles) and follow gently rolling, paved country roads the final 8.3 miles to the finish in Williamsport, Maryland. Yes, the JFK 50 is actually 50.2 miles, but after running 50 miles, what's an extra 2/10 of a mile? This final section is typical country road running, with runners staying to the far left to run against the flow of traffic. There will be cars on this stretch of the course so staying alert is a must. Traffic is restricted to race officials, law enforcement, and local residents so the traffic is light. Most drivers are courteous and respectful of the runners, but I have seen a few that seem frustrated and inconvenienced by the event.

Race organizers determine a time when runners leaving the towpath will likely be finishing in the darkness. At the final aid station on the towpath the officials issue reflective vests to all runners passing after that time. These runners are sometimes referred to as "vesters."

I ran my first JFK in 1999 after hearing about the adventure from a co-worker who is a member of the Reston Runners, a running club comprised of members primarily from in and around the Reston, Virginia area. I had completed seven marathons and finally achieved my goal of a Boston qualifying time. I guess I was looking for another challenge and my friend made JFK sound very intriguing. He said enough to get me interested, then when he introduced me to Anna (now the Reston Runner President and our resident JFK 50 leader / coordinator extraordinaire) the die was cast. Anna is somewhat famous for "convincing" runners to give the JFK a try!

The following excerpt is primarily from an after-action review I wrote after running my third consecutive JFK 50:

> I love this race! That isn't to say I loved every minute of the event (I didn't), but overall the JFK is a great experience. The JFK 50-mile reminds me of a George Sheehan quote; "Running provides happiness, which is different from pleasure. Happiness has to do with struggling and enduring and accomplishing." The JFK 50 certainly involves those elements! So, what do I love about the event? Well, first of all running as a member of the Reston Runners makes it very special. It's great to have the support of the many crewmembers and the inspiration from other runners. It's also pretty cool to be a part of the largest (by far) organized group of runners, all wearing matching singlets so we are readily recognized, that flock to the JFK 50 each year. We can't thank Anna enough for all her hard work and dedication in making this a bigger and better event every year for the Reston Runners members. Reston Runners have been coming to JFK since 1993 (three runners) and now average 45-50 runners and another 50 or so crewmembers each year.

Runners registering for JFK can sign up as individuals or teams of three to five runners, competing in Men's, Women's, and Military Team categories. Running this year as a member of a five-person team, each of us named "Jim," our team had the words "Jim. Reston Jim Team" imprinted bolding on our singlets. I lost track of how many times I was asked, "Just how many Jims are there in the Reston Runners?"

In addition to the camaraderie we experience through the JFK, I also love the personal challenge. Trying to run a smart race, remembering all the good advice from veterans about conserving energy, yet attempting to keep up a good pace and achieve personal goals all make for an exciting adventure.

My running strategy this year:

On the AT: I used pretty much the same strategy on the AT as last year, running the flat sections and down hills and walking up the steep inclines. A friend and fellow Jim Team member and I started together and ran the majority of the AT trading off setting the pace and staying in close proximity. I think we ran the AT a little more aggressively this year, partially due to our strolling a bit too casually from the high school down to the actual starting line. At 7:00 a.m. we were still walking to the starting line having a casual conversation when the gun went off. I guess until that point we were taking the concept of a relaxed start a bit too far. Since we didn't want to be at the very back of the pack getting on the trail, we ran across the starting line and pushed the pace to get past many runners in the first few miles. This was not really the way we had planned to start the day.

C&O Towpath: I decided to try a slightly different strategy on the canal towpath this year. I thought I would start by running between aid stations and walking out for two minutes instead of a timed run-walk strategy. I did this to hopefully achieve a faster time and also to eliminate the mental drill of keeping track of time running and walking. I used this strategy for three iterations and then reverted to running 15 minutes and walking for two minutes. In hindsight, I should have tried to keep the between-station strategy longer. I hope to try that next year. A lesson I learned here is to remember to look at the signs at the start of the station, which state how far it is to the next aid station.

I got a little bored at times on the trail this year, the disadvantage of not pacing with a friend (my fellow Jim Team member and I had separated towards the end of the AT). Talking to other runners along the way helped, as did seeing my loving and supportive wife (Karen) and other Reston Runners crew in the aid stations. This always provides a much-needed mental boost and helps break the JFK into manageable pieces. Even though I love the running surface of the C&O towpath, for a good portion of the towpath I was looking forward to getting off the path, because that means only about eight miles to go!

On the Road: I had forgotten how steep the first hill is when you come off the towpath and get started on the road towards Williamsport. I didn't hesitate walking up that big hill! I told myself to stick with the planned strategy of walking up the hills, running the flats and downs. It's strange how after covering 42 miles every little bump in the road starts looking like a "hill"! I realized somewhere along the road that I was using the slight inclines as an excuse to walk. I was almost hoping for a hill at times. I tried to get over this (sometimes successfully) by telling myself not to be a wimp on those minor up hills. I was doing okay on the road until the 47-mile point. As I was "cruising" along the road, a serious cramp struck in the back of my right leg. It was a knot that felt about the size of a baseball, and I couldn't even walk. I was scared and mad because for the past few hours I had been telling myself that if I maintained a steady pace I could finish in less than nine hours (a PR for me). Now, it seemed with a mere three miles to go, I might blow my chances. As I hobbled to the side of the road to be out of the way of other runners, I looked back and saw a very motivating sight. There was Loretta (a fellow Reston Runner) running strong. She gave me a few kind words of sympathy for my cramp as she pressed on down the road. Great race Loretta!

I knew I needed to keep moving to have any chance at nine hours, so I massaged out the cramp as much as possible and drank the rest of the water I had with me. I ran a bit more until I got a cramp in my left leg. Now I was even more concerned about how this JFK adventure would end. I knew that an aid station wasn't more that a mile ahead and thought if I could get there I could get some POWERade, figuring that I must be somewhat dehydrated and low on electrolytes. So, once again I massaged my cramp, walked a little then started running. The drive to finish under nine hours kept me going. I ran on to the next aid station (two miles to go) and drank three cups of POWERade. I was able to run the rest of the way to the finish, running sub 10 minutes for the last mile. I was very happy to be finished and thrilled that I had achieved my personal goal (I finished 8:57)! I think the adventure of the cramps in the final miles made me appreciate the accomplishment even more.

The JFK finish area was full of excitement, what a motivating place! Sharing the moment with other Reston Runners and crew, watching others push to the finish, and seeing the much-deserved pride and satisfaction on the finishers' faces. What a great experience!

Figuring out what to eat and when is always a challenge for me in the JFK. Before the start I had a bagel, a can of Boost, a banana, and some water. During the AT portion I ate a bagel and a Gu gel packet. Along the C&O towpath I ate a few M&Ms, a couple of bananas, and a GU packet every 40 minutes to an hour. I drank mostly water but also drank a few cups of Coke and a few cups of POWERade. In hindsight, I should have consumed a bit more POWERade or taken some electrolyte tablets. Those cramps were no fun at all! It seems I also learn something new each time about what NOT to eat along the way. Two years ago I had a bad experience with a peanut butter and jelly sandwich. This year I learned my lesson from a harmless little Jolly Rancher. I was moving along the C&O and running low on energy, somewhere in the 24-mile range. I wanted to wait until the next aid station to eat so I thought it might be a good idea to have a piece of candy to trick my brain. I guess the trick was on me! I made it into the aid station but my stomach started flipping like crazy. Several race support folks had the unpleasant surprise of seeing me deal with my sour ultra-stomach. Sorry folks! One friendly stranger was very concerned about me and kept asking if I was okay and how he could help. While I appreciated his genuine concern, that was one time I would have preferred to be alone. It's so great of those many volunteers to spend their days helping us along the way. I felt much better after dealing with this situation. I saw Karen and other Reston Runner crewmembers a few minutes later. I briefly shared the gory details of my experience, ate a banana, and moved on. I stuck with Gu and water the rest of the race.

If you are looking for a challenge, perhaps something different than a 26.2-mile marathon, I highly recommend the JFK 50 mile. It is an adventure, a challenge and when you finish a great sense of pride and accomplishment.

Jim Ashworth's interest in running began when he was attending college at Eastern Illinois University and participating in the Army ROTC program. He was taking a semi-annual physical fitness test, consisting of pushups, sit-ups, and a two-mile run when the most senior officer (a major) came up from behind and passed him. They battled it out around the track. He doesn't remember which one finished first, but he does remember deciding at that moment to start running. He ran his first marathon in 1994, the Columbus Marathon while attending graduate school at The Ohio State University. Now a Lieutenant Colonel in the Army, Jim has completed 15 marathons (PR of 3:09, Lincoln, Nebraska) and five ultra distance races (JFK 50s - 8:57 PR).

Sunmart Texas Trail Endurance Run

huntsville, texas

Web site: www.sunmart.net/Race/
Month: December

Author: Gary Grilliot
Number of Marathons Completed: 25
Number of Ultras Completed: 30
Age Group: 40-44

Prior to running my first Sunmart race I had only run three or four smaller ultras. The largest was the JFK 50, but at that time the field only included 200-300 runners and didn't begin to reach its present popularity. I'd read about Sunmart in *UltraRunning* magazine when I lived in Utica, New York, but never being one to travel too far to race, I didn't think much about it. Sometime after, I moved to Shreveport, Louisiana. Wanting to continue to try some ultras and maybe even run a larger event, I started looking around and soon remembered reading about the Sunmart race. With registration reaching toward 1,000 participants combined for the 50K/50M event, I decided Sunmart was the race for me to try.

Held in early December at Huntsville State Park, approximately one hour north of Houston, Texas, the Sunmart Texas Endurance Run is an incredible race. Great course, plenty of lodging options, and an experienced race director all point toward a fine event. If you could just be certain of the weather you'd have it all, but there needs to be some apprehension ... doesn't there?

I was unable to make the pre-race packet pick-up that year. When you have to work, you have to work! But the next year I found out what I had missed. This isn't the usual t-shirt and a few race applications in your goody bag kind of event. As you walk into the banquet room you're handed an over-sized gym bag and you start walking and stuffing. "What size t-shirt would you like?" "What size polo shirt would you like?" "What color hat would you like?" "What style sunglasses would you like?" "Take a towel, take a water bottle, take a knife, and take a stuffed animal, take, take, and take ....” Wait! Am I supposed to take one of everything? “No, take two PowerBars.”

You’re happy just to have received an incredible swag bag, when they open the buffet lines and you and 1,000 of your closest running buddies are treated to a hearty meal, topped off with cherry cobbler (a la mode if you desire) for dessert, no less. Needless to say, no more missed packet pick-ups for me, forget work!

I was registered to run the 50K, which didn’t start until well after the 50-mile runners began their journeys. Actually, we started late enough to watch as the leaders came through on their first of four loops. To my surprise, Ann Trason was right on the heels of the male leaders, holy cow — Ann Trason! If I’d been a bit more learned in ultrarunning I’d have recognized some of the other leaders such as Tom Johnson, Brian Hacker, and Steve Szydlik (who once won an ultra after breaking his arm during the run), just to mention a few.

After the idol worshipping was done, it was time to line up and get the 50K started. Then race director Norm Klein, who was also the race director for the Western States 100, soon had everyone’s fullest attention (mainly because that was the only way he’d stop blowing his whistle). Norm demands a lot from the runners, but only because he puts his fullest into the race. You can see why Sunmart grew to such heights under Norm, and now continues to be a classy event under the leadership of Roger Solers. The bulk of Norm’s pre-race comments were on course conditions. The previous week had brought multiple inches of rain to the North Houston area. Indeed the rain had only let up in the early hours of race morning. Park officials and volunteers spent the bulk of the night establishing makeshift bridges over newly formed streams. Norm couldn’t give them enough credit for the work they had accomplished on such short notice. After being told of everyone’s efforts I can still remember thinking, no whining!

Time to start the fun, let’s run. Every year Sunmart seems to bring in not only incredible ultra runners, but also road runners looking for their initial trail experience. This mixture has created incredible races and blazing fast times, consider these course records: 50M men - 5:20, women - 6:14; 50K men - 3:12, women - 3:33. “Smokin’” is a very accurate description for the course. In the inaugural years of Sunmart, the marathoners then 50K’ers ran the same loop twice as the 50 milers performed four times, adding on a short three mile out and back to begin the festivities. After this rain-soaked edition though, the 50K course was modified to eliminate duplication of the potentially muddiest areas. One thousand runners, 2,000 feet going over the same trail six times can make a moat out of a mud hole. Now, participants of both races share only the service roads and brief sections of single-track trail.

Personally, those are my favorite parts of both runs. I enjoy seeing how the races play out as the miles add up. As the event continued to grow, other changes had to be made to accommodate the ever-growing starting fields, but eventually the courses settled into their present state. Runners encounter several types of footing and terrain. Solid, packed red-clay service roads, rolling rutted jeep trails, rooted single track trails, twisting sandy paths interspersed with bridges and make-shift pallets all combine to make the Sunmart course interesting, and like Norm, it demands your attention. It'll put you on your fanny if you let your mind wander too far.

Many runners purposely avoid loop races so they don't have to see the finish line more than once. The thought of leaving friends and family behind to be replaced with pain and uncertainty is too much. For me, loop courses are a bonus. At Sunmart your cheering section gets to see you several times throughout the day, not just as you leave and again many hours later as you finish. It doesn't take a million plus people to make up a good crowd. Besides the general activity in the start/finish area, some people will work their way around the course cheering on the runners from unexpected vantage points. You become familiar with runners and spectators you've seen multiple times during the day. Faces illuminate and smiles cheer you on to greater efforts.

You also get to see aid stations more than once. Oh yeah baby, the glorious, incredible, feed your face, take a moment and sample our wares Sunmart aid stations. "Step up. We've got your soups, we've got your melon, your sandwiches of PB&J or turkey, pretzels, M&Ms, potatoes, oranges, water, sports drink ...." A runner can gain a few pounds and lose a few minutes if they don't eat it and beat it at this race. In the immortal words of Jose Wilke "Don't make love to the aid station."

Decisions await the runners with enough fortitude to cross the finish line. After receiving a finisher's medal you get your choice of a colorful Tyvek jacket emblazoned with the Sunmart logo or an ornamental Afghan rug with a design depicting the race and Huntsville State Park. This is only a prelude to the incredible awards distributed to the winners.

As the runners mingle and relate their tales to cohorts, they can replenish their systems with a barbeque meal provided by the race. One race, two meals (or more if you include aid stations) sounds deliciously tempting. In short order, racers are called to gather around for the awards ceremony. Beautiful horse statues on marble bases entitled "Stallion" by P.J. Mene are awarded to over-all and age-group winners alike.

My race went well. I finished, and that's all I really need to be happy. I didn't place well enough at this race to finish in the horses, but I have won several over the years. Of all the awards I've ever received, I value these the most. People have their favorite races for various reasons. Cool shirts, great courses, live bands, etc. … for me I enjoy Sunmart because it's fun.

I'd recommend the Sunmart Texas Trails Endurance Run to anyone looking to have a new adventure. It's an outstanding, well-established, respected ultra distance race. You'll get your money's worth and hopefully enjoy yourself at the same time.

———

A runner with 26 years of experience, Gary Grilliot has completed over 50 marathons and ultras combined. He has a 2:35:57 marathon PR, and a 6:10:12 50-mile PR. The majority of Gary's marathons and ultras are low-key events. The largest events he has participated in are the Boston Marathon, JFK 50 (three times) and the Sunmart Texas Trails Endurance Runs (five times). Gary has completed two, 100-mile runs (Arkansas Traveller) and may never do another.